Glad to Be a Ladd

Glad to Be a Ladd

Marilyn Ladd

cover photo: The Ladd family in 1964. Front row, left to right: Michael, Ralph, Raymond, Frances, Robert, Clarissa. Back row: Harold, Marilyn, John, Suzanne, Dad, Mom, Melvin. The oldest, Marv, age 19, was away at college.

Published by Dagmar Miura
Los Angeles
www.dagmarmiura.com

Glad to Be a Ladd

Copyright © 2019 Marilyn Ladd
All rights reserved. No part of this book may be used or reproduced in any manner whatsoever without prior written permission except in the case of brief quotations embodied in critical articles or reviews. For information, address Dagmar Miura, dagmarmiura@gmail.com, or visit our website at www.dagmarmiura.com.

Names, dates, places, events, and details are described as I remember them and, to the best of my knowledge, are accurately portrayed. The author and publisher do not assume and hereby disclaim any liability to any party for any loss, damage, or disruption caused by errors or omissions.

First published 2019

ISBN: 978-1-942267-98-0

This book is dedicated to my mother, whose loving patience, guidance, and constant support gave me the confidence and courage to pursue my dreams and make them a reality.

Contents

Introduction	1

Part One: Family Life

Francis Marvin Ladd	7
Ellen Regina (Gill) Ladd	35
Marilyn Carol Ladd	81
Birth Order	116
Marv, 1945	117
Mel, 1946	121
John, 1947	124
Harold, 1949	127
Me, 1950	130
Suzanne, 1951	131
Clarissa, 1953	134
Robert, 1954	136
Michael, 1955	138
Ralph, 1957	140
Raymond, 1959	142
Frances, 1960	145
Family Vacations and Day Trips	148
Age Ten and Beyond	170
Teaching and Coaching	198

Part Two: Classroom Techniques

Positive Changes	225
Four Agreements	234
Clarity and Consequences	241
Asking Questions	245
Effective Listening	251
Empathy versus Sympathy	254
Codependent Behavior	255
Commitment	261
Ridding Ourselves of Resentment	271
Epilogue	285
Index	295

Introduction

———◆———

My name is Marilyn Ladd. I was born in 1950, the first girl and fifth born of twelve children to Francis and Ellen Ladd. We were born between 1945 and 1960, generally considered the baby boomer era. My book is part autobiography, part self-help, and because I am a teacher, part supplemental teacher's guide. One of the reasons I wrote this book was to help create positive results for anyone struggling with negative self-talk and feelings of inadequacy; issues I experienced growing up in a large family that eventually led to a series of failed adult relationships. These personal issues often prevented me from achieving my life's potential, from becoming that autonomous, self-actualizing person I wanted to be.

After over forty years of teaching community college health and activity courses, I have put together a guide of proven teaching techniques designed to support those individuals who want to create healthy, meaningful relationships, especially that relationship with the self. The techniques within this book have provided my students, and oftentimes me, with the tools to develop value and positive changes in their lives. Teachers reading this book may find these suggested learning techniques valuable to incorporate into their own classes. The individual reading this book may extract some ideas to possibly address or change your own personal behavioral concerns.

I wrote this book so that others might learn from my mistakes and grow from my suggestions and experiences. My hope for the younger readers of this book is to rid yourself, a lot sooner than I did, of those limiting negative thoughts and feelings that are preventing you from being all that you can be. No matter what kind of upbringing or life's experiences you have had, you can choose to find it in your heart and mind to gain from my book the insight and understanding to love and feel good about yourself. You can decide if what is in this book will be as useful and valuable to you as it has been to me and the lives of my students. As I have learned over the years, your life does not have to be defined by your upbringing.

Most historians conclude that the baby boomer era includes those born between 1946 and 1964. It was a boom as a result of the many children born after soldiers returned from World War II in the mid- to late 1940s. My four older brothers, myself, and one sister were born between 1945 and 1952. We ended up living our teenage years in the 1960s through a time of protest and social unrest. The height of the baby boom occurred between 1952 and 1957, in which three more brothers and one sister were born.

Seventy-six million American children were born between 1946 and 1964. Today, 70 percent of the members of Congress are baby boomers; 58 percent have graduated from college and 65 percent do not or are not sure they have saved enough money to retire. We also take 48 percent of prescription medications, and another 75 percent currently work (http://fiftiesweb.com). It is my hope that those baby boomers reading this book will get the most enjoyment out of it as you identify with our family values and mores. For anyone else reading this book, I would like you to enjoy learning about the safe, progressive, ever-changing world and society that was the 1950s and 1960s.

Little did my dad know, when he returned from the Army in World War II, that he and my mom would generate their own personal baby boom: twelve children in sixteen years. No twins, and yes, we're Catholic. This book is a nostalgic journey down the baby boomer memory lane.

Experience with me what life was like living with thirteen other family members in a two-bedroom, one-bath house. Yes, just one bathroom for fourteen people! Ride along with me and eight of my siblings and our mom on a typical family camping vacation in our reliable, two-door, two-tone green 1950 Plymouth station wagon. You will be amazed and probably a bit frightened at how we experienced and survived family vacations and life's events at home. We had some rather dangerous and harrowing situations and some unforeseen predicaments that ultimately resulted in only a few injuries and broken bones but very little permanent mental and emotional damage. Join the fourteen of us for a typical family dinner in our moderate-size kitchen that was designed for six.

You will gain insight into what a close-knit, loving family our parents created and how our mother's sense of humor and eternally optimistic attitude carried us through lean and challenging times when it wasn't known sometimes where our next meal would come from or if there would be many presents under the tree during the holidays. No matter what happened in the Ladd household, as evidenced in this book, we were taught to never judge others and to love each other no matter what.

You will see what an incredible man of strength and endurance my Father was as he spent most of his waking hours working to support his family. When he wasn't working, he was spending time around the house fixing and repairing things and helping with cooking, housework, and grocery shopping. He may not have always had the time he would have liked to spend with us but we knew he loved us dearly just the same as evidenced by his long hours, days, and years of dedication and commitment to providing us with everything he possibly could. We appreciated the lengths he was willing to go to maintain for his family as comfortable a lifestyle as he was able to provide. He owned a small lawn sprinkler installation and repair business that not only fed and clothed all of us throughout the years but enabled all twelve of us to attend Catholic school and afford a housekeeper for several of our family's early years.

My parents were two amazing, unassuming, soft-spoken, Depression-surviving humble individuals who courageously raised and dearly loved and nurtured, the best they could, twelve intelligent, good natured, hard-working children who became responsible contributing members of society. They made huge sacrifices for us so we could all attend the schools of our choice, compete on sports teams, or buy a graduation dress, suit, or a decent birthday gift, all at the expense of them often going without.

My dad was also a resourceful, diligent, good-looking man who was honest and personable, a man whose major focus in life, for several decades, was to single-handedly support his family of fourteen. His own family taught him to value family, money, honesty, love, and other people's rights, all of which he in turn taught the twelve of us.

What my mother brought to the family over the years was to treat and love us unconditionally no matter what we did or said. She gave us our due well-deserved punishments and always held us accountable for our actions. Her glass was always half full even in the face of adversity or family challenges. She never took herself too seriously, she always maintained a great sense of humor, and she had nice legs!

Enjoy the book. It was written as a clear and compelling testimony describing my childhood recollections that convey to the reader why I am glad to be a Ladd! I will recount how my parents and my eleven siblings became one typical American baby boomer family that successfully navigated the ever-changing face of societal values and the hippie "tune in, turn on, and drop out" drug experimentations of the 1960s, to space explorations, to the often dangerous and volatile Cold War situations of world affairs that surfaced in the late 1950s and into the early 1960s and 1970s. I was raised in a wonderful loving family in which I enjoyed, like my eleven siblings, a fun, carefree, yet disciplined childhood.

Our childhood wasn't without turmoil and challenges that sometimes led to verbal and physical confrontations with each other. The confrontations were typical sibling rivalry situations that were quelled with unfortunately some damage to the psyche and the upper arm, which is where we typically hit each other during our outbursts. To initially survive in this family, you had to be thick-skinned, have a strong sense of humor, and not take yourself too seriously. We grew to respect and appreciate each other with time. Our parents did their best to raise children who would eventually create wonderful, successful adult lives and loving families of their own.

PART ONE

Family Life

Francis Marvin Ladd

Francis Marvin Ladd, born March 22, 1917, Central, Arkansas.

The Ladd name originated in the Scandinavian countries and has a long, rich history that can be traced back to the eighth century BC. At one point Ladds took part in the invasion of France about 900 AD and settled in Normandy after helping conquer that part of France. In 1066 the Ladds joined William the Conqueror when he invaded England. For their service they were granted land in Kent County, England, around the Deal and Dover areas. They were fishermen and farmers, and many of their descendants remain on the land in Kent County today. The Ladd surname appropriately means "servant" or "of service." Other spellings of Ladd are Lade, Lad, and Ladde. The first traceable records begin with John Lade, born about 1478 in Kent County, England.

The first Ladds that settled in America were Daniel and Joseph Ladd, who arrived in Massachusetts in 1634, thirteen years after the Pilgrims landed in Plymouth Rock, which would likely indicate that all the Ladds in America are related. That would also mean that we are related to the famous Hollywood actor, Alan Ladd, who was born in Hot Springs, Arkansas, in 1913, about twenty miles from where my dad was born in 1917 in Central, Arkansas. Alan Ladd was a major Hollywood star during the 1940s and 1950s. He was best remembered as the title character in *Shane* in 1953, considered to be one of the greatest of all westerns.

There is Cherokee on my dad's mother's side of the family. My grandmother's last name was Morris. Her great-grandfather was Dotson Morris, born in 1795, who was part Cherokee and was eventually forced to give up lands he owned on a creek in North Carolina. He eventually moved to Tuscaloosa County in Alabama where he was forced to live out west of town with Choctaw Indians.

My dad was raised on a farm near Fort Smith in Central, Arkansas, with his two sisters and a brother, where they owned a grocery store. He trapped animals for dinner and milked the cows for his family and to sell in their store. His family had a still on their farm in which they sold moonshine during the Prohibition Era. In his teens he became a butcher at the family store and later irrigated acres of cotton and alfalfa on the farm as his first full-time job.

Like many of America's families, his fell on hard times during the Depression and lost their farm and grocery store. Like so many other struggling families from the East, they picked up stakes and moved west. They settled in Raisin City, California, in 1933 when my dad was sixteen. Soon after arriving, his parents were in a terrible car accident, where his mother was not expected to ever walk again and his father was killed. Sitting in the backseat of the car was another couple who were also killed. They were driving on Manning Avenue near the city of Easton when my grandfather, driving them in the infamous San Joaquin Valley tule fog, unknowingly turned in front of a large truck carrying grapes. The truck hit them broadside and spun the car around several times, with everyone in the car being thrown around violently for several seconds.

Tule fog, as it was that fateful morning, is a thick ground fog that had settled as it typically did in the San Joaquin and Sacramento Valleys, which are areas of California's Great Central Valley. The fog usually formed from late fall through early spring after the first significant rainfall. The name *tule* comes from the plant of the same name found in the region (Wikipedia). The fog was usually present traditionally between November and March. The fog has always been hated by motorists but it was a devastating, fatal menace to my grandparents some eighty-five years ago.

She was not supposed to, but my grandmother survived her extensive internal and external injuries and was able to walk again. Her digestive system was never the same from her internal injuries, wand she wore specially made shoes with one sole higher than the other as she was left with one leg a little shorter than the other after the accident. She not only survived the accident when she was forty-five in 1934, but she would go on to live in Southern California and the Fresno area until the age of ninety-four, when she passed away on New Year's Day in 1984.

She always complained to her doctors that she had a piece of glass from the auto accident wedged in her nose. No one ever believed her because glass did not show up on the many X-rays of her head they took over the years. Nearly forty years after the accident, my grandmother once again felt the sharp piece of glass in her nose and went to her doctor to have him take yet another look at it. This time he could see it partially exposed in her left nostril. He removed the piece of glass easily without much pain or blood. She kept that piece of glass for some time and was pleased to proudly show it to us the next time we went to visit her. I am sure, once and for all, that it was a relief for her to be able to finally prove to everyone that she wasn't crazy, that there always *was* a piece of glass from that horrible accident stuck in her nose all those years.

My grandmother often sensed things before or as they happened. When my dad was assigned to the Aleutian Islands in Alaska during his enlistment and was on a landing craft with many other soldiers, about ready to disembark, my dad was accidentally pushed by another soldier when the ramp was lowered, and with the heavy equipment he was carrying, he went under and began to drown. Fortunately he survived, but he received a letter from my deeply concerned but eventually relieved grandmother many days later asking if he was OK, that she felt something terribly bad had happened to him.

I would say my grandmother was a Jill-of-all-trades. I can see where my dad got his many resourceful and inventive skills. My grandmother was very artistic as well as handy around the house. One of her jobs was as a cook and crafts teacher at Camp Trinity in Northern California. There was a lamp she made from manzanita wood that was in use for many years in her mobile home in which she lived for most of the years I knew her.

Grandma Lily Ladd in 1968, age 81.

With a little assistance, she also put in a small shower in her mobile home so she would no longer have to walk to the common showers, located several yards from her twenty-seven-foot 1949 Airstream Trailer Coach. She was an accomplished gardener, successfully growing tomatoes, cucumbers, and squash in the small side yard next to her mobile home. She never drove a car and walked everywhere around the small town of Tustin, located in Orange County, to buy her groceries and small household items. She crocheted beautiful blankets for all of us, several of which I still have and cherish. She was also a healthy eater. Like my father, I never saw her eat anything that contained refined sugar. No wonder she lived to ninety-four.

She had high blood pressure for many years. It was in 1981, at the age of ninety-two, that she was walking to downtown Tustin to buy groceries when her high blood pressure caused her to become light-headed and faint, falling backward hitting her head on the sidewalk. She was taken to the hospital, and recovered somewhat from her head injury, but she was never the same again mentally.

She never returned to her mobile home but was taken to live in an adult care home back in that city in which she had originally resided, Raisin City, California. The facility was just across the street from her daughter Eupha. Eupha visited her almost daily and helped take care of her until she passed away in 1984.

Her death was especially difficult for me to handle as I lived with her from the spring semester in 1972 through June 1974 in her mobile home while I attended California State University, Fullerton. It was a little too far for me to travel the forty miles to Fullerton in Orange County from our family home in South Gate in Los Angeles County, so she graciously allowed me to live with her.

I came home from college one day looking for her. After several minutes and inquiries of her neighboring tenants, one woman in her seventies, sitting on her porch, pointed at my grandmother, who was under her mobile home. There was an opening in the skirting that surrounded the bottom of this woman's trailer, where I peeked in and found my grandmother, who was being paid by this woman to pull weeds from under her neighbor's mobile home. My grandmother was eighty-three at the time.

My dad loved his parents. One of the few times I ever saw my dad shed a tear is when he talked about the car accident that killed his dad. It was the only time I ever remember him talking about the accident. My dad was a very reserved person who did not display his emotions much nor allow himself to be vulnerable. He was given a lot of family responsibility from an early age. He later took his job as parent and breadwinner seriously and did so successfully. I could say that he was a co-parent with his mother, stepping in to parent with her at sixteen when his father died.

My mother's parents died before most of us were born or could remember them. My grandmother Lily, my father's mother, the one who was in the auto accident, was the only grandparent we all knew and remembered until her passing.

My dad had to quit high school in 1933 at age sixteen to support his family financially after his dad's tragic automobile accident. My dad later became a master plumber, journeyman, gas fitter, and electrician. Those skills certainly came in handy when he used all of them to later repair everything from our family cars to fixing or repairing just about any household appliance or fixture, inside or out. We rarely had to call a professional to repair or replace anything in and around the house. He was very self-reliant and self-sufficient from an early age, which saved us a lot of money over the years and taught us to be the same.

He enhanced the entire lower portion of the front of the house that runs under the front windows and along the street side of the porch by cementing it with rocks. He formed and placed a tight-meshed aluminum screen he designed himself over the top of our chimney on the roof of our house to capture any ignitable ashes or hot particles that could possibly escape and start a fire. Local firemen commended him for designing it when they saw it while at our house putting out a small garage roof fire that two of my younger teenage brothers accidently started while smoking pot up on the back edge of the garage roof. An avocado tree just behind the garage allowed them easy access. It was a short climb up through the center of the tree and onto the roof.

My dad modified sprinklers he bought from a local sprinkler company that made watering more efficient and effective for our own lawn and for his customers. He also designed and placed a small water fountain alongside the south fence of our backyard where our other larger, fabulous avocado tree grew. We drank from the fountain every time we were out playing in the backyard, as it saved us a trip into the house. The excess water from the fountain drained under the tree and kept it constantly watered, which resulted in many bumper years of large, beautiful, delicious avocados, some of the best I ever ate, and I *love* avocados!

It was on December 20, 1940, that my dad received his Notice of Classification, 1-A, from his Draft Board. He was inducted into the United States Army in Sacramento, California, during World War II, on March 6, 1941. He was then sent to the Monterey Presidio in Northern California, and on March 11, 1941, he was sent to Camp Roberts, near San Miguel, in northern California, until June 1942.

In June 1942 he met our mother while on a weekend pass at a USO function at Seaside Park at what is now the Ventura Fairgrounds. Ventura County is located on the coast just north of Los Angeles County. Mom said she was attracted to him because "He was such a gentleman and was so handsome!" At Seaside Park that day, my mom needed a partner to play badminton, and invited my dad to be her partner. They spent the next month and a half going to parties and dances and other places of interest until he was sent to Alaska.

He sailed from San Francisco in August 1942 and was stationed at Adak Island in the Aleutian Islands until April 1944. It was there that he nearly drowned as he attempted to disembark from his boat. He was assigned as a cook and baker at the officers' mess hall.

When he returned from Alaska, he proposed to my mother at her sister Margaret's house. They married on May 14, 1944, after Sunday mass at the San Buenaventura Mission, one of the twenty-three California missions founded by Father Junípero Serra in the 1700s. Due to wartime austerity, my mother wore a short light-blue dress and my dad wore his Army uniform. My mom's brother Harold was the best man, and my mother's sister Margaret was her matron of honor. They spent their honeymoon at the Knickerbocker Hotel in Hollywood.

The hotel today is an apartment house for seniors, but back in the 1920s, the Knickerbocker Hotel was at the heart of Hollywood as it played a key role in Tinseltown history for decades. Rudolph Valentino hung out at the hotel bar. Marilyn Monroe honeymooned at the hotel with Joe DiMaggio in January 1954. When he was in town filming movies such as *Love Me Tender* in 1956 and *Heartbreak Hotel*, Elvis Presley stayed at the Knickerbocker in suite 1016 (Wikipedia).

I make it a point when driving up north to visit family to take the 101 freeway through Hollywood so I can see the Knickerbocker Hotel from the freeway. It is located on Vine Street just south of the famous round Capital Records Building. One of these days I plan to get off the freeway and go inside the hotel to see for myself what the attraction was for my parents that they would spend their honeymoon there. I am guessing that its location in the heart of Hollywood, not far from the corner of Hollywood and Vine, was a major factor in their choice. I understand there is a large crystal chandelier in the lobby that I would love to see that cost $120,000 in the 1920s, which would cost over $1 million in today's dollars. It would be fun to stand under that chandelier as my parents did nearly seventy-five years ago and imagine the newlyweds, giddy with joy and happiness, holding hands while walking under that beautiful chandelier in their best nightlife attire, on their way to dinner or a Hollywood hot spot.

Shortly after their honeymoon, Dad left for Camp Hood, Texas, now Fort Hood, and was stationed there from April 1944 until October 1945. Mom drove to Texas several months after Dad was assigned there, and they lived near the base in Temple. I could not find out much detail, but Mom got into an auto accident in July 1944 while in Texas, in the city of Belton. She had X-rays taken at the emergency room that showed that she had broken her nose. One story I heard about the accident is that mom got distracted while looking at a couple of dresses on display in a store window and rear-ended the car ahead of her. The car was damaged but not enough so that my dad could not eventually fix it and drive it back to California when he was discharged from the Army the following year.

While in Texas, Mom became pregnant in January 1944. She stayed in Texas until late July, when my parents decided she should leave for California and move in with my dad's family in Fresno so they could help her through her pregnancy. In late July she boarded a train from Texas back to Ventura, where her family was now living. After a short visit in Ventura, she took a train to Fresno and began living with my dad's family from July 29, 1945, until late October that same year. She wrote many lovely, delightfully affectionate letters to my dad while he was back in Texas, which my dad cherished and kept. I read all of those almost daily letters my mother wrote him between July 27, 1945, and October 9, 1945. That is the day my dad was honorably discharged. She wrote him seventy-two letters in the seventy-five days they were apart. On a few of those seventy-five days apart, she wrote him two letters a day.

Most of her airmailed letters professed how much she missed him, how lonesome she was without him, and how she dearly loved him and couldn't wait for them to be together again. In her letters she constantly prodded him to find out if and when he could get a furlough to be home when she gave birth to their first child, whose due date was September 21, 1945. The average length of her letters was five to six pages. I wondered why she did not keep the letters that Dad sent her, until I read in one of her letters to Dad that said she got rid of his letters because since she was living with his family, she did not want them to find out about what she and Dad were writing to each other. A handful of her letters were never opened by Dad. I would like to think that he just didn't get around to reading them. One letter that was written by Mom just after Marv Jr. was born was apparently read by dad, but resealed for some reason. I never opened and read the resealed and unopened letters.

Mom and my dad's mother, Lily Mae, relied on Dad's monthly allotment checks to live. His mother lived on $50 a month. Because she did not have much money on which to live, Mom's letters were often written on paper used on one side or a mix of different paper sizes. Some were written in pencil and some in faded ink, making some of her letters difficult to read. Because paper was scarce, she wrote on the back of each page and sometimes along the edges. She addressed her letters to him in many sweet and loving ways, such as "My Dearest Honey," "My Dear Darling Pap," "Dearest Sweetness," and "My Sweetest Sweetheart." Her letters indicated that staples like milk, butter, and gas were still difficult to find and buy. She could get a permanent cold wave in town for $12 and a two-piece wool suit for $15 at the local Woolworths in 1945. The minimum wage was $1.30 an hour.

She ran a full gamut of feelings and emotions in her letters, as would be expected of a lonely, newly wed pregnant woman living in an extremely hot unfamiliar place with in-laws she had never met, some of whom are helpful and sympathetic and some, like her mother-in-law, who could be controlling, aloof, and unsympathetic. Grandma had to have things done her way around the house. Mom was uncomfortable as it was and felt she was being a burden and a nuisance to everyone. She was desperate for her and Dad to be together again. Mom helped physically around the house, despite her swollen ankles and ever-enlarging belly. She did dishes, went grocery shopping, and helped with the large amount of canning and pie-making the family did at the time. Other than being physically uncomfortable, Mom seemed to handle her first pregnancy with ease and few complaints. Little did she know she would be going through this same undertaking eleven more times.

It was in her letter dated September 17, 1945, in which she wrote that she went to town to get her cold wave and indicated she was very nervous at the beauty parlor the whole time, fearing she might have the baby. She was starting to get cramps. She managed to get through the cold wave process, but it was at 10 p.m. that evening, on the 17th, that her water broke. She left to go to the hospital the next morning at 6 a.m. She delivered at 1:30 p.m. on September 18. After all the post-delivery pain and afterbirth and baby formalities, she was thrilled with her first child. She described him to my dad in a letter she wrote that evening as "Cute, tiny, with blue eyes and a healthy appetite!" She felt he had her mouth, my dad's skin, and she liked the dimple in his chin. She referred to my brother as "My sweet precious little bundle."

I was amazed at the number of days she was in the hospital given there were no complications or unusual circumstances to my brother's birth. She was discharged after five days. I guess it was a typical length of stay back then. As things played out at her in-laws place in Fresno in the more than two months she was there, she indicated in her letter dated September 24 that she wished she would have stayed in Belton or Temple, Texas, and had the baby there. She felt she was too much of a bother to everyone in Fresno, and she did not get along all that well with her mother-in-law after the birth. Mom wrote that she had cried herself to sleep a few nights, feeling she had become a nuisance and a burden to everyone and was constantly longing for dad. Mom did make it clear in her letter on October 7 to Dad that she was truly grateful for "the Ladd family being so 'swell' to me." Mom never was one to complain.

It was on October 2, 1945, a few months after World War II ended, that mom finally got the news that dad would be discharged soon. He returned home by car via Yuma, Arizona, and arrived in Fresno on October 15. He was honorably discharged on October 12, less than a month after my oldest brother, Marv, was born on September 18. My parents truly had a special bond and an undeniable, beautiful love between them, as evidenced in their loving letters to each other during a rather difficult, trying time for them both.

As I read her letters in sequential order from her first letter to Dad on July 27, when my very pregnant mother wrote him about going grunion hunting on the beach in Ventura on a Saturday night with her sister and sister-in-law, to her last letter on October 9, telling him she received some disposable diapers in the mail from her sorority sisters from Ventura College, I found myself emotionally moved and transported into her letters and became immersed in her journey, even though I would not be making my own appearance in her life for another five years.

I sat alongside her on her initial train ride to Fresno from Ventura, watching her absorbed in thought, feeling her excitement and anticipation, coupled with some apprehension and uneasiness, not knowing exactly what she was getting herself into, but both of us optimistically hoping for the best. I sat on the porch with her as she wrote my dad about how hot the Fresno August evening was and how she was trying to find some respite from the stifling heat. I could taste the refreshing ice-cold tea her sister-in-law, Eupha, brought out to the porch to bring my mom some relief. In some letters, I cried myself to sleep with her, feeling her quiet desperation and anguished yearning to be together again with my dad and start their lives together with baby Marvin. The letter that made her and me the happiest and gave me the most pleasure in reading was the one she sent on October 2, 1945, acknowledging that she had received word in one of his last letters that he had received his discharge papers and would be home soon.

I will always cherish her letters and be forever thankful to my dad for keeping them. Her letters were a thoughtful and touching insight into what I am sure were countless identical situations taking place all over the world at the end of World War II. No wonder my parents' generation has been called the greatest generation. They endured and overcame more difficult and trying times than any generation previous.

Little did my dad know that he ended his military career as a cook in the Army only to eventually become the cook of his own small army! During his military career, my dad did receive many awards for his service: the Bronze Star, an American Defense Medal, a Good Conduct Medal, a Sharpshooter Medal, and three service bars.

After my dad got out of the service, my parents moved down to Southern California and lived from 1945 to 1947 in Huntington Park, a city just northwest of the city of South Gate, where they eventually settled by 1948 and remained and raised the twelve of us until my mother moved up north in 1978 after my dad passed away. We lived in a small house on San Luis Avenue in South Gate from 1949 to 1954, then moved a block east to a much bigger home on San Miguel Avenue in late 1954, when I was four.

The history of the city of South Gate is an interesting one. Francisco Lugo's son, Don Antonio María Lugo, was granted eleven square leagues of land by the King of Spain in 1810 in appreciation for his father's service to the crown. One square league of land is equivalent to 7,628 acres, which equates to just over 500,000 acres of land granted to Don Antonio. It became known as the Rancho San Antonio land grant. It extended from the low range of hills that separated it from the San Gabriel Valley to the old Dominguez Ranch at its south, and from the eastern boundary of the pueblo of Los Angeles to the San Gabriel River. At various times, Don Antonio María Lugo was the mayor of Los Angeles. A little more than a hundred years after the establishment of the Lugo Land Grant, in about 1910, the area at the south gate of the ranch became the city of South Gate.

By 1880, cattle raising had been replaced by agriculture as the most important local industry. By the end of 1918, there were 125 homes that had been constructed to bring the population of South Gate to about 500. Between 1910 and 1940, most of the agricultural land was replaced by homes and factories. It was on January 20, 1923, that the Los Angeles Board of Supervisors formally declared the incorporation of the City of South Gate. The population at that time was about 2,500 people.

The years following incorporation in 1923 were boom years. A residential and industrial base was established and serves as the cornerstone of South Gate to this day. When World War II was over, the city, industry, business, and the people all looked forward to a period of growth and prosperity, as did the Ladd family.

One of the largest local industries was Firestone Tire and Rubber Company, and in 1936 the General Motors plant went into production in South Gate with a thousand employees, which eventually increased to four thousand. Pontiac, Oldsmobile, and Buick were three makes of cars assembled there. South Gate, in the 1950s and 1960s, was considered a lower-middle-class city.

Within the City of South Gate, Tweedy Boulevard was the main street that ran east to west and on which all the mostly commercial stores and businesses were located. It was also the main drag for Friday- and Saturday-night low-riders and local cars to run. As a teenager, I and two of my sisters and sometimes my high school friends would cruise up and down Tweedy Boulevard in my first car, a 1955 two-door Ford Fairlane. We had fun checking out the other cars and trying to avoid confrontations or trouble with other cars, especially those with females in them. Whittier Boulevard in East Los Angeles was the biggest and baddest street for weekend cruising, but Tweedy Boulevard was very popular with the young teens from South Gate and the surrounding cities.

Most of the businesses were small and one-of-a-kind family-owned. There were several original stores like the nationally known Greenspan's Department Store that is still selling hats, coats, shirts, etc. There was a Sav-On store that is now called CVS. There was a Thrifty drugstore, now called Rite-Aid, and there was a Winchell's Donuts on Tweedy and California Avenue that is still there. The only large grocery store in town, where we bought most of our food, was called the Better Foods Store. A smaller family-owned grocery store with a great fresh meat counter was Ashton Brothers located several blocks west of Better Foods on Tweedy Boulevard. Next to the Better Foods store was the South Gate Laundromat, where I worked from the summer after finishing eighth grade in 1964 through my senior year in high school in 1968. That job enabled me to pay for the insurance and upkeep of my first car and pay my tuition fees, totaling about $120, for my senior year at Pius X Catholic High School in the neighboring city of Downey.

For nearly twenty years, the Better Foods Store was our mainstay for any and almost all groceries and sundries we ever bought while living in South Gate. It was located on the far east end of Tweedy Boulevard on the south side of the street. It was the last commercial block of stores before entering a large residential area that stretched about a half mile before ending at Atlantic Boulevard and the South Gate Park. As far as I know, it was a one-of-a-kind independent store that was family-owned. My dad or mom typically spent about $15 to $20 nearly every night buying a day's worth of staples for the fourteen of us. That was a lot of money to spend daily on groceries during those late 1940s and early 1950s.

The daily load of groceries we typically bought and ate included a 49-cent large bag of potato chips or Fritos, a box or bag of 39-cent cookies, sometimes chocolate chip, sometimes ginger snaps or cream-filled wafers. A lot of the items chosen usually depended on what was on sale that day. The three 39-cent boxes of cereal purchased and eaten each day were usually Kix, Wheaties, Corn Flakes, or Cheerios. Sometimes we could buy three boxes of cereal on sale for a dollar. If we were lucky, Trix, Cocoa Puffs, Frosted Flakes, or Lucky Charms were on sale; they were sweeter, but when not on sale, were typically more expensive.

At the height of our increasingly growing and constantly hungry family, about 1962–1963, we went through three to four half gallons of milk every day at $0.39–0.49 a half gallon. The Rockview Dairy deliveryman dragged a large wooden box, containing nine half gallons of milk, up to our porch every other day. We went through three loaves of bread each day at $0.39 each or sometimes three for a dollar. Typically it took us two days to go through a two-pound jar of peanut butter and a package of lunch meat.

Dinner consisted of either two whole chickens or a couple of large steaks or a big roast, a five-pound bag of boiled or oven-baked potatoes, a stick or two of margarine, and a quart-full pan of boiled broccoli, brussels sprouts, or other vegetable. If we had dessert, it was usually either a whole cake, a pie or two, or a half gallon of ice cream. We mostly got Neapolitan ice cream as it had sections of three separate flavors in it: vanilla, strawberry, and chocolate, which satisfied just about everyone's taste in ice cream without having to buy the three flavors separately.

We all loved cheese and went through a large brick of mild cheddar in about three days for $1.89. We ate about three dozen eggs each week at 29 cents a dozen. Our meat or main food for most of our dinners was usually beef or chicken, which again were the two staples everyone liked, were cheap, and could be used to cook a number of different main dishes.

We could have plain old hamburgers one night, then tacos with hamburger the next night, then spaghetti with hamburger another night. Hamburger was about 39–49 cents a pound. We typically went through two or three pounds of beef at each meal. On Sundays, for lunch, we typically cooked or barbequed sixteen to twenty-four hot dogs at 49 cents for a package of eight or fifteen to twenty hamburgers with the buns and condiments. We consumed large amounts of various fruits, which on a daily basis could consist of a dozen bananas or a three-pound bag of apples or oranges. The fruit typically ran from 9 to 29 cents a pound.

All the above did cost about $17 to $20 a day and had to be bought all over again the next day. At one time, there were five growing teenagers, four of them boys, and seven very active younger kids who were hungry all the time. You can well imagine how difficult it was to keep enough food on the table and in the refrigerator and kitchen shelves. We rarely had any leftovers to be enjoyed the following day. My eight brothers were 6' to 6'4" tall and we four girls were all between 5'6" and 5'11". My dad was 6' tall and mom was 5'7". We have two nephews today who are 6'6" and 6'5" and a first cousin who is also 6'6". My dad's dad was 6'5". We were a large family in more ways than one!

We were very fortunate my dad made enough money to be able to spend $17 to $20 a day on groceries, and that's just groceries; that's not including the regular replacement of laundry detergent, dish and bath soap, toothpaste, condiments, clothes, shoes for fourteen that had to be bought on a regular basis, various other sundries, etc.

I worked next door to the Better Foods Market at the South Gate Laundromat full-time during the summer and on Saturdays only during the school year. I worked only as long each day as there were clothes to separate and wash. Most days I worked an average of five or six hours. I always called home using the phone at the laundromat on those Saturdays as I was getting off work to see if Mom needed anything I could pick up at the store next door. There were a few occasions when, believe it or not, she did not need anything, but inevitably there was almost always some food item or household product she needed and was grateful to me for buying it for the family.

Next to the Better Foods Store was what was called a five-and-dime store, equivalent to our 99-cent stores of today. It was a variety store that sold a wide assortment of inexpensive personal and household items formerly costing 5 or 10 cents (Dictionary.com). It had been there for many decades, but that particular chain store was going out of business in the late 1950s and it was soon replaced by what was then a Sav-On Store, which later became Osco and what is today called CVS.

Both the Better Foods Store and the South Gate Laundromat eventually went out of business in the early 1970s when commercial laundromats were replaced by neighborhood coin-operated laundromats. Brand-name food stores became popular and a commercial boom moved many stores and businesses a few miles west on Tweedy Boulevard, which was more centrally located rather than on one end of town. The Sav-On moved from the east end to the new, more commercially successful section, where it remains to this day.

When it was a Sav-On drugstore, I remember being able to buy a scoop of ice cream in a cone for 5 cents. Some of today's candy bars are smaller and much more expensive than when I bought them at Sav-On. A Big Hunk or Abba-Zabba, a box of Good & Plenty, a Hollywood Bar, a Cherry-a-let, or any number of other popular candy bars, and I knew and ate them all, could be bought for 5 cents. Some days I scored when they were on sale three for a dime! Those were the days. Those same but smaller candy bars are anywhere from 99 cents to $1.99 each today. Now I understand how the 5-cent price of a candy bar I paid as a kid was so disconcerting to my aunts and uncles, who told me they bought similar types of candy for 1 cent when they were kids back in the 1920s and 1930s.

There were some other well-known chain stores that were originally located in South Gate but most of them eventually went out of business, changed names, or moved to another city. There was a Thrifty drugstore, a Mode-O-Day women's clothing store that was located a block west of the original five-and-dime store. There is still a nationally known Greenspan's Clothing Store located on Tweedy Boulevard near the west end of town in South Gate.

Greenspan's, a family owned clothing store, opened in 1928 in the city of Watts, and another soon after in South Gate. The Watts store closed but the original store in South Gate continues to sell hard-to-find old classic styles from the 1940s, 1950s, 1960s, and 1970s. The original Greenspan family has and continues to provide wardrobe clothing for many classic movies, such as *Stand by Me, Sandlot, Stand and Deliver, Boyz n the Hood* and several others. Ice Cube used to shop there before he was Ice Cube. It continues to hold the name as the "Last Original Clothing Store" (YouTube).

One establishment we grew to love and patronize was Ziegler's Hardware, located on Tweedy Boulevard and San Luis Avenue. Our house was the first house located behind the hardware store on San Luis. Only a vacant lot separated us from Ziegler's parking lot and the back of their store. We spent many raucous and carefree times in that vacant lot. It allowed us a much needed overflow play area that replaced our rather small, inadequate backyard. The vacant lot was about fifty by one hundred feet with a large eucalyptus tree growing in the middle of it. My four older brothers, to no avail, spent a lot of time trying to climb that tree and build a tree house in it.

There was a small, dangerously precarious, and well-worn shed next to the tree that made a great clubhouse and climbing structure for us until it collapsed completely one day. Before it collapsed, when I was four, I was over playing with my brothers in the lot and watched as my brother John kicked out the weakened door from the inside, and it inadvertently fell on top of my brother Harold, who happened to be standing on the other side. We were stunned that John didn't realize that five-year-old Harry was struggling underneath the door when John, who was seven, began to walk out onto the door with a huge proud smile on his face that he had the strength to kick out the door all by himself. He continued to walk several steps onto the door until we all screamed, including Harry, "Get off, you're standing on Harry!" Fortunately, Harry made it out from under the door unscathed but for a few scratches, and a little embarrassed. Since Harry's body language indicated he was OK, we figured that gave us permission to laugh at and tease him for how frightened and surprised he was, and the look we all saw on his face not only when the door initially fell on him but the even worse look he had on his face when John started to unknowingly walk out on top of him.

It was just one of the many scary, potentially dangerous early childhood situations we experienced, sometimes purposely created, but we always felt, for the most part, or at the very least, that we would survive. We could eventually look back at these incidents with laughter and rarely, but sometimes, a little remorse. For good reason, we did not mention to our parents that day this incident nor most of those harrowing, often dangerous incidents to follow.

Because we lived so close and were always walking by the Ziegler's Hardware store and sometimes buying items there, we got to know the owner and his son Bill personally. We kept in touch with the Ziegler family long after we moved away and they sold the store. The store is still located at the same place on San Luis Avenue and Tweedy Boulevard with the same name and is doing well. A block west of the hardware store is Larry's Liquor store, on the southeast corner of Malison and Tweedy, where we bought candy, gum, and sodas. It is still in its same location.

There was also the Allen Theater a few blocks west of Larry's Liquor, located on the north side of the street. At eight years old, I saw my first movies ever at the Allen Theater; they were double-feature scary movies. I saw the *Invaders from Mars* and *Attack of the Crab Monsters*. I had never seen anything so scary and frightening in my life as those two movies. I had nightmares for weeks! The theater is still there but is not in use.

The original Tweedy family was headed by R. D. Tweedy, who played an important part in South Gate's history. Mr. Tweedy was born in 1812 in Illinois and came to California by ox-drawn cart in 1852. Mrs. Tweedy rode across the prairies perched on her rocking chair on the ox cart. The family was large, and several generations have lived in the city. The family members bought some two thousand acres of land on which most of South Gate was built. The downtown buildings on Tweedy Boulevard I just described were named after the Tweedy family. It is now called the Tweedy Mile.

Soon after he married my mother in 1944, my dad started his own lawn-sprinkler installation and repair company in 1949, the year he received his first business license from the city of South Gate after moving there in 1948. He installed and repaired lawn sprinklers not only in the greater Los Angeles area but in areas south of Los Angeles near San Diego and eventually east in Victorville, California, and in a few cities in Arizona.

Several of my brothers and one sister worked for him over the years in the family business until they began college or started their own careers. After my dad passed away in 1977 at age fifty-nine, five of my brothers continued to run the business, adding irrigation and drip systems, landscaping, and lighting. The business continues to be run to this day, seventy years later, by my two oldest brothers, Marvin and Melvin. They stay in business because they continue to do good honest work at a fair price, just as my dad did for over thirty years. Most of their customers, as was the case with my dad, are from word of mouth from other satisfied customers. They have done very little professional advertising for the past ten years. My brothers continue to carry my dad's professional notion that "If a job is worth doing, it is worth doing right."

Some of my dad's customers over the years included famous singers Karen and Richard Carpenter, who lived in the city of Downey, just east of South Gate. Other customers were actor Steve Allen and his wife Audrey Meadows. Maurice McAlister, the cofounder of Downey Savings and Loan, was another of his longtime customers. Mr. McAlister was a resident of South Gate, at one time attending South Gate High School. He later attended my father's funeral and visited our family at our house afterward to give his condolences.

My dad left quite a legacy behind to his children as an example of what hard work and perseverance looks like. Many of us went into careers that allowed us, like him, to be of service to others. He was a man of honesty and integrity. He was tall, had tan skin with high cheek bones, piercing blue eyes, and broad shoulders. His hairline receded very little as he aged, and he kept his hair cut short on the sides and had what was called a butch cut on top.

GLAD TO BE A LADD

My dad, as I mentioned, was a cook in the Army for the officers' mess hall while he was stationed in Alaska. He did not cook anything fancy during the war because the available food was typically military. He could turn out some surprisingly great meals with very little to work with, which is why he was the *officers'* mess hall cook. Over the years he continued to cook delicious meals for his twelve children, who in birth order are: Marvin, 1945; Melvin, 1946; John, 1947; Harold, 1949; yours truly, Marilyn, 1950; Suzanne, 1951; Clarissa, 1953; Robert, 1954; Mike, 1955; Ralph, 1957; Raymond, 1959; and Frances, 1960—eight boys, four girls. My mother gave birth to four boys in a row, then three girls in a row, then four more boys in a row, and then our youngest sister, Frances, who was born last.

My mother was a good cook also, but it was always fun to wake up to the pleasant smells and sounds of Dad on an early Sunday morning before church stirring pancake batter in a four-quart aluminum bowl and hearing a large spoonful of batter sizzle as it hit the hot griddle that was located in the middle of our gas stove between the four outside burners. I could smell and hear the sound of bacon or sausage cooking in one of our well-used cast-iron frying pans. One by one, emerging from our beds, the twelve of us eventually ended up in the kitchen, each trying patiently to wait for our personal batch of pancakes. In a warm pan of water, dad heated the Log Cabin maple syrup that came in a large-size glass bottle or a big two-quart tin that you may remember was made to look like a log cabin. The chimney top was the lid you removed to pour the syrup. We also typically went through two half gallons of milk, a quart or two of frozen canned orange juice, a stick of butter, a half dozen eggs, and a pound of bacon or sausage links on those remarkable, memorable Sunday mornings. Those breakfasts often took an hour or two from start to finish for everyone to get their fill of pancakes and bacon. Many often returned later to see if there was anything left in hopes of getting another helping of bacon or batch of pancakes.

Over an hour's time, he probably cooked a total of forty-five or fifty big, delicious pancakes. Something he learned as a cook in the Army that made his pancakes unique in taste was to add some orange juice to his pancake batter. It made them rise more than a regular pancake and gave them a nice zesty taste. There was the strong smell of percolating coffee on the stove for my parents in our old aluminum coffee pot. My poor mom, tired from her weeklong family and household workload, would usually join us once she was fully awakened by the noise of several sets of feet running outside her bedroom door through the house and down the hallway on our way to or from the kitchen, enjoying our hearty Sunday morning breakfast.

On rainy days, when he wasn't installing lawn sprinklers, and who wants to buy lawn sprinklers when it is raining, we often came home from school to find him cooking long, thick noodles on the griddle. He boiled the noodles in a pan first and then fried them in butter on the griddle. It doesn't sound really appetizing but they sure tasted good to me. He also made us the best grilled cheese sandwiches, which we thoroughly enjoyed on those cold rainy afternoons after a long day at school.

When one of us got sick, we all got sick. I remember when I was nine I got the chicken pox and stayed home with three of my brothers and a sister who also had chicken pox. I remember on one of the rainy days we all stayed home from school, and mom wanted us to put calamine lotion on our red itchy areas affected by the chicken pox. Since dad was home, he put the lotion on us. I remember waiting in a line with one brother and one sister ahead of me. When it was my turn, he dabbed on the lotion with a cotton ball that soothed the itching and afforded me a rare bonding moment spent with my dad.

Dad always loved to go camping and prospecting for unusual rocks or gems. He took my four older brothers on numerous camping trips near the desert communities of Lancaster, Palmdale, and the Mojave Desert, located in southeastern California and southern Nevada, where he could teach them about prospecting. He kept a rather extensive rock and gem collection along with a fluorescent light on the shelves in what we called "the front kitchen." It was the original kitchen that was too small to be of any functional use to fourteen people. Another, much larger kitchen that we called "the back kitchen" had been added on to the back of the house before we moved in. We had a much needed second refrigerator in the front kitchen, and my dad put in a gas dryer in that front kitchen where the gas stove used to be.

When he shined his fluorescent light on rocks containing certain minerals or crystals, to our delight they would glow different iridescent colors. He knew all the different types of rocks and gems he had collected, and we were always thrilled when a rare occasion presented itself, like relatives visiting, where we could all run up to the kitchen, turn off the light, and ooh and aah at the shimmering, shiny rocks and listen to the stories behind his finds.

On those treasured occasions, when he was willing to show us his prized collection, we were always mesmerized all over again each time by what we saw, even if we had seen them many times before. We looked over his shoulder, sat on the counter around him, and the younger ones stood in front of him on their tiptoes with their fingers clinging onto the edge of the kitchen counter, with their eyes fixed just above the tiled counter edge. No one was to get into or touch his precious treasured exhibits but him. He was very proud of what he had accumulated, but I am not sure where or who has his collection now.

Between 1959 and 1961 my dad took my four older brothers to a couple of Dodger games when the Dodgers were playing at the Los Angeles Coliseum after they left Brooklyn and before Dodger Stadium was built. I was about nine or ten then and wished he would take me with them to a game. My parents acted like it was no place for a little girl. They had SRO (standing room only) sections at the Coliseum, which is where my dad and brothers stood during one of the games they attended. He paid a dollar a piece for the tickets.

In 1962, when I was twelve, I was finally able to talk my dad into taking me to a Dodger game with my four older brothers. That first year the Dodgers played at their new stadium in Chavez Ravine was 1962. We sat well above home plate near the first base bag, and as young as I was, I remember being impressed with how fast the Dodger pitcher was pitching, and that he was left-handed. It was several years later that I realized that it was Sandy Koufax and how privileged I felt that I had gotten to see one of the greatest baseball pitchers of all time when I was just twelve; at my very first-ever Dodger game.

My dad took us to the beach a few times, and I vividly

remember him wearing these faded blue swimming trunks that looked like and fit him like a pair of underwear. I think they were the first, last, and only pair of swim trunks he had ever owned. He waded into shallow water with us and had a sibling swinging from each arm, screaming with delight as the small waves crashed underneath them. I treasured every moment of my times spent with my dad, even though those times were few and far between. I am sure he cherished those rare moments with us also and wished he could have spent more time with us as well.

Dad said that at age fourteen he started smoking unfiltered cigarettes with his brother Roger and continued to smoke daily over the next forty-three years. He quit at age fifty-seven after learning he had, and started receiving treatment for, throat cancer. He never smoked on the job or during dinner, but he did chain-smoke on the weekends when he wasn't working and during the work week from the time dinner was over until he went to bed. He probably smoked close to a pack a day and more on weekend days. On many occasions, I remember walking through the kitchen at night on my way to the bathroom from the den where we watched TV and where he drew his sprinkler plans for customers and listened from late spring through late summer to the Dodger games on the radio, which was located on the kitchen counter next to the bread box. Each evening, he smoked an endless number of Tareyton or Viceroy cigarettes and usually drank a six-pack of the tall cans of Lucky Lager beer.

He bought his six-pack at the Better Foods store or from the liquor store just a few blocks away on Tweedy Boulevard and McNerney Avenue. He brought home his beer and began drinking it usually after, but sometimes before, dinner. As you walked in the back door, the kitchen was located to your left, our refrigerator was located directly in front of you just inside the den, just outside and to the right of the kitchen. It was placed in the den because there was no room for it in the kitchen and it wasn't convenient to run up to the front kitchen several times a day to bring refrigerated items back. Besides, the refrigerator hid the double bed located behind it in the den. The bed had no headboard or sideboards; it was just the frame and the mattress.

I mention the refrigerator only because I clearly remember,

even before entering the kitchen after working all day, Dad placing his beer in the refrigerator first thing after coming through the back door. The door of the fridge opened from left to right, away from the kitchen, and dad did not like any of us keeping the door open any longer than necessary, which he constantly complained would allow a lot of valuable cold air to escape. So to lead by example, he hooked the inside of his right knee on the outside of the door so it would not open any further than necessary, which allowed only a minimum amount of cold air to escape as he placed his six-pack onto a shelf.

My dad had throat cancer surgery in 1976. He stopped smoking cold turkey only to start drinking more alcohol. It became obvious to me at that time that he did, as did some of his siblings, possess addictive behavior. He usually just drank beer, but after the surgery I noticed he was often drinking a mix of whiskey and a grapefruit-lemony-tasting soda called Squirt, maybe because the sweeter taste of the Squirt was soothing to his irritated throat. In those days, doctors did not caution against drinking alcohol after sensitive throat cancer surgery and radiation. In my dad's case, the alcohol irritated the still raw and healing surgery site in his throat. It might also have been that his doctors did not say anything to my dad about drinking after his extensive throat surgery because maybe they did not know he drank or assumed he wouldn't or didn't.

Recently, one of my older brothers also had throat cancer from smoking and was told not to drink any alcohol after his surgery because they knew it was risky to the rest of the body to do so. That brother did live a lot longer after surgery by not drinking.

My dad almost lost his voice after the throat cancer surgery and the follow-up radiation treatments. The surgery left him with a slightly raspy voice, but we were able to understand him. Because of his increased drinking, within a year he developed cancer in the nearby lymph nodes in his neck, near the surgery site, that quickly spread to his lungs and brain. My dad was always so healthy that even he could not believe that he was terminally ill. This was difficult for me to have witnessed. I remember the last time I saw him in the hospital, weeks away from death. I watched him as he was trying to scoot down and out the bottom of his hospital bed. He indicated that he was anxious to go home because all he wanted to do was get back to work.

He did unfortunately succumb to the cancer on February 23, 1977, just a few weeks shy of his sixtieth birthday. If it weren't for his smoking and drinking, I truly believe that my dad would have lived well into his nineties. It was difficult to lose a hard-working, driven man like my dad at such a young age. He had many good productive years ahead of him yet to live.

After he passed away, an autopsy was performed to determine if the original throat cancer surgery was successful or if it was not completely removed and contributed to the spread of the cancer he later developed that eventually ended his life. The autopsy report found that the original throat cancer treatment was successful in removing all the initial cancer. The report suggested that it was his increased drinking after the surgery that irritated the throat before it could heal and led to cancer developing in the local lymph nodes in his neck and then spreading eventually throughout his body.

At that last hospital visit, I saw my dad in denial about the seriousness of his condition. He was hopelessly looking beyond his illness and just wanted to get his life back to normal and do what he had been doing nearly all his life: selflessly providing for others. I am very grateful to my dad for all he did for me and my family. My mother was devastated by his early death and had difficulty adjusting to life without him. On one occasion when my mother and my sister Sue and I visited him in the hospital, Sue and I started putting lotion on his dry hands and arms. I remembered at that moment how soothing and comforting it felt when Dad was putting that calamine lotion on me when I had the chicken pox those many years earlier, and hoped my dad was feeling the same comfort as he went in and out of consciousness during our visit. Shortly after we started, he did awake briefly, lifted his head up to see who it was, smiled at each of us, and then lay back down. I was happy that he was able to acknowledge our presence, and I would like to think that he enjoyed the pampering, as that was the last time I saw him alive.

He is buried at All Souls Cemetery in Long Beach, California. My dad, rest his soul, had more inner and outer strength than that of three men. He spent most of his years working ten- to twelve-hour days, sometimes seven days a week, to keep enough food on the table and clothes on our backs and the ability for all of us to attend Catholic school. I don't remember him missing a day of work and I never saw him sick or ill, but for a few colds, until he was diagnosed with cancer in early 1976.

My dad was placed in a position of responsibility at an early age. At sixteen, when his dad was killed, he replaced his dad as the head of the family. He had a lot of say, and people did what he told them to do. His older brother Roger was the rogue son who did not want the responsibility of taking care of his mother and siblings. Often, Dad did not have time for himself; he was busy doing and making things happen for his family and others. It would make sense that he, as the early breadwinner and provider for his family, would be attracted to and later marry the "babe" of her family, my mother, a person who was used to getting attention and being pampered and looked after. He ended up the breadwinner and provider for his family of fourteen, where he always did his level best to be the best husband and dad he could possibly be.

As our family grew larger, my dad understandably became somewhat removed as a parent because he worked so much. I noticed in my mid-teens, about 1965, that he began to become more occupied and engaged each night with his drinking. Many nights, after a long day's work, he often quietly drank himself to sleep and interacted very little with the rest of us. Throughout the years, when he came home from work, he did constantly complain about the condition of the house or was unhappy with the way my mother cooked or took care of us, or why wasn't the trash taken out yet, or the dishes washed and put away. For the first several years my mother would argue back. She indicated that she was doing her best but that it was difficult for her to keep the house clean and keep up with the antics of twelve very active, growing, needy young children and all that goes with raising them.

Eventually, in the mid-to-late 1960s, my mother stopped arguing back when my dad came home and started complaining. It was only then that since my dad was not getting the response he normally received from my mother, he apparently realized it and, given that his complaining was not changing anything anyway, stopped. I believe he thought since he was so highly productive and competent on a daily basis, my mother should be able to do the same. I don't think he realized that as the baby of her family, she probably did not have a lot of responsibility at a young age, and nothing close to the responsibilities he shouldered as a youth, and therefore was not as accomplished as my dad at getting things done as effectively and efficiently as he did.

My dad came home from an eight- to ten-hour work day, and after buying groceries on the way home or after dinner, often took out the trash because he insisted my brothers couldn't do it or didn't do it right, according to him. Unlike my mom, he did not always hold us accountable for our actions. He did not follow through on punishment or reprimand that we deserved. Instead he did the work for us and then complained the entire time he was doing our work or chores. Some of it was that he did not hold us capable; if it was going to get done right, he was going to have to do it because no one else could. He could be impatient and quick-tempered at times—behaviors I would guess he learned during his childhood. I believe he was made to feel that he was never good enough and spent the rest of his life proving he was. I feel that he stayed so busy all the time so he didn't have to feel. He kept his emotions to himself as if it was not OK for him to be openly sensitive or vulnerable, that he would be considered less of a man if he did. Later in my life I discovered that I also stay busy to avoid feeling. Over the years I did end up developing some of his negative traits that later on affected my personal and professional adult relationships.

It was about 1966 that I noticed an added increase in his nightly after-work and weekend drinking. His drinking seemed to become an easy escape and a regular routine from the long work week and household challenges. It was also an inherent family addiction. Fortunately, my dad was not an ugly alcoholic. He did not get into arguments or physical confrontations as he drank and, to my knowledge, never drank and drove. His drinking was excessive but always under control as I never saw him stumble or fall while drinking. Nonetheless, I considered him am alcoholic.

I understood how difficult it would be for my dad, as a former Army cook, to come home to a messy house and yard and what he considered a less than adequate meal. My dad set high standards for himself and expected others to do the same. Because of his family dynamics, all my dad knew to do, in childhood and as an adult, was to physically provide for his family day in and day out, and he did so successfully with earnest and dogged determination. He took his job as father, husband, and provider very seriously. What he had difficulty understanding was that it was impossible for my mom to keep a house of fourteen clean with all daily household chores completed in the time and manner that he expected. No matter how often the house was cleaned and chores completed, it would be dirty and cluttered again within hours.

We, and especially my mother, loved and cherished him dearly and appreciated and respected him for the wonderful man and provider he was, despite some of his shortcomings. He was an extremely honest man who taught us that our purpose on this earth is to leave the world a little better place for the next person. I miss him still.

Ellen Regina (Gill) Ladd

Ellen Regina "Babe" (Gill) Ladd, born August 4, 1919, at St. John's Hospital, Oxnard, California. In 1942 at Oxnard Beach, age 23.

Mom was called "Babe" because she was the baby of her family, the last of seven children born to Gregory and Margaret Gill, who were among the first founding families and farmers of Oxnard, California. Her father was born in County Longford, Ireland, in 1874, and her mother was born in San Francisco in 1872. Her family name was Gilligan, and they originally came from County Roscommon, Ireland. Her father came to the United States in 1887 at the age of fourteen and initially stayed for a short time with his relatives, the McGraths, for whom McGrath State Beach in Ventura is named.

Her parents first settled in the La Colonia district of Ventura County, on Lewis Road, after marrying in 1904. After they married, they bought and moved, in 1908, to the eighty-two-acre ranch on Laguna Road in Oxnard, located near the current Highway 1 that runs north and south near the coast through Port Hueneme and eventually merges with Highway 101 in Oxnard. The city of Oxnard is located within Ventura County.

The first-born sister, Martha, tragically died at eight months old. Martha was just learning to walk when she reached up and pulled a boiling pot of water off the stove on top of herself and scalded herself so badly that she died soon after from her burns. My grandparents did go on to have six more children. I understand that my grandmother was never the same after the accident that killed her firstborn. My grandmother died in 1949, a year before I was born, so I never got to know her.

The farm where my mother was raised was originally part of the Rancho El Rio de Santa Clara o la Colonia Mexican land grant in present day Ventura County. The land grant was given in 1837 by Governor Juan B. Alvarado to Valentine Cota and seven former Presidio of Santa Barbara soldiers. The grant extended from the Santa Clara River south to the present-day Point Mugu Naval Air Station, and east from the Pacific Ocean to the present-day Highway 101. La Colonia comprises the current cities of Oxnard and Camarillo (Wikipedia).

Before the arrival of Europeans, the area was inhabited by the Chumash Indians. The first European to encounter the area was Portuguese explorer Juan Rodríguez Cabrillo, who claimed it for Spain in 1782. The area was settled in the 1850s by American farmers who cultivated barley and lima beans.

Mom grew up on the ranch, which they purchased in 1910, with her four brothers and a sister. The first crop they grew on the ranch was tomatoes. After my grandfather had a stroke in 1943, they moved into the city of Ventura. My Uncle Harold took over the ranch and began growing lima beans. Several years after Uncle Harold passed away in 1964, another uncle, Lewis, who was considered one of the best citrus growers in Ventura County, began growing lemons on the ranch. The ranch currently grows lemons and avocados. After over three generations and more than a hundred years later, the ranch is still farmed by members of the Gill family.

All six of the Gill children attended Springville School between 1912 and 1931. Springville was a thriving rural community founded before Camarillo or Oxnard became cities. It was a challenging two-and-a-half-mile walk to school. They gathered classmates as they went and eventually came across the all-important sugar beet dump before reaching school. Sugar beets were the main crop grown in Ventura County at the time.

The city just south of Oxnard was Camarillo, named after Adolfo Camarillo, who founded the city. The Camarillo family had an injured parade horse that was no longer considered for show. They gave the horse to my Aunt Margaret, and she rode it to Springville School for three years. The school had horse stables where my aunt fed and watered her horse at recess. The school consisted of one classroom and one teacher for all eight grades.

One story Mom told me was, when walking to school alone one day, she encountered a stubborn, menacing bull. After several frightening moments in which the bull would not move, a young man came racing up in his car and shooed the bull away. She later learned that it was Robert "Bob" Oxnard, one of the four Oxnard brothers after whom the city was named in 1903. Thomas Oxnard, their father, was a French-born sugar magnate. In 1860, the Oxnard brothers moved out west and started a beet factory in Chino, California.

Henry T. Oxnard, another of the four brothers, became interested in Ventura County when he learned that locally grown beets could yield better than average sugar content. He built a sugar beet factory in an industrial area next to what is now called the Five Points intersection in Oxnard, the same area mom and her siblings and friends passed on their way to school. In 1899, the American Sugar Beet Factory opened and became one of the largest sugar producers in the country. The factory became the nucleus of what eventually became the city of Oxnard.

Mom graduated from Oxnard Union High School in 1935. She attended one of the last reunions of that class, their sixtieth, in 1995 with four other surviving students. She graduated from Ventura College in 1937, and soon after began working for Winemans Department Store in Oxnard as an office clerk.

She also worked from 1940 to 1944 at Camarillo State Hospital as a typist. It was a hospital for the mentally ill that today is a satellite campus of California State University, Channel Islands. After marrying my dad and moving to South Gate, and after having twelve children, she brushed up on her secretarial skills again at Los Angeles Trade Technical Community College. She began working at Locke High School in Watts, from 1967 to 1969, as a stenographer. She was a stenographer at South Gate Intermediate School from 1969 to 1979. Several of my younger brothers and sisters attended South Gate Intermediate School while my mother was the secretary there for the Dean of Students.

A few years after my dad passed away in 1977 my mother moved about 120 miles north of South Gate to Lompoc, California, where she worked for the Santa Barbara County Air Pollution District as a clerk from 1980 to 1982. The city is located a few miles from the Pacific Ocean. In 1983, she worked as a secretary at Lompoc Middle School until her retirement in 1986. After retiring she was able to travel to several places throughout the world before settling into a lovely home in Vandenberg Village, just north of Lompoc. In 1992, at the age of seventy-three, she was given a certificate from Meals on Wheels for picking up and delivering meals to shut-ins and the elderly of Lompoc.

In 1992 she became a senior volunteer at the Catholic Charities Thrift Shop in Lompoc and volunteered for the Democratic Party in Lompoc that same year. I remember going door-to-door with her collecting for the American Heart Association when I was younger. She instilled in us the importance of volunteering and giving back to our communities. She was also an OR—original recycler. She began recycling glass and aluminum in the mid-1960s before it became commonplace. Wherever she lived in Santa Barbara County she always had a compost pile surrounded by chicken wire in which she dumped yard waste and house garbage to be used eventually as fertilizer for her many lovely gardens. To volunteer, to recycle, and to be environmentally conscious and friendly was instilled in us all early on and continues today.

Lompoc was inhabited by the Chumash Indians, who lived off the sea and the land. *Lompoc* is Chumash for "lagoon" or "little lake." The translation suggests the lakes and lagoons that resulted from spring flooding. Their first white contact was in 1542 with explorer Juan Cabrillo. In 1787, Mission de la Purísima Concepción was founded as one of California's twenty-one missions.

By 1837, the Lompoc area was divided into five ranchos. The town was originally called Temperance Colony by a lawyer from Santa Cruz who established the town as a place where he could raise his children in a peaceful atmosphere, where no liquor could be made, consumed, or sold. Today Lompoc is considered the Flower Seed Capital of the World, in which it grows five hundred varieties of flowers for seed for the world. Its rich soil, cool ocean breezes, and long summers allow flowers to grow exceptionally well. The sweet pea is the city flower. The population today is about 45,000 people. It is a perfect, lovely city for a perfect lovely person like our mother to have lived.

After living in a condominium for the first several years in Lompoc, my mother moved into another lovely condominium that had two bedrooms and two baths in the neighboring city of Vandenberg Village, located on the far edge of one of the greens of the Vandenberg Village Golf Course. It was after we had all graduated and moved away from home and the recession of the mid-1980s occurred that the ranch property my mother's family owned began to generate a lot of income from the newly planted acres of lemons. The Japanese are the biggest importers of lemons and were buying lots of them from the West Coast at the time. That income during the recession allowed Mom to buy several homes and travel extensively. Too bad the ranch didn't make that kind of money when we were growing up!

In 1992 she moved for the last time about a half mile south into a large, beautiful four-bedroom, three-bath hillside house on the golf course, facing east, overlooking one of the fairways and the course waterfowl and goldfish pond. Vandenberg Village is located within Lompoc Valley, at the downstream end of the Santa Inez River Basin, in Santa Barbara County. Much of its approximately 6,500 inhabitants are current or former Air Force military from nearby Vandenberg Air Force Base. Vandenberg Village is a lovely, quiet city with lots of flat plateaus, surrounding hills, and moderate weather. It was a perfect place for my mother to have lived out her life. She loved that home. The neighborhood was quiet and safe, until we all showed up for a visit!

Vandenberg Air Force Base is located on the central coast of California, about 160 miles northwest of Los Angeles and just north of Vandenberg Village, where my mother lived. It is the only installation in the United States from which unmanned government and commercial satellites are launched into polar orbit. Its coastal location allows missiles to be launched into the Pacific Ocean without population overflights. It was in December 1958 that Vandenberg successfully launched its first missile. Part of the reason my mother bought a house in Vandenberg was because of how safe it was, and so many of the residents were older retired Air Force personnel from the base who made great golf partners and fellow canasta players.

Since I was a teacher, I had summers off and I spent several days staying at her place and visiting her and a few family members living in the area. The wonderful times spent with her those summers and holidays were pleasantly reminiscent of the time we spent together in South Gate. We shopped at the many small local antique stores in the surrounding communities and would eat lunch at one of the lovely little nearby cafés or restaurants. We often went for lovely walks around the golf course after dinner.

She and I absolutely loved watching the Miss Universe pageant together. A few times the pageant was on TV while I was visiting her. We lay together in her bed, each with our own homemade judge's sheet, and picked who we thought would advance to the finals. It never mattered to me who won; what mattered was spending that precious time alone with the person I loved most in this world.

Mom was an avid UCLA fan, especially during football season. She loved watching their games on TV, getting excited at those game-changing plays, jumping up and down at a fumble or a last-minute touchdown. It was fun being in the same room with her while she was watching those games, as her enthusiasm and vivacity were infectious. She was nearly as avid a basketball fan as she was a football enthusiast. She admired and respected John Wooden and loved how cool and calm he always remained despite the nail-biting, nerve-racking game situations. I liked that Mom gave herself permission and the precious time to thoroughly enjoy and immerse herself in UCLA sports each season, especially since my brother, Harold, graduated from UCLA.

She loved the Lompoc and Vandenberg Village area. She picked a perfect place to move to get away from those constant nostalgic reminders of the many years spent in South Gate married to our dad. Within ten years after she moved north, she was pleased when two of my brothers and three sisters moved to cities near her. I have so many pleasant memories of times spent with my mother in her lovely home and condominiums in Lompoc and Vandenberg Village. She hosted many a Thanksgiving and holiday get-together as well as several of her own birthday celebrations.

She had this long-established habit of going around her two-story house at dusk closing the blinds before going to bed. She repeated the process each morning before making her breakfast. She appeared to fully enjoy her self-imposed task. It was for her like the final closure of each day, and the embracing of the next as she happily went from window to window opening or closing each in her slow and methodic way. She performed this task she loved so much until she was no longer able to get up and down the stairs easily. She suffered from osteoporosis and her bones were becoming thin and brittle.

Shortly after turning ninety in 2009, it was while she was in the middle of her window-closing routine one night that my youngest sister, who was her caretaker in her later years, called to my mother to ask her something. In her fragile state at the time, she turned her upper body quickly to face my sister and ended up falling to the floor, breaking her hip. As my mother would have it, she was in such pain that she did not want to be moved right away. She spent several hours on the floor in as comfortable a position as my sister could get her. She finally consented to go to the hospital and received treatment the next morning for her broken hip. She recovered from the incident, but her gait and mobility became further limited. Soon after the fall she began to use a walker to get around and had to stop driving.

She showed a tremendous amount of pain tolerance during her broken hip incident and throughout other incidents in her lifetime. One time she took a broom to try to break up a fight between two of my older teenage brothers. Just as she got between them, one of my brothers accidentally hit the broom, knocking it out of my mother's hand but breaking her baby finger on her left hand in the process. She found out it was broken when it was put into a cast two days later only because it kept causing her pain. Of course, my brothers felt bad and begged for her forgiveness, but the damage had been done. She recovered fully from the incident but never tried intervening in a fight between her sons again, and they never fought like that again.

There was another instance where she was learning self-defense at about age sixty and interlaced her fingers improperly. Instead of keeping her fingers wrapped around the outside of her palms to hit an assailant, she was practicing with her fingers interlaced. She ends up hitting herself on her own knee when she was practicing and hit herself so hard that she fractured the outside of her left hand. She did not appear to be in any pain and did not know it was even fractured for a few days. I guess if she could survive twelve full-term pregnancies, three miscarriages, and a hysterectomy, she could easily survive the pain of a broken hand.

In her early forties, she suffered for several agonizing months from vaginal bleeding caused by uterine tissue that was slightly torn from all her pregnancies and miscarriages. At the time, our family doctor, Dr. Carmody, did not want her to have a hysterectomy, but did try to control the bleeding with birth control pills. In the early 1960s, birth control pills were just being made available to women. She continued to bleed to a dangerous level and finally consented to a hysterectomy. I don't believe it was Dr. Carmody who wanted to delay the surgery. I believe it was my parents, who did not have family insurance and could not afford the procedure. She was such a physically and mentally strong woman. She developed such a tremendous capacity to endure pain that, in this case, almost killed her.

Days before her hysterectomy I remember my mom lying on a cot we brought just outside the back door for her to lie on so she could be in the sun and rest. She had been in bed for several days before that, slowly bleeding the entire time, hoping it would stop. As I walked out the backdoor and stood over her, I was taken aback at how jaundiced she was and what little energy she had. She was lying on her right side in a fetal position with her hands together in a praying position under the right side of her head. As I was looking down at her, she looked up at me with this meek half smile before putting her head back down. It was a few days later, and not a day too soon, that she finally had her much needed life-saving hysterectomy. It was terrific to see her recovered several weeks later and back to her fun, energetic self again.

My mother was a good athlete and an avid sports fan. While living on the Vandenberg Golf Course, at about the age of eighty, she learned to play golf and bought a club membership. I am not sure why, but the club pro had her buy right-handed clubs and had her play right-handed when she was a lefty in everything she did. She played pretty well for her age.

My last vivid precious memory and moment I had with my mother was while I was up visiting her a year or so before she became too frail to golf. She and I decided one late afternoon, in about 2007, when she was eighty-eight, to each grab a couple of irons and a putter from her closet and walk down to the course from her house onto a nearby fairway. As we had done in the past, she and I each whacked a ball around and played the four holes that were closest to her house. We just had to golf late enough in the day and make sure no other golfers were on the course. I hit the ball ahead of her and was walking toward where my ball was lying, and I looked back at her, where she was clearly visible, about seventy-five yards slightly downhill from me, squarely in the middle of the fairway. She had her back to me and seemed to be frozen in time, leaning on her club with both hands clasped over the top of her club, looking up toward the sky and the trees immediately in front of her. She appeared to be taking in and thoroughly enjoying this rare reflective moment. It looked like she was allowing herself to acknowledge and absorb all that was before her; to thoroughly relish all that she had achieved, created, and amassed in her life, including her beautiful home just yards away, knowing what it had taken for her to get to this moment in time in her life.

The weather at that moment was perfect, with a bright blue sky and a few light clouds and the beginnings of the sun setting over the local mountains to our left. There was a slight breeze blowing through the large trees along each side of the fairway and several birds and fowl were chirping and carrying on in the small course pond just to her right. She remained in that spot for several seconds, then turned and walked several steps toward me with her head down, still deep in thought, before she finally raised her head and brought herself back to the golf course, where I was eagerly waiting for her to hit her next ball. I will never forget that moment as long as I live. It was such a well-deserved retrospective moment for her, and an unforgettable intimate moment with her for me.

She remained active to the end of her years. She often endured hiking with us while on vacation in her younger years, up into the steep hills above Soledad Canyon Campground, and walked barefoot downstream with nine of us to a swimming hole near the campground. Even with a walker, at ninety-one, she insisted on walking around the Vandenberg Village neighborhood and getting out of the house, even if it meant just taking a few steps.

Christmases spent at Mom's were memorable and festive. Even with four bedrooms, several of us had to stay in local hotels. If everyone from the immediate family showed, it meant having about twenty-five of us spending the day at her house. Speaking of presents, as it had while we lived in South Gate, it usually took us about three to four hours from start to finish to open the 175 to 200-plus presents we brought. The challenge was to find enough room and chairs for everyone to sit while opening presents and to later eat. Sometimes some of us had to stand for a while until several of the presents had been given out before having enough room to bring a chair into the living room and sit with everyone else. It was just as challenging to find enough places in the house to sleep. We were used to both challenges growing up.

About twenty of us often went walking after Christmas dinner into the local Lompoc neighborhood. We walked a lovely easy little one-mile loop hike locally, usually around sunset, to a place called Muffin Mountain. It was an easy hike that everyone, including my mother, could climb. Muffin Mountain was about two hundred feet high with partially sandy soil and about a 20-degree angle to climb. At the top, it was fairly flat and had a 360-degree view of the Lompoc Valley with all its beautiful flowers, farmland, and ocean views, not to mention fantastic sunsets. It was a great way to end a wonderful family holiday together. We followed that walk back to her house, where we ended the day taking family photos on her front lawn.

In early May of 2011, at the age of ninety-one, she suffered a slight stroke at home and was taken to a local hospital. At the time, she was beginning to develop bouts of dementia and could be very lucid one minute and confused and disoriented the next. I am sure the dementia was partially a result of old age, and the vessels in the brain becoming occluded or blocked. Because of her dementia, a few times she tried to get out of her hospital bed unattended without realizing how dangerous that was for her to do. An alarm to notify the nurses would go off if she did leave her bed, and they would guide her back to her room. The staff also knew that she was a fall risk.

Because of the mild stroke she had, her words were slurred and difficult to understand, but after putting her on blood thinners, she was speaking more clearly and was on the road to recovery with what appeared to be little permanent damage. The alarm was turned off when she was taken to physical therapy, but when she returned from therapy, the alarm was not turned on again. Later, when no one was around, in her dementia she got out of bed and ended up falling back on her head, suffering a severe fatal injury. She immediately went into a coma and never woke up again. She was declared brain-dead. Because she was on blood thinners, she bled into her brain after the fall, which ultimately eventually caused her death. We were all devastated because she and all of us knew she was on the road to recovery.

The entire immediate family from all over California happened to be in Lompoc attending a memorial for my sister Suzanne's husband, Gill, who had passed away from cancer a few months earlier. We had just finished his memorial when we got a call from the hospital, a few miles away, letting us know what had happened and to get over there to say our good-byes. They did not expect her to survive the night. We did all rush over to see her for what we thought would be for the last time. She did survive the night, and since they could no longer do anything for her, they sent her home the next day to die at home under hospice care.

All we could do was make her last days at home as comfortable as possible. We all knew how much she meant to us and how much she sacrificed for each of us throughout our lives. Throughout her life, anytime any of us were around her, we fell all over ourselves to wait on her hand and foot to make her comfortable and content; as we did to the end.

Unfortunately, since she was brain-dead with no hope for recovery, we were not able to feed her or give her any liquids through an IV. Everyone who could stay and help did. Those who needed to go home did but came back to continue to help as soon as they could. Several of us took three hour shifts 24-7, moving and turning her often to prevent bed sores, changing her adult diaper and combing her hair and holding her hand and talking to her, even though we knew she could not hear or understand us.

The hospice caregivers were wonderful. They were very understanding and kind to our mother in her final days and hours. Unbelievably, she lived eleven more days without food and water before she died on May 23, 2011. It was very difficult to watch her slowly die over those eleven days, knowing there was nothing we could do for her, and never got to say a conscious good-bye, and further to know that her demise was caused by the hospital's negligence. I knew she was an extremely enduring and endearing person, never complaining much about anything, ever, so I was not surprised that she was able to endure living nearly two weeks without food and water before passing away at ninety-one.

Sitting with her in the middle of the night on about the seventh day of her death journey, during one of my three-hour shifts, was both frightening and deeply personal as I worried much of that time without answers about what she was going through physically, and maybe what she might be going through mentally. I reflected back through the years about the many, many good times she and I experienced together and how much I had wished I had told her what a positive influence she had been on me all these years. I told her that night how much I loved and admired her and how grateful and blessed I was to have had such a close, harmonious relationship with her. I told her she was the single most influential person in my life and that I hope I can live up to a fraction of the upstanding, kind, and generous person she was. I am sure she heard every word.

There were about seven of us in the house on May 23, the night she passed. My sister was on her three-hour shift from 9 p.m. to midnight. It was at about 10:45 p.m. that she woke me in the guest room where I was sleeping and said she felt the end was near for my mom, as her breathing had become more labored. She woke up the others in the house and we all gathered around her bed. I was standing to the right of my mother, nearest her head, and my sister was to my right, then it was my sister-in-law Janice next to her and her husband, my brother John, at the end of the bed. My brother Harry was across from me on my mother's left.

Her labored breathing continued. It was shortly after 11 p.m. when my mother suddenly sat bolt upright in her bed. Her head turned slightly to her right, she took one last gasping breath, then fell dead, back against her pillow. She was looking directly at me when she took that last breath! I will never forget the look on her face. Her eyes were wide open, her head and chin were rigid and tilted slightly downward. I could not tell if the look on her face was fright or something else. All I know is that, of all the people surrounding her bed that night, she looked directly at me while taking her last breath. That was the first and I hope the last time I ever experience a loved one take their last breath.

My brother John, the one standing at the end of my mother's bed when she passed, said just as she passed he felt a strong presence and a gentle wind go by his face and upper body. He said it gave him the chills and believed it was my mother's spirit leaving her body. I believe it too. It was so hard to believe that she would die this way. She probably only had a few good years left, but it was still difficult to accept how others' negligence led to her early death.

Since it was nearly midnight, the funeral home said they would pick her body up early in the morning. We closed her bedroom door and got a little bit of sleep, woke up early the next morning, and watched her body being loaded into the hearse and taken to the funeral home in town. Given how close I was to my mom through the years, I thought I would be more devastated by her passing, but surprisingly, and without explanation, I initially accepted her death rather easily. Maybe it's because we had such a loving, fulfilling relationship together that it made it easier for me to let her go. In some ways, I feel she has never left me, which may explain why I have not grieved her passing that much. I did seek grief counseling a few months later at a hospital near where I live that helped me understand my feelings and allowed me to grieve in my own way.

I continue to constantly feel a close, personal presence of my mother to this day that is of great comfort to me. I feel my life is still being guided by her. Even as I write this book I feel her peaceful presence. When I am searching for just the right word or words to enhance my writing, I feel she helps me find them. The words seem to come to me out of nowhere. I especially feel her presence during those moments when I am feeling the most calm and serene. I sense that she is there supporting me in creating that serenity. I am so blessed.

I believe my mom is now represented on earth as a dove. Like her, a dove is considered a quiet, peaceful bird with strong maternal instincts. Its quiet, pleasant cooing voice can carry far, especially at dusk or dawn, which is when I hear her soothing cooing the most. It was the next Thanksgiving, about six months after her passing, that I had a family gathering at my house out on my backyard patio. I have a telephone pole located smack in the middle of the wooden fence in my backyard. For most of the afternoon there was a dove that sat on a wire just to the right of the telephone pole. It rarely left its perch the entire time everyone was there. We all noticed and began to talk to the bird as if it were our mother. Since then, similar dove appearances have happened on a few other occasions when family has been present.

Each subsequent year since, I have had four different sets of dove families hatch their babies in as many months each spring in a nest they share that sits on a support bar under a protective aluminum awning just outside the sliding glass door of my back bedroom. I feel close to those doves, as I believe they represent my mother's presence and her nurturing nature and prolific output! Each day I get to hear their soft, gentle dove cries that remind me of the soft and gentle voice of my mother. My mom normally spoke just above a whisper and rarely raised her voice, just like my new precious dove tenants.

The one and only time I ever heard my mom raise her voice and swear in the same sentence was when I was about five years old. I remember that I was upset and went to look for her to complain. I found her in the washroom, where I could see that the washing machine was overflowing, and soapy water was beginning to run out onto the floor. She had one of my sisters on her left hip, and a younger brother was crying and tugging on her dress for attention. She was also pregnant at the time. Just as I started to whine and complain about being hungry, she suddenly turned and looked at me, making a fist with her right hand and raising it up. In what was her loud voice she said—"Oh, damn!" And that was the extent of her anger at that moment. And even at that, as close as I was to her, her so-called rant was still not that loud. It was at that moment, at five years old, that I realized it would always take a lot for my mother to get angry, and when she did, it would be short-lived but direct and warranted.

As the years passed and I looked back on that memorable scene, I realized that, given all the unsurmountable challenges she faced at that time as a young developing-experience mother of, at that time, eight children, she had every right to cuss and raise her voice. She commanded and received respect and obedience from us all with that rather soft, quiet voice. When we got rambunctious and on the brink of either hurting someone or breaking something, she would yell out to us, "You kids stop that!" It usually took about five of those "You kids stop that" before we actually did. Either that, or we only stopped after someone did get hurt or something did get broken.

After her funeral, the family discussed whether or not to sue the hospital for negligence, especially because they admitted wrongdoing by not putting the fall risk alarm back on when she came back from physical therapy. We explored several options and a possible course of action and decided that our mother would not have wanted to sue but would have wanted to make sure that the same thing that happened to her did not happen to anyone else. That was our mother, and we all agreed to not sue. A few months later, several of us arranged a meeting with the hospital administrators and laid down what we would like to see happen in the future. They agreed and said they had already put a lot of our requests in place after the incident and assured us nothing like what had happened to our mother would ever happen again to anyone else. To my knowledge, it has not.

I am glad to say that one of my younger sisters and her husband bought my mom's house on the golf course when it was offered to us to buy. They have done a lot of lovely refurbishing of the roof, windows, lights, walls, etc., and it is a joy to continue to visit the home where so many wonderful cherished family memories were made.

I look back at when it was that I first developed a close bonding relationship with my mother. I remember when I was in fourth grade, my mom had just given birth to my youngest sister and the last born of the family. My teacher, Mrs. McKintigh, after hearing of our latest birth, pulled me aside and said to me, "You are going to have a lot of responsibility now." I wasn't quite sure what she meant, but what she said stuck with me, and it seemed shortly after that, I did begin to step in and help mom more.

My dad was often removed as a husband and parent, especially in those years when he worked a lot and we desperately needed every penny he made. When he wasn't working, he was doing chores around the house and shopping for us. And when he wasn't working or shopping and doing chores, he removed himself further by drinking each evening. It was shortly after that last birth that I stepped in as a co-parent with my mom. I, in essence, replaced my dad. It wasn't anything I had planned; it just seemed to naturally happen. Maybe because I was the first girl in the family, I knew Mom needed help with the youngest five or six kids changing their diapers, helping them get to bed at night, and sometimes feeding and bathing them.

I was a second mom in the family for many years. There were a few times when my youngest brothers and sister called me "Mom." Quite often Mom was confined to bed because she was so rightfully tired at times and needed much deserved rest, especially after her last pregnancy, when she began to experience episodes of heavy bleeding. From the blood loss and an extremely hectic, busy life, she developed severe anemia. It was so bad that, at twelve years old, I learned to give her daily iron shots by needle in her arm to give her energy. I was not very good at giving her the shots, even though I practiced on an orange, because she often winced when I gave them to her. I felt bad, but it did help. I gave them to her for about two months. By then, we were both having a lot of continuing difficulty in me giving and her receiving the shots, so I quit. I don't think at that time that there was anything that would have helped her to gain the energy she needed to raise twelve children, who in 1962 now ranged in age from seventeen to two.

By the time I was thirteen and in eighth grade, which was the last grade you attended before graduating on to high school, at St. Emydius Catholic School, in 1963, I helped get five of my younger brothers and sisters ready for school each morning. Sometimes Mom got up early and drove two of my brothers to St. Don Bosco High School in the city of Rosemead, about a twenty-minute drive northeast of South Gate. When it rained, my dad would often drive them so my mom could sleep in or drive the rest of us to school.

On those mornings when she couldn't get out of bed or she had to drive my brothers to high school and dad was already gone from the house for the day, I typically woke up my five younger siblings, helped them get dressed, fed them breakfast, made sure they had their lunch made, and then the six of us all walked about one mile to school together, and hopefully got there somewhere near on time. When it was time for us all to be ready to leave the house and get walking, I yelled out, "Forward ho!" which was my rallying cry for "let's get going." I think it was a saying from the beginning credits of the TV show *Wagon Train*.

I remember one time when I was in eighth grade I was called down to my brother Mike's first-grade class by his teacher. She walked him over to me, handed me a comb, and told me to take him to the restroom next door and comb his hair. Obviously, I did not do a very good job combing it that day. When I put a little too much water on his head to comb his hair, I could see several small streaks of water that had run down his neck. His neck was so dirty that the only clean part of his neck you could see was where the water left clean streaks. Yikes! I had a lot to learn about hygiene at thirteen. I made sure they all had clean necks and combed hair after that incident. I never got called down to his or any of my other brothers' and sisters' classrooms after that.

There were still two more siblings under six at that time who were not in school yet and of course stayed home with my mom. My dad always left early to work, usually before 8 a.m., and my four older brothers were all in high school and did not help their siblings in the morning much because they had to get themselves to school. One brother had a car and drove himself to school and another of my four older brothers walked or rode his bike to South Gate High School or whichever school he was attending at the time. He got kicked out of several different high schools for fighting and misbehavior.

The Catholic school we attended, called St. Emydius, opened in 1950. It was then and still is one of the largest Roman Catholic parishes in the archdiocese of Los Angeles. School started, as many schools did then, at 9 a.m. and we got out at 3 p.m. It was located a little over a mile from home in the city of Lynwood, located just south of the city of South Gate. It originally had first through eighth grade classes, but in about 1962, with the baby boom and so many more children going to grade school, the school added not only another grade of each class but four more classes that were combinations of two grade levels. So there were two classes each of first through eighth grades, making sixteen classes, and then four other classes that were a first and second grade combined, a third and fourth grade combined, a fifth and sixth grade combined, and a seventh and eighth grade combined, to make twenty total classes.

There were four bungalows constructed on the south side of the playground that housed four classes. We had an annex to the school that was the old church. A big, new beautiful church was built in 1954 that was located on the north side of the playground. When school started in the fall of 1959, my fourth-grade class was one of those four bungalows that were not quite ready yet to occupy, so all four grades were taught in the annex. For about a month and a half, until the bungalows were ready, four poor nuns tried to teach in that annex without anything separating the four classes. It was loud and chaotic, but some learning did take place. The classrooms were soon ready, and my class moved into the last classroom, farthest from the rest of the school, in the far southeast corner of the playground. When I last drove by my old school, those bungalows were still there in the same location.

I started first grade at St. Emydius in the fall of 1956 at the age of six. My four older brothers were already attending there. The oldest, Marv, was in sixth grade, Mel was in fifth grade, John in third grade, and Harry was in second grade. We were fortunate that the school charged $10 a month for the first child and then only $5 a month for any subsequent child. One year there were six of us attending the first through eighth grades, costing a fairly affordable tuition fee of $35 a month.

At the time, large Catholic families were not uncommon. I went to school with the same students from first through eighth grades. To this day, I can still remember and name just about everyone I went to school with those eight years. Some of them also came from large families. I attended school with the Bybees, who had eleven children, the Kosslers, who had eight, and the Lundbergs, who had the most, with thirteen children. The Bayans, who owned the local dairy, had seven, and the Hamrocks had seven or eight.

I remember the very smart, studious, and talented Mary Jo Hepplar, who wanted to be a nun, lived in an apartment just across the alley from the school playground. I remember that Eugene Foss and Robert Brough were the class troublemakers for the entire eight years at St. Emydius. My good friends for eight years were Susie Lopez (Dave Lopez from the channel 2 news is her brother), Debbie Miller, Barbara Gernazio, and Marie Smith. My two best friends were Nancy O'Connor and Monica Velarde. In the fall of 2018, I attended our fiftieth-year Pius X High School reunion in Seal Beach, California. I had a lot of fun seeing my classmates and elementary school friends who attended Pius X after going to St. Emydius. Debbie Miller and Judy Lake were instrumental in organizing the event, and they did a great job. They also were my classmates throughout my eight years at St. Emydius.

Over the years I continued to work alongside my mom, helping her raise my seven younger brothers and sisters, keeping the house clean, helping her get everyone ready to go to school in the morning, attending church and school activities and events with her, and eventually nervously sitting alongside her in the critical care recovery room at Queen of Angels Hospital in Los Angeles in 1976 while my dad was having his throat cancer surgery.

My mom and I did everything together that had to do with the family. At eight years old I watched and tried to entertain four or five younger siblings outside in the car, often for an hour or so, sometimes in the heat of the day, while she was inside at her many doctor's appointments. I welcomed those opportunities and the responsibility that came with it. I treated my mom in the same way my dad did, by taking charge and giving constant support and help in many areas of the home and heart, which is why she and I had such a great relationship.

As a co-parent, I grew up fast and took on a lot of responsibility at a young age. I became the go-to person in the family, the one who could be depended upon to get things done and make things happen. By age eleven I was baking birthday cakes and arranging birthday parties for my siblings. I was often assisting her in helping to cook dinner, washing and drying clothes, giving baths to and babysitting the younger ones, changing their diapers, and feeding them. Everyone pitched in and helped; it was a total family effort.

As time went on, I took my level of responsibility and self-confidence that I developed growing up into creating a level of success in my personal and professional life. I was often the captain of many of the teams on which I eventually played. I later held positions of responsibility as a college administrator, athletic coach, and chair of a few faculty committees. I continue to help arrange family reunions, camping trips, and family social get-togethers, and serve on campus and local community committees where I volunteer my time and energy to help in planning and carrying out various projects and events.

What came with the level of responsibility I shouldered at a young age was a controlling, commanding personality in which I got used to everyone listening to me and doing what I told them to do, whether they liked it or not. After a while, I gave them no choice. I became a bully, and my behavior was not always discouraged. Even if my bullying was discouraged, it didn't stop me. I wasn't consciously developing into a controlling bully at the time, but I eventually realized it when that behavior continued to show up in my adult relationships, which led to many breakups. It unfortunately took many broken relationships to finally understand that it wasn't them, it was me who needed to change. It took a lot of years of therapy and a number of personal and professional development workshops and seminars over the years to recognize and change that behavior, which has led to more effective, meaningful relationships with everyone in my life.

I thoroughly enjoyed every minute of the time I spent with my mother throughout the years. We worked well together and I am grateful for all that she taught me. Unlike me, she did not take herself seriously and was able to laugh at herself and was willing to admit any wrongdoing and quickly make amends for it—things that took a long time for me to learn. I took myself and life far too seriously, and unlike her, I had a lot of difficulty admitting wrongdoing and making amends for it. Those shortcomings led to a lot of failed relationships with family, friends, students, athletes, and faculty.

She never lied to us. I did. Because of my position in the family and a genuine desire to stand out, I developed this need to look good even if it meant lying, stealing, or cheating. All of which, I am ashamed to say, I did in my younger years. I don't think my mom could lie if she tried; she was that honest. I was always more than happy to help her. I loved the attention I got that came with the work and help I gave her. She made me feel appreciated for my efforts. Unfortunately, my need for recognition and acceptance later led to developing a severe case of codependent, enabling behavior that ruined many of my adult relationships.

I wish I could have had half her patience and eternally calm demeanor. No matter what the evolving situation or unfolding drama that was taking place, she kept her head and handled everything with poise and controlled reserve. Like my dad, I wanted to, and did, get things done quickly and efficiently. I often lost my patience around her and others when I felt she or they were not doing things the way I wanted things done, or they weren't doings things as fast or as quick as I could. Unfortunately, my impatience turned up in my early years of coaching and teaching, leading to some hurt feelings and resistance to learning from my athletes and students.

My need to please others and the accolades that came with my giving is what eventually led me to become an enabler (doing for others what they can do for themselves). I began to give all my time, energy, and money to others, whether they wanted it or not, to please them and be recognized for my giving. After a while I felt that I was being taken for granted by others until I was finally able to understand that I was doing things for them that they did not ask me to do. I did not hold them capable and had difficulty accepting that they did not have to thank me or in any way owed me for something they did not ask me to do. I put myself last on my list time after time and got upset that I was last on my list, even though it was my choice to put myself there. My enabling got me into troubled and failed relationships time after time throughout my life. I was then and continue to be generous to a fault, but I am working on it.

One relationship I wished I had better developed in early childhood was that relationship with my teeth. Yes, I am embarrassed to say, my teeth. At St. Emydius school I was in fourth grade when I got a dental checkup that the school provided every so often. I remember the dentist was telling his assistant the work my teeth needed. Frightfully and a little embarrassingly, I could hear the dentist continue to give her his list of suggested extractions, fillings, etc., long after I left the exam chair and the next student had already sat down. I did eventually, in my teens, when my mom was working and her insurance kicked in, get all my teeth fixed. I regret now not having taken better care of my teeth given how often I was encouraged to do so by family, school, and dentists over the years. I am good at learning the hard way; most often during my life's experiences, that learning was too little too late. I may be a late bloomer, but when I get it, I get it. It's everybody out of the pool, here comes Marilyn! I was a stubborn all-or-nothing person, which has unfortunately been detrimental to my achieving success in my life sooner.

It was not only difficult to keep our teeth healthy, it was also difficult to stay injury free while living in a large active family. The one sibling that sustained more injuries and broken bones than anyone else in the family was our oldest brother, Marv. One of the earliest injuries I remember that he sustained was when he was attempting a backflip off the high dive at the Lynwood City Plunge and hit his head on the diving board on the way down. He had to have several stitches to close up the wound. Luckily Mom was not at the pool watching but ended up meeting him later at the emergency room at St. Francis Hospital in Lynwood.

Marv subsequently sustained several other injuries over the

years. He is 6'4" and could jump up and grab the rather low roof at the back of the house. He was swinging on it when one of his hands slipped and went through a kitchen window, breaking the window and cutting a nerve on the inside of his upper left arm. Luckily, we were not back there eating dinner at the time. He was walking barefoot on top of a small glass greenhouse in which we grew vegetables in the backyard. His foot went through the glass because he missed stepping on the wooden frame part of one of the glass panes and broke the glass instead. He had several stitches in his foot on that one.

Harry broke his arm playing on what we called the monkey bars in the backyard that consisted of sprinkler pipes connected together for climbing, walking on, and swinging from, which were erected at two different heights, that my dad put together in one corner near the back fence. Harry got pushed into one of the poles by another brother while playing touch football in the backyard. Harry also got hit in the eye at school during lunch by a baseball that a student carelessly threw into a crowd just as Harry happened to turn and look. His bruised eye healed but his eyesight was compromised and he had to wear glasses after that incident.

I cut my head open when Harry and I were climbing on a steel ladder propped up on the palm tree located just inside the entrance to the backyard of our home on San Miguel Avenue. He climbed the palm tree just beyond the top rung of the ladder and accidently kicked the ladder as he climbed higher, hitting me in the head while I was underneath him holding and balancing the ladder for him. That was my first but would not be my last trip to the emergency room for stitches or X-rays.

I got upset at my younger sister Sue one time for beating me in a foot race from the front of the house to the backyard, and I regretfully pushed her into a window that broke and nearly severed an artery on the inside of her left wrist. Mom really panicked on that one. We created a *lot* of fires for my mom to put out. Not literally; well, maybe a few! I could go on and on. Over the years and after several harrowing incidents, Mom learned to remain calm when a mishap occurred and handled injuries and cuts like a seasoned paramedic.

We weren't the only ones who got hurt while playing in the

house and backyard. Two neighborhood kids ended up with injuries that required stitches for one and a big black eye for the other. They were accidents! Their mothers limited them from coming over after that. In fact, word got around to the other mothers in the neighborhood, and they began limiting their children's visits to our house as well. We were just a bunch of very active risk-taking kids, who easily became bored with routine play. Among twelve roughhousing kids actively playing sometimes at three different locations in and around the house, you're bound to understandably have a few mishaps; right?

My cousin Gerry remarked recently how much he protested to his parents when they said they were going to visit the Ladd family. He was a quiet, shy child and an only child at the time at home with his parents. They made him visit us anyway. One time on one of his reluctant weekend visits, when he and his parents knocked on the front door and one of us opened it, he said most of us were in the living room playing a game to see who could walk all the way around the living room the fastest—without touching the floor! I usually fell right around the mantel as I did not have the strength to support my entire body weight by my fingertips and walk hand-over-hand across the top of the mantel to the chair on the other side. As I got older and taller, I was able to pull myself up onto the top of the mantel and just walk across to the other side like all my brothers could. Of course, we quit playing when my dad told us to, but it didn't do anything for our poor cousin Gerry to quell his worry and hesitancy in visiting. It was Cousin Gerry who suggested the title for this book. Naming the book at his suggestion was the least I could do for him given what he went through on those tortuous visits to our house.

For many years my mother was one of the few parents who drove players on my and my two sister's sports teams to and from our away games. I played three different sports at St. Emydius in the seventh and eighth grades; volleyball, basketball, and softball. She was one of the busiest parents compared to all the other mothers or fathers, but she still managed to drive to almost every away game during those two years I competed. She often had to bring a few younger brothers and sisters with her, and most of the time she was missing time at home with my other siblings. She often stayed and watched the games rather than go all the way back home just to return in a short while when the game was over. It was usually about 6 p.m. when we returned home, and then she had to start cooking and taking care of the family again. I felt I owed her for her time and energy driving me and my teammates to the away games. One of the ways I repaid her for her time and effort was to help around the house.

Mom was always easygoing and pleasant to everyone, even if they were mean or unpleasant to her. She operated from that "turn the other cheek" philosophy when someone wronged her. She did, however, have every right to be upset and angry at our crazy neighbor Elsie Bacchino. She lived in the house to our north with her husband and son, Charlie. We all felt she was schizophrenic and obsessive-compulsive. I was in her house about two or three times over the years when we were on a more friendly basis. I was surprised how extremely neat and tidy the house was, but maybe that was because I didn't know what extremely neat and tidy really looked like, not having witnessed it in my own home.

Every day she was constantly cleaning, dusting, vacuuming, etc., much more so than I thought was warranted given there were only three of them living there. Her bathroom window was feet away from our driveway, which my family walked up and down many times a day. From her open bathroom window, we had to listen to her rants and raves that we could hear, loud and clear, that seemed to be directed at no one in particular. During some of her bathroom window rants, she complained and criticized how my mom was raising us and that we weren't keeping the outside of our house as clean and neat as hers. This really bothered and upset my mom. She did her best to defend us against Elsie's comments by jawing back at her, but to no avail.

After several years of her banter and "crazy talk," my mother decided to ignore her and told all of us to do the same—something she probably should have done from the start. After a while, since she was getting no response, Elsie slowly stopped her verbal assaults. We rarely ever saw her husband and never heard him say a word when we did see him. He seemed resigned to allowing her to do and say whatever she wanted. She was going to anyway. I think he tuned her out years ago and was just going through the motions of husband and father. They were such polar opposites. I guess that's why they were able to coexist successfully. She did everything, he did nothing; just the way she wanted it, just the way he allowed and was content to have it.

Elsie kept any ball that we accidentally kicked or hit over into her backyard. Sometimes she purposely popped the ball and then threw it back over the fence. Unfortunately, her actions would put an end to our kickball game, as we usually only had the one plastic ball. We then just played hide-and-seek, red rover, or climbed in the avocado tree until our parents could buy another ball.

We were elated when they finally moved away in 1965 and a lovely young family of four moved in. Even when she moved away, for whatever reason, crazy Elsie didn't want us to know. They moved pieces of furniture and boxes a little at a time, mostly at night, thinking that we wouldn't know they were moving. We did notice and waited and watched until the last of everything was moved. About ten or twelve of us were watching them as they got ready to drive away for the last time. Just as they pulled away from the curb, we all ran out onto the front porch and whooped and hollered and clapped as loud as we could and waved our hands good-bye. We were pleased to see the look on her face as she sat in the front passenger seat as they drove away in front of our house. If looks could kill. It was very satisfying to have gotten the last laugh, especially for my mom.

My mom did her best to put up with Elsie. She knew that Elsie had lost her daughter, Connie, years earlier to polio and always wanted to be as kind and understanding to her as she could. Losing her daughter may be what caused Elsie to become emotionally unstable. She could often be heard loudly calling out her daughter's name during those times when she was feeling the most distraught and upset. Things got back to normal in the neighborhood after they moved out. Mom had her warm smile and kind demeanor back and was her usual reserved but optimistic self again. We got along well with the family that moved in.

I am sure my mom did not do much cooking growing up, given that she was the youngest of her family with two older females doing much of the cooking and housework. My mother spent most of her time running around the farm playing with her dog and pet hen Tippie, watching her brothers and father do the plowing, planting, and harvesting. She eventually got pretty good at cooking dinners for us, which were rather simple in nature and were pretty much the same dinners week after week. The only problem she had sometimes was leaving things in the oven too long or cooking one side of our hamburgers or chicken on the stove too long. This meant one side was more well-cooked than the other. These things happened sometimes because she placed the meat or chicken in the pan or oven and then intended only to go lie down for just a few minutes to rest, and then fell asleep instead and woke up to find the meat smoking or one of us kids yelling at her to get up. She made sure that she served the less burned side up. Also, understandably, my mom preferred to keep all the knives in the house dull to prevent any bad accidental cuts.

She did the same thing in the middle of the night sometimes when she had to warm up a baby bottle for yet another crying baby. She put the bottle on the stove to boil and then intended to come back in a few minutes to test it for warmth before giving it to the baby. On a couple of occasions, she fell back asleep and did not return. The glass bottle got so hot it broke in the dry pan because all the water boiled out of it. Luckily, she never caught the house on fire, but there were a few hungry babies that went unfed in the middle of the night.

Despite her cooking ability or lack thereof, we became very hardy eaters. We could stomach just about anything. At times, we ate weevils in our cereal (when the industry wasn't as regulated as it is today). We got used to the taste and had no choice because sometimes it was the only cereal left to eat that morning. Besides, Mom said they were a good source of protein for us! We also sometimes drank sour milk, not always at the same time we were eating the weevils in our cereal. We drank the sour milk because there was no more in the refrigerator and we were hungry and could not wait for someone to go to the store to buy more. After a while, just like the weevils, we got used to the taste.

We had a bread box on the kitchen counter to the left of the stove that was sometimes filled with near empty loaves and broken pieces of various types of bread, and some of it sat in there long enough that it began to get moldy. Every time one of us complained about the moldy bread that was piling up in the breadbox, inevitably the next morning the moldy bread was gone, and for breakfast mom was serving us French toast! No wonder our immune systems to this day are so strong and healthy. Everybody should eat weevils in their cereal, drink sour milk, and eat French toast made with moldy bread.

My mother was easygoing. It took a lot for her to get upset enough to turn off the TV or kick us out of the house to go play. For the most part, she gave us a lot of rope, but when we hung ourselves with it, she made us pay the consequences. If she said you were going to get a spanking for misbehaving when we got home, you got a spanking. If we had to get spanked, we wanted to get spanked by her because her swats didn't hurt that much, but we acted like they did. Sometimes we got surprised when we got home and Dad was there; she told him what we did and he spanked us. Now, his swats hurt! When we did get spanked, it was well deserved. Spankings in the 1950s were a common and accepted form of discipline. The spankings I got certainly taught me to stop repeating those actions and behaviors that led to the punishment.

What ended up being worse than the spanking itself was the teasing by siblings that took place after exiting the bathroom where our spankings took place. While I was crying, I could see one sibling mouthing the words, "You got four swats!" Another one could be seen holding up four fingers for the number of swats I got. Still another was snickering with a smile on their face. However, it didn't stop me from doing the same to them when they got a spanking.

Sometimes when we really got on her and each other's nerves, she piled us into the car and drove us a couple of miles down to the South Gate Park for an hour or so to burn off some energy. When I was thirteen, I had just scrambled out of the car with six other siblings when I took out the bat and golf ball I had brought with me and proceeded to hit the golf ball straight up in the air. I was so proud that it was such a good, solid hit that went pretty high. I watched it as it unfortunately came down about thirty yards away, hitting my younger brother Ralph square on the top of his head as he was running away from the car headed for the swings. What a bummer! It almost knocked him out, and he cried for several minutes. It left a lump on his head the size of a golf ball, no pun intended. Unfortunately, my mom was standing right there and saw the whole thing. Needless to say, I not only spent the entire trip to the park in the car for punishment, but I also got a spanking when I got home—from Dad.

Another time that I got myself into trouble was with my brother Harry, when he and I and the rest of the family were at Salt Lake Park in the city of Huntington Park. Our other brothers and sisters were playing over at the three-stage, wire-frame rocket ship with the second-story slide. Harry and I were over near a street that bordered one edge of the park. We sat at the base of a ten-foot slope and would throw small rocks at the cars that drove by on the street at the top of the slope and then duck down at the bottom of the slope to avoid detection. My Mother saw us and was on her way over to tell us to stop when one of us hit a car. Of course, we each claimed that we were the one with the golden arm who hit the car until the guy we hit backed up, got out of his car, and was looking for us. Of course, we both now claimed it was the other one who hit the car with the rock.

Fortunately, my mom was now standing behind us and apologized to the guy. Harry and I both got a spanking when we got home. The spanking itself wasn't as bad as the anticipation of getting it. We were dreading getting the spanking from the time it came out of my mom's mouth until we eventually got it that evening. I think she purposely waited until after dinner to give it to us just to cause us more agony. I remember Harry and I talking nervously in the backyard around the tetherball pole hoping she forgot. No way. No sooner did we say that when she called us into the house to face the music. Luckily it was her that gave us the spanking and not Dad.

Still another time when I got into similar trouble was while at home. You'd think I would have learned from the previous incident. A couple of us were shooting these big leftover rubber bands from one of my brother's paper route at the cars that drove by in front of our house. We hid behind the back end of a parked car and ran up the driveway to hide if we thought we had hit a car. We all ran up the driveway after I had unbelievably hit a driver on the left side of his face. He stopped, backed up and knocked on our front door. He was irate to say the least. Mom as usual apologized and promised him she would reprimand us. She did. We got a spanking once she found us hiding in the garage. I tried again to blame it on my other sibling, but Mom wasn't buying it; the guy told her he saw me do it.

One other childish prank I and some of my brothers and sisters used to do was to climb high up into the large jacaranda tree on the curb side in the front of our house to hide in the branches and wait for either the Helm's Bakery man or the Good Humor ice cream truck to drive by. As they passed under us we yelled, "Stop!" Of course, they stopped and got out and looked around, waiting for several seconds, only to find no one approaching them. We waited long enough for them to get back into their vehicle and yell "Stop" again, just as they began to drive away. A few times the driver stopped directly under me. They eventually caught on to our prank and either didn't exit their vehicle or didn't bother to stop at all. Looking back, I believe I did these pranks out of boredom and a need to see how far I could push the limits of dangerous, sometimes risky behavior before getting caught. What I did not take into consideration was that somebody could have really gotten hurt by my childish actions.

Helm's Bakery trucks operated from 1931 to 1969 selling fresh breads, doughnuts, and pastries in Helm's vehicles in neighborhoods throughout the Los Angeles basin. We did run out front and often actually bought ice cream from the ice cream man and bread and doughnuts from the Helm's bakery truck when we heard its distinctive whistle blow twice. We legitimately yelled "Stop" on those occasions.

Good Humor ice cream trucks sold a wide range of novelties throughout the United States beginning in the 1920s in Youngstown, Ohio. Good Humor ice cream became a fixture in American popular culture, and at its peak in the 1950s the company operated two thousand sales cars and trucks (Wikipedia).

What I loved most about my mom, which I believe made her the fantastic mother she was, and what I believe is the key to the success of any person in authority, whether a parent, teacher, boss, police officer, etc., is that she was always *firm* but *fair* and never sarcastic. She treated us all the same. She was clear with what we were supposed to do or what she wanted from us, and if we broke any of her rules or agreements, she always held us accountable with an appropriate punishment or disciplinary action. We could never say to her as she was handing out her punishment that "We didn't know," or "You didn't tell me."

If she didn't have the whole story or wasn't sure who did what, she weighed the facts at hand and the evidence of the two stories and did what she felt was fair in the situation. Sometimes both parties got punished. As the go-between, she quelled arguments, heated discussions, or disputes in a fair and reasonable manner. I rarely felt I got a raw deal after she arbitrated or intervened in a situation unless I was determined to not admit guilt, even if I knew I was the one who did wrong.

Mom never belittled us or called us names; she never made us feel bad about ourselves or went out of her way to embarrass or shame us. Yes, there were times when she let us have it with direct, well-deserved comments, especially if we were not doing well in school or not doing our chores or were causing trouble because we were cranky or tired. Her talks with us were aimed at getting us to listen and learn from our mistakes and not to make us feel bad because we made one. Now, if we kept making the same mistake over and over again, she knew there was nothing she could do to change that about us. She knew we would change eventually after we had suffered enough consequences for that behavior. She had to let us learn the hard way sometimes.

Those three attributes she possessed, of being firm but fair and never sarcastic, are what I have always liked best about her. What I have also always loved about her is her endless capacity to love others unconditionally. There were many times when I know her feelings got hurt by my dad or one of us or Elsie, and she never got angry about it or sought revenge or retribution. She quietly absorbed the slight or unnecessary comment with stoic dignity.

The one sibling that I believe hurt her most was one of my younger brothers, Mike. He was estranged from the family and society in general at an early age and carried a lot of anger and hate toward others, and got into trouble often. Although he loved her dearly, he was not very kind or nice to my mom at times because of his later addictions. It hurt her deeply that she was not able to help him with his demons and character flaws and his verbal abuse toward her. She always blamed herself for the way he turned out. She was sick a lot and absent as a mother for a while when he was a newborn, and Mike ended up being raised partly by her and partly by the rest of us, which I am sure affected his behavior in a negative way, none of us having the proper nurturing and a mother's special love that is much needed by any child. She also felt that the fact she was not feeling well and was not able to breast-feed him very much was another reason why he turned out so emotionally different from the rest of us. Like others who wronged or disappointed her, she still genuinely loved him without reservation.

Mike as a child was defiant and obstinate, and later was a very aggressive adult. He was born with scoliosis, a curvature of the spine, that gave him a slight twist of his upper body. The curve was located just above the middle of his back. The curvature did not seem to affect his ability to lead an active life, as he surfed and played youth baseball and the guitar. He never complained about his condition, and it did not seem to cause him much pain, nor did he seem to be the least bit conscious or embarrassed about the slightly obvious curvature.

His defiance and anger began at an early age. I remember when his first-grade teacher told his class that, if they did not like something she said to them, they could just leave. The first time she said something Mike didn't like, he got up and walked home. His rebellious, insolent behavior concerned my mother enough that she sought therapy for him from a psychiatrist. She stopped taking him after two sessions because Mike never opened up and refused to say anything the entire hour. We didn't help his situation any by teasing him when we found out he was seeing a therapist.

Mike was very bright and did well in school until he went to South Gate Intermediate School. He quickly fell into the wrong crowd and began smoking pot and not performing well in school. He went to South Gate High School, where he continued to smoke pot and hang out with other potheads and pretty much did what he wanted, including getting into arguments and disagreements with students and his teachers.

In the summer of 1972, when Mike was seventeen, unbeknownst

to the rest of us, he began to grow a few pot plants in a four-foot easement that ran between the back of our yard and the neighbor's backyard behind us. It was just before Labor Day in early September when we were all home after returning from one of our summer family vacations. I had been staying at the house off and on that summer. I was twenty-two and attending Fullerton College and about to return to live with my grandmother in Tustin, as school was starting the following Tuesday. Because we had been gone for several days camping, Mike needed to water his pot plants.

So at about 8:30 a.m. he waited for several family members to leave and made sure the rest of us were in the house before jumping over our five-foot back fence and watered his pot plants. Well, a neighbor happened to walk into his backyard and saw Mike watering his plants, which were located just beyond his back fence in the easement. Mike quickly jumped back over the fence into our yard and promptly headed out front, and walked two doors over to one of our neighbors, who were Mike's friends and classmates, I am sure in hopes that he would not be found. The neighbor who saw my brother watering these obvious-to-him pot plants called the police after he saw Mike jump back into our yard.

It was about 9 a.m. when I started to wake to one of my younger brothers and youngest sister watching TV in the living room, where I had slept on the couch that night. The other youngest brother was still sleeping in the back of the house in the den where I thought Mike was still sleeping as well. Everyone else had gone to work or school and it was just me and my three youngest brothers and sister at home. I got up to go to the bathroom when I heard a loud knock at the side door. I continued past the bathroom down the hall through the girls' room and unlatched and opened inward just the top half of the door, which was screened, to see a rather large Hispanic male flashing a badge in my face and telling me to open the door. I had to wake myself up quickly and asked him to repeat himself. He said, "I am here on a narcotics investigation; open the door!"

I told him that the door does not open, which was true, the lock was broken, and for him to come around to the front door. When I was about to open the front door I told my brother, who was still lying down in his bed in the living room, "Get up, Ralph.

I don't know who this guy is that wants me to open the door." I no sooner opened the door and put my foot behind it to block the door to prevent his entry when he grabbed me by the neck and pulled me out onto the porch. As he grabbed me, I kept my right hand on the side of the door in an attempt to close it behind me to prevent him from getting in to possibly do harm to my brothers and sister still inside.

As I was trying to close the door, Ralph, who heard the initial scuffle, has now jumped up out of his bed and pulled the door from the other side toward him as I was trying to close it. Ralph was trying to help me with this unknown guy, who had now dragged me out onto the porch and had me in a chokehold. All I could manage to quietly mutter to my brother as I was being choked was, "Call the police." Ralph let go of the door and began to run to our parent's room to call the police when he told me later that another smaller white guy appeared in the hallway with a gun in his hand and stopped him from entering my parents' room. At the same instant, my other brother Ray, asleep in the den, was now awakened by all the ruckus and was running up from the back of the house to the living room to help us. The white guy, who apparently entered through the back door and did not see Ray still asleep, turned and stopped my brother from advancing any farther from the other end of the hall. He got my two brothers to come back into the living room and sit down. While all this was going on, my twelve-year-old sister was screaming and crying hysterically in the armchair she was sitting in while watching TV. I couldn't go to her to comfort her because by now the two guys had the four of us calmed down and sitting down on the couch in the living room.

I did not know that our neighbor behind us had called the police about an hour earlier and that these two guys were undercover South Gate police officers who responded and were investigating who it was that was seen watering the pot plants. It was only *after* we had all been sat down in the living room that a black-and-white unit with a uniformed police officer showed up at the house. Had the uniformed officer showed up at the beginning of the initial response, I would have opened the door and let all the officers in. But because I resisted opening the door, and Mike was not in the house, and I had no idea who these guys were, *I* was arrested for growing the pot and interfering with the duty of a police officer, even though the neighbor said it was a young boy he saw watering the pot plants and observed jumping over the fence.

I was told to stand and put my hands behind my back, and the two undercover officers handcuffed me and put me in their unmarked car, not the marked unit, and I was told to sit between them on the center console in handcuffs behind my back while we rode to the police station, leaving my brothers and sister alone in the house. As we took off down the street, Mike was now walking back to our house from the neighbors, watching me being driven to the police station. Mike *never* acknowledged nor apologized to me for being arrested for his pot-growing, nor for the subsequent problems I endured as a result of my arrest for something he did.

As soon as I was driven away, Ralph called my mother at work, which was at South Gate Junior High School at that time, and told her what happened. I soon found myself, after being fingerprinted, in a jail cell at the police department with three other older, surprised women asking me why a healthy young girl was sitting in the same cell as them. My mother and another sister showed up in about an hour to bail me out. They knew I was innocent but bailed me out anyway because they did not want me to stay in jail any longer.

My family ended up hiring a lawyer, and about a year after the arrest we went to court with the South Gate Police Department to prove my innocence. My two younger brothers and sister were outside the courtroom ready to testify. The judge quickly threw out the case after the Hispanic officer testified. The judge did so because he could see that I did not resemble the boy that was described by the neighbor, and the undercover officer did not wait for the black-and-white unit to show up before knocking on our door and forcing his way into the house. The judge did not believe him when he said that when he was walking from the side door to the front door, he could hear us flushing the toilet to get rid of evidence.

My family then sued the city of South Gate for false arrest. We won the case, and I bought a new car with the settlement money. Unfortunately, the arrest meant I had to declare I had been arrested on my California state teachers credentials application. This meant having to go to Sacramento, where the credentials office is located, hiring a lawyer up there, and have him explain my case to a panel. They were convinced that it was false arrest, and in the summer of 1974 gave me my California teaching credential. Today most applications ask if you have been arrested *and* convicted of a crime or felony. My record was expunged many years later.

After graduating from South Gate High School in 1973, Mike continued to work with my dad for our family sprinkler business, doing the repairing and replacing of broken sprinklers or water pipes. After my dad passed away in 1977, four of my brothers, including Mike, continued the family business until Mike went off on his own years later to do nothing but sprinkler repair work. He was one of the best in the business when it came to repairing and replacing sprinklers.

Unfortunately, his increased use of alcohol and drugs led to him losing everything. He eventually lost his driver's license, his work van, the house he was renting, and soon found himself on the streets, homeless. He was hospitalized numerous times when he was found unresponsive in public. He was arrested on several occasions for public intoxication, driving while under the influence, and other minor altercations and infractions.

I lived in the same city as Mike and spent many a day and night for nearly seven years looking for him on the streets to see if he was OK. I spent money putting him up in a hotel room for a night or two on several occasions, bought him food at times and alcohol when he was in severe withdrawal. There were several hotels that stopped allowing him to stay there as he would sometimes, for a small fee or for some drugs or alcohol, allow other drug users or prostitutes to stay in the room with him after he was told not to allow them in.

When my Mother passed away in 2011, it was in her will for Mike to have housing, as she did not want to see him on the streets any longer. The family felt it would be better for him to live in a hotel rather than rent a house, as we figured it wouldn't be long before he would be evicted from a house, and it would be much more difficult and expensive initially to furnish. I found some great local hotels that he stayed in before that allowed him extended stays, but he was getting kicked out again for his misbehavior. He continued to allow drug users and prostitutes to stay in his room.

He was getting free hotel stays provided by my mom and had money for food and alcohol he bought with his Social Security monies that he was allowed to collect at fifty-five. I thought things would turn around for him, but he became more and more emaciated and sickly from his continued alcohol abuse.

It was on April 17, my sixty-third birthday, in 2013 that I got a call on my cell phone from my oldest brother, Marv, who had just received a call from the manager of the latest hotel in which Mike was staying. He said Mike had passed away in his hotel room the night before from a massive heart attack. He was fifty-seven.

I believe Mike had a tortured soul and a broken spirit early on, if that is possible for a person to have. I believe his broken spirit is what led him to lose himself in drugs and drinking, which temporarily took away his pain and emotional hurt. When he wasn't drinking, he had a side of him that was charming, smart, and fun, with a talent for playing the harmonica and guitar. When he was drinking, he was extremely angry, antagonistic, and easily incensed or provoked into fighting, name-calling, or offensive language to anyone and everyone. I always felt bad for Mike and wanted to help him as much as I possibly could. I can say today that I believe I did do everything I could over the years to help him deal with his demons.

I am embarrassed to say that I often hurt my mother's feelings or disappointed her with my behavior and actions at times over the years. I felt guilty when I said or did things that hurt her. After an incident, she talked to me about what I did wrong, and sometimes she didn't say anything at all, which often worked as a reprimand for me. She spoke to me in a quiet yet firm and straightforward voice that clearly indicated her hurt and disappointment in my behavior. There were times when I should have apologized to her after these incidents, but I was a proud person and had to look good no matter what. Admitting wrongdoing or apologizing would not make me look good. I defended or made excuses for my behavior instead of taking responsibility for my actions, or played the victim to other people's actions and blamed them for what happened. I displayed that same proud look-good-at-all-costs behavior in many of my adult relationships, which later in my life cost me dearly.

I was more inclined to change my ways after those hurtful incidents when she did not talk to me about what I did. By not talking to me, she left me to stew and think about my actions. At any rate, I respected her and eventually stopped hurting her with my inappropriate behavior and words. She was a *very* forgiving person.

Mom had a warm smile, a funny laugh, and a great sense of humor. Her laugh would start out quietly, as a near silent chuckle. It got louder the more she thought about the joke or the more the rest of us laughed. You knew something was really funny to my mom when she threw her head back and laughed so much that she would then lean forward, holding her stomach. She always maintained her sense of humor and optimism throughout the good or bad times. I loved that about her.

One odd thing she started doing around 1964, when I was fourteen, was yelling "Help" in her sleep. *Loudly* yelling "Help" in her sleep! The first time it ever happened, at the time I was sleeping in a single bed in one of the corners of the living room with our homework study table close to me on my left. There was a large world globe on the table one of us had been using for geography homework earlier in the evening. It must have been about two in the morning when I began to hear the quiet word "Help." I was half awake and wondered if it was a dream. Then I heard it again. This time the "Help" was a little louder and a little longer; the *e* in "help" each time now was being emphasized and held longer than the other three letters; like "He-e-elp!"

When I finally became more wide awake and realized I was not having a dream, all I could see at that moment was what I thought was the head of a man sitting on the table next to me. I froze in terror and at that very second heard the word *"He-e-elp"* again. It was even louder and longer than before. It took me several seconds to recognize that it was not a man's head sitting on the table, but to my relief it was that globe we were using earlier for our homework. Whew!

At about that same moment, I hear several people running down the hall toward my parents' room, which was next to where I was sleeping in the living room. Now I was thinking people were running to attack my parents. Turns out it was three or four of my brothers who came from the back of the house and were running down the hall to come to my parents' aid. I got up and ran to their bedroom, where nearly everyone in the house was now standing, and found my mother just waking up out of her "Help" nightmare.

It was about that time that my dad woke up. He slept through the whole thing! My mom looked surprised and didn't know why everyone was standing around her bed in the middle of the night until we told her what she was yelling in her sleep. After a few more minutes of questions with no answers, we all left their room but had difficulty, rightfully so, going back to sleep that night. We were hoping to chalk it up to a onetime incident. It would happen several more times over the next several years, probably about six or seven altogether. Each subsequent time we initially woke up, realized it was her again, ignored her, and went back to sleep. We usually made fun of her the next morning by imitating her haunting yell. She took it in stride, and we felt bad that she had these awful dreams, where she was obviously in need of help.

We felt the night cries for help had a lot to do with, to say the least, the extremely busy and hectic life she led. She probably desperately wanted to and probably often thought about yelling "Help" many times each day, but knew it would be to no avail. We did help her out around the house a lot more after those first few "Help" nightmares. We took her cries for help literally.

Her "Help" nightmares began happening several years after we had to let our housekeeper, Ernestine, go. We did not have enough money to pay her anymore. It was in 1957 when I was seven that she stopped working for us, which meant Mom, by herself, was now going to take care of ten children. I believe she was pregnant with the eleventh child, Ray, when Ernestine left.

Things did begin to improve for her. Shortly after the last child, Frances Ellen, was born in 1960, mom wisely decided to assign one of the six older children to begin to help take care of one of the younger six children to shift some of the heavy workload to us older children. The older sibling that was assigned to a younger sibling helped her or him with things like their homework, getting them ready for bed, help them make their lunch for school, etc. It worked well for quite a few years. She did this just at a time when she needed our help the most. It wasn't too long after we started taking care of each other that her "Help" nightmares subsided. Who knew?

As far as I remember, my oldest brother, Marv, was assigned to my younger brother Mike; Harry helped take care of Ralph; John had my youngest brother Ray; and Melvin was assigned to Bob. I took care of my little sister Frances. The only drawback was that, especially the younger ones, we were each missing the natural parental nurturing necessary for a healthy, complete upbringing. It was what worked fairly well at the time, given the limited amount of love and care Mom was able to give us. The lack of maternal nurturing did impact many of us later in our lives. I believe it is why my brother Mike developed severe emotional problems and extreme anger that eventually led him to drugs and alcohol abuse in his teens and an early death.

What I remember of Ernestine, our housekeeper, is that she was very soft spoken, moved slowly but deliberately, and had a great relationship with my mom, who trusted her completely. We all loved her and did what she told us to do with her quiet, soothing voice. She had beautiful medium dark skin with black straight hair that curled under at her ears and just above her shoulders. She was about 5'3" with a round figure. She wore dresses that were neatly pressed and of a light color that ended at the middle of her shins. I believe she was our housekeeper for about four years, from 1956 to 1959.

My mother and Ernestine (by the way, what a great name for her, as she was an earnest person) kept in touch with each other long after she stopped working for us. She lived a few miles away in Watts, and since she did not drive, my mom often picked her up or dropped her off after a day's work. I remember visiting her several times at her home over the years, especially during the holidays, and always looked forward to those pleasant times with her.

Nearly thirty years after she worked for us, her sister called my mom in the summer of 1988 to let her know that Ernestine was in a rest home, suffering from dementia, and thought it would be nice if my mom were to visit her to celebrate her birthday. I went with my mom to Riverside to the facility where she was staying. Her sister and a friend were there in a fairly large, busy recreation room. I don't remember what year we were celebrating, but I believe she would have been in her early nineties. Ernestine did not recognize my mom but we had a nice celebration anyway.

However, there was this brief, room-stopping, jaw-dropping moment of cognizant recognition of my mom from Ernestine that I will never forget as long as I live. My mom was looking down at Ernestine as she sat in a chair opening my mom's present to her. As she was handed her present from my mom, Ernestine looked up and their eyes locked. Ernestine's previous confused, bewildered look disappeared into a look of joy and delightful recognition. They looked at each other as if they were back in our kitchen standing face-to-face in an old familiar pleasant encounter thirty years earlier. It was then that Ernestine totally recognized and remembered my mom. Everyone in the room quietly watched their silent connection unfolding before them, and all eyes were on Mom and Ernestine. The room remained suspended in time as they reconnected for those brief few precious seconds with each other one final time. There was not a dry eye in the room. Their kind mutual smiles and familiar looks of affection and love for each other are what I remember most about that captivating, unforgettable moment. Most of the way home that day mom sat in reflective silence with her head slightly lowered and a contented half-smile on her face.

It was several months later that Ernestine's sister called to tell my mom that she had passed away and how extremely thankful she was that my mom was able to attend her last birthday and reconnect as they did. How blessed we were to have had such a wonderful and kind person enter our lives and make such an impact on us all in those brief few years she was with us.

My mom ran the house the best she could, given there were twelve of us and one of her. Getting us all ready for anything was a major production. One of the most difficult was getting ready for Sunday church. The mass we attended depended on when we all finished breakfast that morning or if enough clothes got washed that week so that we all had enough clean clothes to all go to the same mass at the same time. On a few occasions, I had to go to a later mass than my sister just a year younger because for a time we only had one dress to wear between us. When my sister got home from church, she quickly changed out of the dress and I put it on just as quickly, and off to the next mass, hopefully on time.

I was almost always the first one dressed and on time and in the car ready to go before anyone else. It usually took another ten minutes before everyone was in the car and on our way. We had the usual nine or ten people as my three oldest brothers were trusted to go on their own. They usually went to an earlier mass than the rest of us just to get it over with. If they brought home the dated weekly Sunday bulletin that was handed out at the end of mass, they passed the attendance test, and they were good for the rest of the day.

We were inevitably and notoriously late for church nearly every Sunday. A lot of the time Monsignor McGuiness was already at the pulpit, ten minutes into the mass, giving his lengthy sermon for the day. Unfortunately, most of the empty pews left were way up in the front of the church. So here we went, nine, ten of us, a few crying, a few dragging a few others by the hand, trapesing up the center isle in front of everyone with the monsignor glaring at us.

The church did eventually have two soundproof baby rooms added onto the sides of the church that we often used when we could get there early enough that they weren't already full. These rooms had a large, thick, double-paned soundproof window and each held about twenty-five people. My mom usually sat in there with the two or three youngest, and the rest of us found other seats outside in the body of the main part of the church. Mom watched where I sat, and when she went to Communion she would drop off a kid in my lap, and then pick it up on her way back to the baby room. Usually she had a sibling old enough with her in the baby room to watch the others while she went to Communion.

Sunday-night dinners were special. We were usually treated to a roast or a sirloin steak. There were some lean times when we were limited to the amount or number of pieces of food. Once in a while, especially in the winter, Mom would tell us there was only enough chicken for us to have one piece each, or there was only enough dessert for the youngest six. Just like her, we learned to take those situations in stride. We got used to the word *no* so much so that after a while we just stopped asking. We knew we wouldn't get that toy, candy, or ice cream cone we wanted when shopping with her, so we knew it wasn't going to do any good to ask.

One vivid memory I have occurred when my two sisters and I were invited to our neighbor Beverly's tenth birthday party. We wanted to buy her a Barbie doll at the Sav-On drugstore on Tweedy Boulevard next to the Better Foods store. Mom gave us her last three dollars to buy the Barbie. It was two one-dollar bills and the last of her change. We were five, seven, and eight years old.

The three of us walked the mile to the Sav-On only to find out that we did not have enough money to buy the Barbie. There was another doll at half the price but it was only wearing a diaper and didn't even come in a box. We had about a dollar left over and spent it on ice cream cones and some candy on the walk back home. When we showed up with the cheap doll and handed her the few cents we had left; she launched into one of the angriest "How could you do this; what were you thinking" reprimands I ever remember getting from her. She was bent over at our height level and was raising her voice as she reamed us. She was especially angry at me because I was the oldest and should have known better. She made it clear that those three dollars were all she had and the doll we bought was not even presentable to Beverly as a decent present.

She ended up reluctantly leaving a chaotic and busy house that day and drove back to the Sav-On and bought the Barbie Doll with a check that she knew would overdraw my parents bank account. It wasn't the first time she did that nor would it be the last. Needless to say, I learned my lesson and decided after that incident I would not be, on any possible future troublemaking endeavors, the oldest one in the group who should know better. The only problem was, it was rare that any of my older brothers ever let me go anywhere with them so one of them could be the one who should know better and would be the one to get into trouble.

My mother was pregnant every year for sixteen years giving birth to my oldest brother Marv at age twenty-five and gave birth to our youngest, Frances, at age forty. She unfortunately had three miscarriages in those sixteen years. That may sound like a lot of miscarriages for one woman, but on the average, miscarriages occur in one out of every five pregnancies. She had one miscarriage between my third and fourth brothers, John and Harry, in 1948, another one between the second and third sisters, Sue and

Clarissa, in 1952, and the last and most difficult miscarriage was between the second and third youngest brothers, Mike and Ralph, in 1956. I was six years old when she had the last miscarriage.

She was changing the sheets on one of the beds in the girls' room, and just as she was lifting and extending both arms to spread the top sheet, she grabbed her stomach in pain. Two younger brothers, Bob and Mike, were playing nearby. My dad had already gone to work. There were five or six of us outside in the backyard playing kickball; my mom was in agony inside, now lying in the bed she was attempting to make. Bob, who seemed to sense, even at two, that something was seriously wrong, started to get alarmed and afraid.

She became concerned about the amount of bleeding she was suddenly experiencing but could not get up to call Dr. Carmody, our family doctor. She asked Bob to go outside and tell everyone she needed help. I remember when he came out the first time and told us Mom wants us, we figured she wanted us to do a chore or something, so we basically ignored him and kept playing. He went back inside and told her no one was coming in to help. She then tells him to go back outside and yell "Help" as loud as he can. He came out the second time and yelled "Help" at the top of his lungs, and everyone froze. We instantly knew something was really wrong, so we all bolted for the house and saw her in a lot of pain and agony on the bed.

Mel, who was eleven at the time, quickly called Dr. Carmody, who arrived at the house in about thirty minutes. She was bleeding a lot by now, and the blood was getting on the sheets. She asked for a towel to put between her legs to help stop the bleeding. Mel took the six of us who had been playing outside into the living room and asked us to pray while Dr. Carmody was trying to stop the bleeding. Fortunately, he was able to expel the fetus with some physical manipulation of her uterus just before the ambulance arrived.

We all watched as she was wheeled outside to the ambulance. She appeared to be in some pain and she was very pale. We were just thankful that she survived and were grateful to our doctor for probably saving her life. We had to wait until dad got home from work several hours later to tell him what had happened. He was very concerned and went to the hospital immediately. To this day, anyone who was home and experienced her miscarriage has been profoundly affected by the event. We were all frightened and terrified as to what was happening, and what made matters worse was the not knowing if she would live or die given the amount of blood we all saw on the sheets and towels.

She was in the hospital for a few days but looked good when she came walking back into the house. The hospital was the only place she ever truly got some rest! My dad had gone out to Tustin to bring his mother back to help us until mom got back on her feet. Grandma usually did help us for several weeks after a child was born, but this time it was under very different circumstances. We really appreciated her help all those years and especially her support after mom's painful, difficult, and thankfully last miscarriage. All we knew is that we were eternally grateful to Dr. Carmody, Bob, and the fact that so many of us were there at the time of the incident. Otherwise, who knows what may have happened if Mom had been home by herself with a one- and a two-year old. There was no 911 nor cell phones to use to notify dad when the incident happened.

As usual, as she did with other family challenges or setbacks, Mom took the miscarriage in stride and went on to have three more children in the next four and a half years. She was an amazing woman to say the least. At first appearance, she seems fragile and meek; she was anything but—she had the physical capacity to endure just about anything. She never complained about any of the pain or agony she endured and suffered over the years.

I remember when she was headed to the hospital to give birth to what would be her last child, she walked around the house from room to room just before bedtime letting each of us know that she was on her way to the hospital and would be back in her usual few days. When she got to me, I was lying in bed with my two sisters, and I could hear her saying to everyone as she made her rounds for us to name the baby. Because we didn't know its sex, we thought we would name it our dad's first name, Francis, or Frances if it was a girl, and Ellen would be its middle name, which is our mother's first name. We felt those two names were appropriate because it represented the first names of both our parents. Turns out that she was the last born, and having both our parent's names was fitting.

Mom was a woman who persevered and triumphed through

many difficulties and challenges countless times as a mother of twelve. She had tremendous strength, endurance and stamina to survive twelve pregnancies, three miscarriages, and a hysterectomy at forty-five. She lived to the age of ninety-one. It says a lot about her strong will and the dogged determination she always exhibited. What a wonderful example she was to the rest of us.

She was in good spirits at the hospital when I picked her up after her hysterectomy in 1966. I thought maybe that was because she knew she would never have to be pregnant again! I am sure she was elated that she would never see the inside of the maternity ward again. When I brought her home, and got her in bed, the rest of the family gathered around to welcome her. We were all smiles and happy to see her when nine-year-old Ralph yelled out, "Where's the baby?" Every time before, when she got home from the hospital, there would be another sibling in the bassinet. We all had and still get a good laugh over his comment.

She was a warm, caring, tender-hearted mother and wife who was dedicated and devoted to her husband and children. She was always considerate and concerned for others. She was even-tempered, sensitive, and always supportive of the twelve of us. She treated us all the same. I am sure she never dreamed that by forty years old she would be the mother of twelve, considering she was the "babe" of her family.

I consider myself very fortunate indeed to have been blessed with having a long, close, and loving relationship with such a beautiful person. She was perfect in every way to me. I admired and idolized her and wished I could have had half her level of honesty, integrity, and patience.

Much of the historical information I have garnered for this book has come from a large 530-page book put together by my cousin Kathy Gill. She found volumes of forgotten information, pictures, and materials in a large trunk on her parents' ranch. She put together a big blue book that has the letters GILL written in gold on the cover. It can be found in the Ventura County Historical Museum on Main Street. When the Gill family gathered to receive a copy and sign each other's books, this is what my Mother wrote on page 337: "Marilyn, to my most dependable, hardworking helper all her life. Love, Mom."

Marilyn Carol Ladd

Marilyn (Marylyne) Carol (Carole) Ladd, born April 19 (17), 1950, St. Francis Hospital, Lynwood, California.

When I was about to turn sixteen in 1966 and ready to go to the DMV to get my California driver's license, I had to have my birth certificate to show proof of my age. When my mom handed it to me and I looked at it, to my horror it had a different spelling of my first and middle names and a different birth date than I had been celebrating for the last fifteen years. When I ran to my mom to clarify the discrepancies, she looked at it, looked at it again, looked back at me, shrugged her shoulders, and simply said; "I guess I got you mixed up with one of our neighbors." What?!

Turns out, our next-door neighbor, Mrs. Lang, had a daughter,

Nadine, born at about the same time as me. That may have explained why I celebrated the wrong date of birth all those years, but what about the misspelling of my first and middle names? She had no explanation for that. When I came home from my first day of first grade, I had a cardboard name plate strung around my neck with MARILYN on it. She never said that wasn't the correct spelling, so I went through the next sixteen years of my life with the wrong birth date and spelling of my first name.

I was named Marilyn after my aunt, but my aunt spelled her name Marylyne, which is the way it is spelled on my birth certificate. Now, not even my dad said anything about the way I spelled my name early on, given he knew I was named after his sister. Maybe he didn't know how she spelled her name. Luckily it didn't stop the DMV from giving me my driver's license. I didn't even ask about the spelling of my middle name, and I have kept the spelling Marilyn. I had to get used to celebrating my birthday two days earlier than I had previously. What didn't surprise me was Mom's nonchalant reaction to the whole thing. Turns out I was not the only one with surprises on their birth certificates. Mel found out that the first name on his birth certificate is not Melvin; Melvin is his middle name. My mom again had no rhyme or reason for the mix-up. He continues to go by Melvin.

My earliest childhood memories are from living in the house we owned on San Luis Avenue. It was two separate but identical small houses on the same property. The house we lived in was a two-bedroom, one-bath house with my parents and now seven siblings. I was too young to remember, but I am sure living there with that many people must have been difficult to say the least. We had tenants that lived in the other house. My parents and four older brothers moved into the house in 1949. We lived there until 1954. They lived in the city of Huntington Park before that. One of the few memories I had of what we called later the "old house" on San Luis was my grandmother not letting my sister Sue and I out of the front bedroom unless we took a nap. She was there to help us after my mom had given birth to my sister Clarissa. I probably remembered this incident because we were typically not forced to take naps.

The only other memory I had of living at the old house was

when I, at four years old, and my sister Sue, at three years old, still in our pajamas, wandered away from the house just after my four older brothers left for school. Upon discovering that we were gone, my parents panicked and began looking for us right away, and found us about two blocks away, up on Tweedy Boulevard. We were marched back to the house, being reprimanded the whole way, and were each given a spanking. What I remember most about the spanking is one, we got it from our dad; two, he used a long, thin stinging switch; and three, I didn't have any underwear on when I got the spanking. As he approached me with the switch in his hand, I tried pulling my mid-thigh length pajama gown down over my butt. My dad was so surprised when he saw that I had no underwear on that he stopped running me around the living room with the switch and stopped swatting me. We never wandered away from the house again.

The oldest six at the "old house," 1954. Front, left to right: Mel, Sue, John. Back: Marilyn, Harry, Marv.

Outside those two memories and the one where John walked on Harry when the shed door fell on top of him in the vacant lot next door, the next memory was excitedly running around an empty house a block away that I was just told was going to be our new house. It was originally a two-bedroom, one-bath home. Three rooms were added onto the back of the house to the original six to make nine total rooms constructed in a big square. The front of the house faced east and was located in a typical, at that time, all-white neighborhood with a mix of young and old established families.

Two steps led up to the long, covered fifteen-foot-long by four-foot-wide front porch that ran from the driveway, located on the north side of the house, to the front door. As you walked up to the house from the street, a kitchen was the room on the right of the front of the house, a small dining room was the room in the middle of the front of the house, and on the left was the fourteen-by-fourteen-foot living room you walked into upon entering the front door. There was that side door from my incident with the South Gate police, located on the driveway side of the house, that, upon entering, if you could get it open, was a small six-by-five-foot room that housed the washer and water heater.

The second row of three rooms, from left to right, were our parents ten-by-ten-foot bedroom, the seven-by-eight-foot bathroom in the middle of the nine rooms of the house, and the ten-by-ten-foot girls' room, located next to the bathroom and nearest the driveway side of the house. My two sisters and I resided in that bedroom along with a crib that housed whomever the latest toddler was at the time. Everyone had to pass through our room to get from the back of the house to the front of the house or vice versa. This meant a *lot* of constant traffic, with fourteen people traveling through at all times of the day or night. The west door in our room was originally the back door of the original house, which had three steps that had led to the backyard but now led to the three added-on rooms that were constructed prior to us moving in.

The first room at the base of these steps was another, much larger twelve-by-eight-foot, more functional kitchen than the small one in the front of the house. On the other side of the kitchen was the large twelve-by-twelve-foot den that had a fireplace and led to the ninth and final room, the back porch, which was a long twelve-by-six-foot room that was covered with ivy on the outside, and on the inside were large thin sheets of plywood nailed together. There was absolutely no insulation in that room. It was originally supposed to be a patio or back porch. There was always a set of bunkbeds along the far wall, and two hardy brothers usually slept in there. The room was very cold in the winter and warm in the summer, and since there were more boys than girls in the family, usually it was two brothers who were the ones to sleep there.

There was also a single bed on the back porch that I did sleep in for a short while when I was about ten. The bed was placed along and outside the wall that bordered a small corner of our parent's room above. There was a window about four feet above that single bed that was originally the back window of the house. We did a lot of crawling in and out of that window between the back porch and my parents' room over the years. I and several others crawled in and out of it on that day we were all there checking out the house before we moved in.

There was a chest of drawers and a desk for studying on the back porch that were the only other pieces of furniture there. It could get to 38 or 39 degrees in there in the middle of a cold night in the winter. We had to open the door to the den to let some warm air in from the fireplace that we kept burning late into the night, which was the only method of heating in those back three rooms. The back porch had a screen door on the northwest corner that opened onto the backyard. The lower half was made out of wood and the upper half was screened. That back screen door was kept locked most nights with a simple hooked latch—the kind of latch where the hook part is connected to the door and the small round metal hole it fits into when locked is connected to the door jamb.

All three add-on rooms were built on a four-inch-thick slab of cement. I believe those three rooms were originally meant to serve as a large entertainment area and were not meant to house half a dozen kids. The kitchen had linoleum on the floor over the cement, and the cement floors of the den and back porch were painted red.

As soon as you walked into the kitchen from the back door of the house, there was a long seven-by-four-foot wooden dinner table on your left that was placed in the northwest corner of the room. The west side of the room faced the backyard, and the north side was built along the driveway. Those two sides of the kitchen had 1-by-1-foot-square windows that started eighteen inches from the floor and stopped about two feet from the ceiling. A four-inch-wide wooden bench was constructed that ran along the base of the windows. The big table was placed against the corner, and at times eight of us could fit around the table while sitting on that four-inch ledge. We could eat, entertain company, celebrate birthdays, or do our homework on that multipurpose table.

A stove was on your right as you entered the kitchen from the back door, leaving only about a foot and a half between the table and stove to walk through the rest of the kitchen to the upper rooms in the house. Next to the stove in the southeast corner of the kitchen was a counter and sink with upper and lower shelves for our dishes, pots, pans, food, etc. With all the constant foot traffic walking on that narrow eighteen-inch swath of floor between the stove and dinner table day after day, year after year, we eventually wore a path through the linoleum and the coat of red paint, which exposed the original layer of cement.

Unbelievably, in the worst possible place, a leak from the ceiling eventually developed in the kitchen that dripped onto that highest-trafficked area directly in the middle of that eighteen-inch path between the front of the stove and the dinner table. Until Dad could get up there and fix it, every time it rained we had to put a pot down to catch the rainwater, and inevitably someone would forget the pot was there and in the middle of the night, on their way to the bathroom, would kick and spill the water all over the kitchen floor. That person was usually not about to clean up the water in the middle of the night, let alone admit it was them that forgot it was there and kicked it over. Fortunately for us girls, our room was above the kitchen and just a few steps down the hall from the bathroom.

Because the windows were constructed to look like French windows that stopped at the four-inch bench we used to sit on while eating, we were constantly breaking the lower set of one-foot-square windows. Sometimes just sitting our butts down on the small fixed wooden bench at the bottom of the window pane caused a window to break. The busy gate entrance to the backyard from the driveway was right next to those low kitchen windows. It was easy to break a window from a ball or object kicked, thrown, or hit from our backyard while playing, or from someone carrying a large object through that back gate.

My dad solved the problem by installing clouded white

quarter-inch sturdy plastic sheets over the inside of the lower three-inch portion of the windows. We could still easily see from inside or outside the kitchen through the windows left above the plastic. After that, we only broke an occasional window from the backyard side. Like the time I broke a kitchen window when I was in the backyard waiting for dinner to be ready. I was playing in one back corner of the yard near the tether-ball pole with a golf club and golf ball. Never in my wildest dreams did I think at twelve years old I could accurately hit a golf ball that could break a kitchen window from thirty-five feet away, shattering glass all over the kitchen table into the ready-to-eat dinner. It took me, and those who were in the kitchen at the time, a few seconds to realize what had happened. At first, I thought I had hit the side of the house and not a window, so I just stayed where I was. It was when six bewildered, frightened, and then angry brothers and sisters came outside with my parents yelling, "What was that?" "What did you do?" that I realized I had broken a window and was in big trouble. I was the only one in the backyard, and the only one standing there with a golf club in my hands, so there was no talking or lying my way out of that one.

As I remember, there was glass in the mashed potatoes and the broccoli that had just been placed in the middle of the table. There was no telling if the chicken on the stove had glass as well. Nonetheless, everything had to be thrown away. I got the evil eye and a lot of guff from everyone for the rest of the evening. I did get dessert, which was spared from any glass, and I didn't get a spanking. The only good news is that my dad drove to the Lucky Boy fast-food place on Otis and Firestone Boulevard and bought us all hamburgers and French fries. By the way, I found out that I had just missed hitting the house instead of that window by three inches.

After our first initial run-through of the new house in the summer of 1955, my next memory was of standing just outside the back door, at five years old, playing with a bottle of bubbles my parents gave some of us younger ones to keep us busy and out of their way. My dad was taking another trip to the old house to bring more items back. I wanted to go with him, so I set my open bottle of bubbles down just outside the back door. I started to run toward my dad to get in the truck when he said I couldn't go. It was bad enough that I didn't get to go with him, but just as I ran back to get my bottle of bubbles, someone opened the back door and spilled them! I stomped my feet in hurt and anger and started to cry. To make matters worse, because I made such a scene, I was told to go take a nap. Not a fun way to remember one of my first experiences in the house I would live in for the next fifteen years.

I am not sure why, but I did not go to kindergarten like many of my brothers and sisters. I began the first grade in the fall of 1956. The nuns who taught us were from the Sisters of St. Joseph of Orange, California. They started in Le Puy, France, in 1650. France was experiencing many terrible wars in which many pious widows

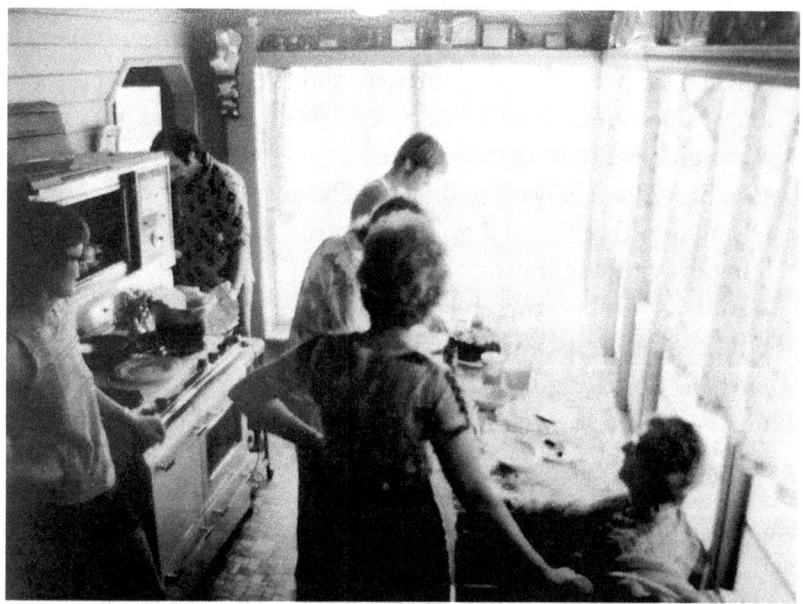

The "back kitchen," 1971.

cared for the sick and orphaned who had no social structure to care for them. In 1652 they were officially organized into a religious congregation and became known as the Sisters of St. Joseph.

The Sisters of St. Joseph of Orange were established in 1912. A group of eight nuns originally settled in Eureka, California, where they opened a hospital and became nurses to respond to the needs of the many thousands affected by the great influenza epidemic of 1918. They are still in existence today. Many of them currently provide support to patients at St. Joseph Hospital in Orange, and others continue to teach at various Catholic schools in Southern California, like they did for us while we attended St. Emydius Catholic School.

My earliest memory of first grade was the location of the classroom. It was on the busy southwest corner of the school, at California Boulevard and Norton Avenue. It was the place where the school buses and parents picked up their kids before and after school. The intersection at the time was a four-way stop. There were windows on both the south and west sides of the classroom, providing plenty of sunlight each school day and plenty of things outside for me to see instead of paying attention to my teacher.

Unfortunately, it was the same intersection where my classmate Cheryl Rottino's brother was run over and killed by a car when he stepped out from behind a school bus and started to run west across the intersection to catch up with Cheryl. After that unfortunate incident, the school moved the pickup and drop-off place to a less busy part of Norton Avenue, east of the previous intersection.

I also remember walking down the Norton Avenue sidewalk single file from the playground and lunch area several times a day in two lines, boys in one line and girls in the other. Once the bell rang to signal the beginning of school or the end of recess or lunch, my classmates and I found our predesignated lineup area and walked back to our first-grade classroom. One memory was of a boy named Roger who had polio that affected his right leg. He used crutches, and his affected right lower leg was bent at the knee and held in place behind him by a thick green army-looking belt that went around his right ankle and was hooked to the top of his pants at his belt. When he sat down he would remove the belt from around his ankle and waist and take his seat.

Polio affected a lot of people in the 1950s, including neighbors, friends, and classmates. I was about twelve when the disease was thankfully nearly eradicated worldwide. It had no cure and no identified causes. No one had the slightest idea where polio had come from or why it especially paralyzed so many children. Nobody has ever discovered completely how it is that polio is spread.

Those who were diagnosed with polio recovered with little

or no disability. In 1952, the worst epidemic year, three thousand people died from polio. In 1950 a man named Jonas Salk was certain that he had developed a cure and wanted to begin testing it on children. It took several years to convince the National Foundation for Infant Paralysis (NFIP) that the vaccine was safe. The vaccine was finally given to children in 1954. Once this vaccine was proved to be an effective cure, polio was basically wiped out in our nation (Charles Wills, *America in the 1950s*).

My family received the polio shot in 1956 when our family doctor told my mother that she could get shots for all of us at $3 a family. The shots were being given in the gym at neighboring Lynwood High School the next evening. She decided to take advantage of the $3-a-family offer by taking all twelve of us over to each get a shot. I remember when we arrived at the empty gym that the staff was pleasantly surprised to see a dozen or so people show up all at once to get a shot, not realizing we were all from the same family. We learned that the shots were $3 a person, not $3 a family! My mom realized Dr. Carmody had misunderstood the price of each shot. She only had $7 on her, and after a few phone calls to their superiors, the staff thankfully accepted her money without turning us away. I was grateful that we got our polio shots and that we were never affected by polio, as so many others were.

In 1956 each grade at St. Emydius, first through eighth, had two classes. There were two first-grade classes, 1A and 1B, two second-grade classes, 2A and 2B, and so on, through eight grades. While in first grade I experienced, on several occasions, a rather loud and rough lay teacher (not a nun) next door to my classroom who frightened me and others with her booming voice and strict ways. She was Mrs. Schneider. She was big, overweight, bow-legged, walked with a limp, never smiled, and had the jowls of a bulldog and a five o'clock shadow to boot. She was a scary, formidable figure to just about everyone. She was also one of the two second-grade teachers I could possibly have the next year!

I prayed all summer that I would not have her as my next teacher. My prayers were answered when I learned my second-grade teacher was a newly arrived Irish nun named Sister Mary Patricia. I was never so happy in all my life that I did not have Mrs. Schneider. I loved Sister Mary Patricia and her soft, pleasant Irish voice. My sister Sue, just one year younger than me, cried for two days when she found out that she would have Mrs. Schneider for second grade. After she found out she had Mrs. Schneider, Sue told my mom that one year of school was enough for her, and she felt that she didn't need to go to school anymore. Turns out she did just fine in Mrs. Schneider's class and was none the worse for wear. She was too frightened to misbehave!

My only unfortunate memory of second grade was when Sister Mary Patricia was working with a small group of students with their reading, and the rest of us were working on an assignment. I had to use the restroom, and unfortunately, I approached her at a time when she was getting very frustrated with the poor reading performance by those students. I had hardly opened my mouth when she dismissed me back to my seat. It seemed forever before the next recess would come, and I knew I could not hold it much longer. Sure enough, I peed in my pants while sitting at my desk just minutes from the next recess and drew the attention of the surrounding students as the pee leaked onto the floor.

It was then that Sister Mary Patricia came over to see what was going on and saw the shamed, embarrassed look on my face. Her face was one of anger until she realized what had happened. Her stern look then turned to pity as she told me to go to the restroom and clean-up and bring back some paper towels to clean up around my desk. Thank goodness the bell to go to recess sounded while I was in the restroom, and I was able to clean myself and my desk area by myself instead of in front of my classmates. Everyone was pretty kind to me upon returning to class. I was relieved that no one made fun of me or made things any worse than it already was.

Sister Patricia felt so bad that this had happened to me that she told the class the next day that from now on, if anyone had to use the restroom during class, to raise one finger if you had to go and she would let us. Some students took advantage of the new rule, as many more students suddenly had to use the restroom during class time than before my incident. But all in all, I believe at least a few students were saved the possible future embarrassment of peeing on themselves in front of everyone else because of me. She also called my mother that evening to apologize for the incident and told her about her new rule. My mom did talk to me that night after the phone call from Sister Mary Patricia to ask if I was OK. I was pleased that my teacher took the time to call and apologize and felt she was truly sorry that it had happened and would take steps to see that it did not happen again.

My most pleasant experience of second grade was making my first Holy Communion. It was in the spring of 1958, just before my eighth birthday. There was a woman with no children in the parish who wanted to buy a Holy Communion dress for someone.

I was informed by my mom that I was the one picked to receive it! It is required by the Church that the Holy Communion dress be white. The woman went with us to the dress shop and not only bought me a Holy Communion dress but a beautiful pink dress as well. I was thrilled! Both dresses were high quality and lasted through my next two sisters for their Communions and other various events: to church, for Easter, to birthday parties, and family gatherings. I was so thankful to that woman for making my Communion so memorable. I still have my Holy Communion individual and class pictures from that Sunday in the spring of 1958.

Once we arrived home from school each day, we were expected to change out of the one and only set of school clothes we each had, get a snack, and start our homework before going out to play or watch TV. It was very difficult to wash eight or ten sets of uniforms in the middle of the week. It was tough getting one uniform to last a week without it getting too wrinkly or dirty. I must have done well to make my uniforms last all week all those years. It was not until seventh grade when my teacher, Sister Mario, took me aside one time as I was exiting the cloakroom to ask me why my blouse was gray instead of white. I just gave her this puzzled, devastated look because I didn't see my blouse as gray. I did after that! I told my mom when I got home, and she bought me another blouse as soon as she had money. Thanks a lot, Sister Mario!

The first family picture taken in black-and-white in 1964 shows most of us wearing some piece or pieces of our school uniforms. That's because our uniforms were often the best pieces of clothing we owned at the time. We often wore our school blouses or pants to church or birthday parties. We were usually given a new uniform at the beginning of each school year or hand-me-down uniform clothing from an older sibling, depending on whether or not the sibling just older than you was the same gender. Sometimes there was enough money to buy two uniform blouses, shirts, pants, or skirts. Our new Buster Brown shoes we got at the beginning of each school year were expected to last a full year. To make that one pair of school shoes last, we went barefoot a lot, even during the wintertime. I still like going barefoot a lot, and not because it saves me from buying a new pair of shoes.

We were fortunate at the beginning of each school year that school supplies were fairly inexpensive. For about $5 our parents could buy a good amount of our needed supplies for any given school year. They bought Pee-Chee folders for 10 cents apiece. Packs of pencils were ten for a dollar, and a two-hundred-sheet pack of binder paper was 99 cents, which lasted at least four or five of us older kids about a month or two of school work. Erasers were 10 cents apiece, and a box of eight crayons was 39 cents, with a box of sixteen crayons a reasonable 69 cents.

The third and fourth grades were uneventful. The only thing that stands out to me in third grade was getting the measles right in the middle of learning my twelve times table. To this day I know all my multiples through eleven, but I still struggle to remember all the twelve times tables after 12 × 5. The only other thing that stands out from third grade was when I was helping my teacher, Sister Michael Arthur, to open our classroom door after lunch to let my classmates in. She looked at me and said, "Why can't you be as smart as your brother Harry?" She had my brother Harry, who is a year older than me, in her class the previous year. That made me feel good. No teacher ever asked any of my younger brothers or sisters who ended up with the same teacher after me why they weren't as smart as me!

I had Mrs. Meyers as my fifth-grade teacher. She was very strict, but I did learn a lot in her class, especially geography and math. I was never very good at math, but she made learning decimals and simple equations easy. It helped me later in high school when I took algebra as a sophomore.

My favorite grades at St. Emydius were the seventh and eighth grades. It was early in the seventh grade that I was standing on a bench that was cemented to and ran along the outside walls of the house where the nuns lived. Students sat on those long sets of benches to eat lunch. Even if we finished eating early, we had to stay on the benches until a bell rang to let us play for a while before returning to our classrooms. If one of the patrolling nuns caught us off our bench before the bell, we were made to sit for five minutes after the bell rang while everyone else was playing. It was a large blacktopped playground with a big five-inch white line painted down the center of the playground that separated the girls' yard from the boys. We played separately from each other. In the boys' yard, which took up the east side of the playground, there were painted bases on the blacktop to play kickball and several basketball courts. In the girls' yard, which took up the west side of the playground, there were the painted lines of a volleyball court and several hopscotch game squares, along with a few areas painted for playing four square. The school yard was where cars parked on Sunday while attending church.

Since there were about a thousand students attending the school in 1962, there were two lunch periods in which about five hundred students in each ate. The younger four grades ate first, and the older four grades ate second. We got twenty minutes to eat and twenty minutes to play before returning to class for the afternoon.

I was standing on that corner of one of those long benches after school waiting for my mom to pick me up when a woman who was coaching the girls' basketball team at the time approached me and stopped and said, "Do you want to play on the school's girls' basketball team?" Her name was Elaine Stanley. She had several of her six children attending St. Emydius at the time, and her daughter Pam was a year older than me and was already competing on the team. I said I would have to talk to my mom and, if she said I could play, I would stay the next day. My mom said yes, and the rest is history.

Little did I know then that Mrs. Stanley would be the catalyst that changed my life and put me on an eventual personal and professional career path that saw me compete athletically at the state, national, and international levels, prompted me to become an instructor of physical education activity classes, and eventually serve as a college coach and athletic administrator for more than twenty years. I had no experience competing on sports teams at the time. It turns out that my mom's tardiness in picking me up late that day led to my participation in six different sports over the next twenty-five years.

I didn't know it at the time, but I took to athletic competition naturally. It helped that I was used to competing at home for everything from playing outdoor games to competing for food and attention. After all, at this point in my life, I had four older brothers and four younger brothers. When I wasn't running *away* from one of my four older brothers, I was running *after* one of my four younger brothers. Sports turned out to be a way for me to get the attention and accolades I yearned for at home. Sports were also an opportunity for me, unlike at home, to stand out from others.

Mrs. Stanley was a great coach for her time. I incorporated her methods of coaching into my own eventual teams. She emphasized the basics, conducted repetitive drills, and was a great motivator. I loved every minute of my first two years of competition. I went on to compete on the school's volleyball and softball teams as well. Mrs. Stanley also coached the volleyball team. Her daughter Pam and I went on to compete in high school together on the girls' basketball team.

Before 1962, girls' basketball was played with six players. Three were guards who could only play on one side of the court and only played defense, and three played on the other side of the court and could only play offense. You were limited to three dribbles, and then you had to pass the ball. In 1963 the game evolved to allow two of the six players to be rovers, which means they could "rove" across the center court line and were allowed to play both offense and defense. In eighth grade, in the spring of 1963, Mrs. Stanley had me playing in one of the rover positions. I liked being able to run the full length of the court and play both offense and defense.

In eighth grade, my sister Sue was now playing on the team with me as a seventh grader. She had big hands and arms down to her knees! She made a great defensive player. All she had to do was stick one arm up full length when our opponents were shooting. She easily blocked their shot, then passed the ball on to me, and off I went to the other end of the court to score.

The very first trophy I was awarded was in seventh grade at the St. Joseph's Girls High School Annual Basketball Tournament in Orange. I made the all-star squad, which very few seventh graders made. I still have that trophy stored in my garage. I am very proud of it. Earning that first trophy taught me from an early age that I am capable of achieving anything I put my mind to and that I will be rewarded for my efforts provided I am willing to put in a lot of hard work, learn from my mistakes, be a team player, and always give it my best.

Those first two years of competition taught me that results in life cannot be accomplished without the commitment and dedication of the entire team. I had already experienced time and time again how important team work is in my own family situations. No family, team, business, or any unit can succeed without the cooperation and collaboration of everyone involved. That concept served me well over the years as my athletic life and sports competition progressed.

My seventh-grade teacher was mean Sister Mario. She was thin as a rail and never smiled. She seemed to have it in for me because she was always on my case about one thing or another, like drawing my attention to my gray blouse. It seemed to me that she was always waiting for me to slip up so she could call me on the carpet. She knew I was excelling in sports and wanted to make sure I was also excelling in my academics. I understood and appreciated that about her. I rarely missed turning in my assignments; you just didn't do that in Catholic school, or you were made to believe that you would end up on the cross like Jesus.

One time I missed turning in a math homework assignment in the middle of our softball season. Sure enough, Sister Mario asked me to stay after school the next day. I wasn't used to someone telling me I did something wrong, so as she was telling me that "All work and no play makes Jack a dull boy," it made me feel so bad that she hardly got the first few words out of her mouth when I started to cry. When she saw my tears, her voice softened and trailed off to barely a whisper by the time she got to "a dull boy." After a brief explanation of what she had just said and why she said it, which I wasn't hearing because I was focused on my crying, she then let me leave the classroom.

It took me about a week of thinking over and over about what she said when it came to me that her quote didn't apply to my missed assignment. "All work and no play" means you are not going to have any fun in life if all you are doing is working all the time. That means I was doing the right thing all along by playing on the school's sports teams, because the playing didn't make me dull—it was doing all that homework that could make me dull! I wanted so badly to ask *her* to stay after school and tell *her* that her "makes Jack a dull boy" quote was not what she should have said. I think that's why her voice trailed off that day toward the end of the sentence, because she knew she had picked the wrong quote to get her point across. At least that's what I would like to think. Needless to say, I did not miss turning in any more homework assignments for the rest of my seventh-grade school year, and Sister Mario stayed off my case after that.

I loved my eighth and final year at St. Emydius. It was fun being the head honcho of the school and a recognizable star member of the school's sports teams. It was now 1964 and the baby boomers were in full swing as many schools nationwide were bulging at the seams with students. By then, St. Emydius had twenty instead of sixteen classrooms. Four classes were added that were combinations of two class levels. I was in the class that was a mix of seventh and eighth graders. I do not remember my eighth-grade teacher's name, but she did a great job juggling two grades. I sat next to Eddie Escobedo most of the year. We sat in one of the last desks in the last two rows, nearest the back door, where we could get away with talking while the nun was teaching at the front of the classroom. He was the most popular guy in school. He was smart, funny, handsome, had beautiful dark skin and the most beautiful white teeth. We got along great in class, especially when our eighth-grade side of the class was doing an assignment while she was working with the seventh-grade side of the class. He and I shared our art supplies and continued to be good friends through high school, where he continued to be the most popular guy on campus.

One vivid memorable part of school was listening to Carmen Dragon and his orchestra on the radio every Friday morning at about 10 a.m. as part of our weekly music lesson. His music played in all the upper-level grades over the intercom. We were expected to listen and discern the various instruments being played and at times just to enjoy the music. I was never good at music and was glad that it was never an important part of our learning nor carried much weight on our report cards. I am a terrible singer and to this day I listen to the melody more than the words.

When I wasn't attending school, I was watching a *lot* of TV as a child. We got our first TV when I was six in 1956. It was a small black-and-white TV with a fifteen-inch screen. There were only a few local and national stations at the time; seven channels were available in the Los Angeles area. These shows only ran from 6 a.m. to midnight each day. When the shows signed off at midnight, the screen went to a picture of an Indian in full headgear with a background that had a radio tower and several large circles behind him that were radio waves. This picture remained until 6 a.m. the next morning. Everything was pretty much live TV, like *The Lawrence Welk Show, The Ed Sullivan Show,* and the news, of course. The first and only news anchor at the time was George Putnam. He came on at 10 p.m., and my dad would not miss him. I remember that George would sign off each night by saying about tomorrow's newscast, "See you at ten—see you then."

Televisions had several knobs that adjusted the horizontal picture, the volume, and the brightness. We were always getting up to fix the horizontal picture on the TV, which, out of the blue, would just start jumping or flipping, making it difficult to watch. We also had to get up to change the channel. It was tough having one TV because we all had to agree on what one program we wanted to watch, and then find a spot in the room among thirteen other people where you could see the show. On Sunday nights, we all agreed to watch the Walt Disney show and Mutual of Omaha's *Wild Kingdom*.

On Saturday mornings, we looked forward to watching Mighty Mouse cartoons (about a Superman-type mouse), *My Friend Flicka* (about the adventures of a horse), and *Sky King* (the adventures of the pilot of a small plane). Other programs we watched during the week were *Highway Patrol, The Twilight Zone*, Bugs Bunny, and *Lassie*. Other weekly shows we watched back in the 1950s were *Leave It to Beaver, The Donna Reed Show, What's My Line?*, and *Concentration*, to name a few. Many of these original shows can still be seen on local cable stations. Some nights we watched roller derby and wrestling from the Olympic Auditorium in Los Angeles with announcer Bill Welsh. One of my current friends that I met through a college classmate many years ago is Sally Vega, one of the best roller derby skaters of all time. There has been a resurgence of roller derby competition and popularity in several large cities of late where Sally has been asked to appear. Sally is also a great badminton player.

Sometimes in the early evening while eating dinner, we gathered in the den where the TV was located to watch Engineer Bill. Between cartoons and commercials, we played Red Light, Green Light with Engineer Bill. It was a way to get kids to drink their milk. He prefaced the game by saying that "On the green light, you go, and on the red light, you stop, because no good engineer would ever run a red light." He had two child guests on his show who competed against each other to see who finished their glass of milk first. Each with our full glass of milk ready, Engineer Bill would say "green light," which is when, of course, you would begin drinking your milk, until he said "red light," at which time you stopped drinking. If you didn't stop drinking after he called "red light," you were out of the game. The winner was the first one who finished their glass before anyone else. On the show, that person would win a prize. At home, we often played, but usually just ended up arguing about who won.

Some of the popular commercials, with their catchy tunes, I remember watching during those early 1950s were for Alka-Seltzer, Ipana toothpaste, Charlie Tuna, and Dr. Ross Dog Food, that had an especially catchy jingle I remember to this day:

> Dr. Ross Dog Food—do him a favor
> It's got more meat and it's got more flavor
> It's got more meat to make him feel the way he sho-o-ould
> Dr. Ross Dog Food is dog gone good ... Woof!

We watched Sheriff John, who came on in the middle of the day during the summer and early afternoon during the school year. He showed cartoons and had guests on his show. One of the things he did was sing "Happy Birthday" to a member of his home audience who wrote in. It was not the traditional birthday song but a fun tune that was different and appropriate.

In my early childhood years, what I remember about our typical dinner routine was first hearing my mom yell, "Dinner is ready!" and then, no matter where we were or what we were doing, we usually made a beeline for the kitchen. If we were outside playing in the backyard when she yelled that dinner was ready, and you tripped while running in with everyone else, you might as well get up, turn around, and keep playing, because you weren't going to get any dinner that night. It was important to get to the dinner table as quickly as possible. There were a few times that we ran out of food before everyone had a chance to eat. There was always something in the fridge or in the food shelves to fix and eat if someone did miss dinner or did not get enough to eat during dinner. I remember being hungry after a light dinner and eating raw uncooked spaghetti out of the package, which was the only thing I could find in the kitchen shelves to eat.

Typically, upon entering the kitchen for dinner, we grabbed a paper plate and eating utensils, which were all placed in a pile in the center of the table. There were a few stacks of plastic or metal cups for everyone placed in the center of the table as well. These items were placed there by whoever's turn it was to set the table that evening. We then turned around to the stove and filled our plates with whatever had been cooked.

At first, we used to use glass plates, bowls, and cups, but it only took a few years of use before most of the glassware got chipped or broken. That is when we bought plastic bowls and cups and started using paper plates. We did get these nice brightly colored twelve-ounce aluminum drinking glasses that came free inside the large bags of Tom Sawyer potato chips. The most fun part was getting to be the one who got to open the bag first and find the cup. We used those cups for quite a few years.

A favorite dinner was spaghetti and a vegetable with oven-baked French or sourdough bread. The only problem with having spaghetti was the way it had to be prepared to satisfy the various ways everyone liked it. Some of us did not like meat, so the hamburger was cooked separately. Some did not like spaghetti sauce, so that was warmed up separately and left in a pan. The spaghetti itself was left in its own large four-quart pot after boiling and draining the water off it. Everyone could now help themselves to a satisfying dinner by mixing one or all the ingredients together or separately.

Sometimes Marv, who was the oldest, tallest, and the quickest, was the first one to enter the kitchen and stick his finger in a piece of chicken or meat and claim, "This one is mine!" Some of the rest of us started doing the same thing until Mom put a stop to it. We older kids did help the younger ones fill their plates. As we all got older and bigger and sometimes had friends over to eat, the kitchen seating space became more difficult and limited in accommodating everyone. Sometimes a few of us sat and ate on the steps leading down from the girls' room to the kitchen. Someone could pull out the cutting board next to the stove and eat there. There were a few occasions where the only place left to eat was to find an unoccupied place somewhere in the kitchen to stand and eat or go into the den and find a bed or chair where you could sit and eat.

With eight or nine people sitting around the dinner table, having to go to the bathroom during dinner was difficult. The only way to leave the table was to either crawl under or try to get three or four people to move out from behind the table, which wasn't likely, and then ask them to move out again when you returned. It was wiser to use the bathroom before dinner or just hold it until you were done eating. However, washing your hands and using the bathroom before dinner would most likely make you late, and you ran the risk of not getting a good seat or choice picks of food. We did often use the kitchen sink to quickly wash our hands before dinner, which gave a person a few steps' advantage and a better chance of a good seat and ample amounts of food.

When we finished dinner, we simply threw our paper plate in the trash and our aluminum cup and eating utensils in the sink. One of us three girls was responsible to wash the dishes, depending on who was assigned to wash the dinner dishes that week. We rotated weekly washing breakfast, lunch, and dinner dishes. I washed breakfast dishes one week, and then lunch dishes the next, and dinner dishes for a week after that, then started again with breakfast the following week. My older brothers rotated mowing the lawns and taking out the trash, and we were all responsible for keeping our rooms clean ... yeah, right!

One of the games that most of us played during dinner was guessing state capitals. One person would say a state, and the first person to give the correct capital got to have the next turn. We also played "I Went on a Picnic," where one person starting by saying, "I went on a picnic and I took ..." let's say watermelon. The next person would say, "I went on a picnic" and had to say what the people ahead of them said in the order they said it, and then say what you would bring. If you said the picnic items out of order or couldn't remember, you were eliminated from the game. The person with the best memory, who named all the picnic items in order, was the winner.

One other game we played during dinner was to give everyone, when it was your turn, the first letter of a bird you had in mind. If someone guessed the name of that bird, it was their turn. I remember these games fondly and always looked forward to playing them. It was educational and an enjoyable intimate time with family.

Our next task after dinner was to clear the table and use it to finish our homework and make our lunches on it before going to bed. It was like an assembly line, with all the lunch items placed on the table, starting with a pile of brown paper lunch bags and plastic sandwich bags. What was next on the table was a loaf of bread, a jar of mayonnaise, a package or two of bologna or salami, a jar of peanut butter, and a large bag of some sort of chips or Fritos. Next was the fruit for the next day, and lastly there was a package of cookies from which to choose and pack two or three in a plastic bag. No one regulated how much we took, but we knew we had to make sure everyone got enough, so we regulated ourselves—most of the time. We had to make sure that we put our names on our bags before putting them in the refrigerator. We grabbed a small carton of milk at school the next day from the back of the classroom before exiting to go outside and eat lunch. Milk was provided to those who paid their $1 "milk money" at the beginning of each month.

We were expected to brush our teeth in the morning and at night, but I don't remember brushing my teeth on a regular basis as a child, and I know my mom was not about to check on twelve people twice a day to see if we did. Most of the time, if I did decide or felt forced to brush my teeth, I used whatever toothbrush was available or looked good in the toothbrush rack. Those toothbrushes that did not fit in the four-brush holder were tucked into the top left-hand drawer next to the bathroom sink. I think I only got caught and yelled at a couple of times for using someone else's toothbrush. I was a young teenager before I remember having a toothbrush that I and only I used on a regular basis. Now I know why, when one of us got sick, we all got sick. I was probably one of those that got us all sick.

Mandatory bedtime was staggered by age. The younger ones went to bed at about 8 p.m., the middle kids at about 8:30 or 9, and the older ones at 9:30 or 10. Someone slept in a single bed in the dining room in the front of the house because we did not use that room as a dining area. The bed was set under a window that faced onto the front porch. The only other piece of furniture in that rather small dining room was a desk against the back wall.

The living room, the "front room" to us, had a single bed in the far left corner as you stood looking in from the front porch doorway. There was a long, large, sturdy couch and several chairs in the front room, in which we used to watch TV when the TV was housed there. There was the large round, wooden, six-person dining table next to the bed that we used for homework and playing board games. We often sat on the bed and used the bed as chairs while at the table. I slept in that single bed in the front room for a stint when I was a teenager. I vividly remember sleeping in that bed under the open window next to that round table and hearing one summer night the frightening burst of gunfire coming from the city of Watts, about three miles away, during the unfortunate Watts riots of 1965.

It was on August 11, 1965, that racial tensions reached a breaking point in the predominantly black Watts neighborhood of Los Angeles. Two white policemen scuffled with a black motorist suspected of drunken driving. A crowd gathered near the corner of Avalon Boulevard and 116th Street to watch the arrest and soon grew angry by what they believed to be yet another racially motivated abuse by the police.

A riot soon began, spurred on by residents of Watts who were embittered after years of economic and political isolation. The riot eventually ranged over a fifty-square-mile area that at that time was called South Central Los Angeles. The rioters were looting stores and torching buildings. Order was restored by thousands of National Guard troops on August 16. The five days of violence left 34 dead, 1,032 injured, nearly 4,000 arrested, and 40 million dollars of property destroyed (History.com). It was difficult to watch the riots on TV each evening, but I understood the frustration and pent-up anger that is often seen in many of our larger cities that unfortunately continues today.

My parents had their own room, of course, and they slept in a double bed. If one of us in the late afternoon got cranky or misbehaved, we were often banished to their room, with the door closed, to take a nap or take a time out. If you wanted to try it, you could sometimes sneak out of their room via the window that led to the back porch and blend in unnoticed with the rest of the family hopefully for a while. Often you were discovered by another sibling, who knew you were being punished and supposed to be in her room, and who told Mom, she'd send you right back to her room for twice as long a period of time as she originally did. It was usually worth the risk to try escaping.

Their room housed the one and only telephone in the house, which sat on a small table next to my mom's side of the bed. It made it difficult to have any semblance of an intimate conversation with anyone if she or dad happened to be in bed when you got a call. Our number in the 1950s was originally LO-93103. The *LO* stood for "Lorraine," which determined our location before area codes. The LO letters were dropped in the mid-1960s and turned into seven numbers, as seen on the corresponding rotary phone dial. Our phone number then became 569-3103. Then eventually the area code 213 was added as a prefix to our number in the late 1960s. It became our area code when the population of Los Angeles County exploded, as did the demand for more phone numbers than were available. The 213 area code was eventually split into the 323 area code.

After our nasty neighbor Elsie complained to the Better Business Bureau that my dad was running a business out of his house, we were forced to add another telephone line and number to be used for business only. That phone was housed on a desk next to my dad's side of the bed. It worked out well after all to have that second phone, even though it was a small financial burden. There was a bassinet next to mom that housed the latest baby. There was a chest of drawers and a file cabinet in which mom kept a file on each of us and other important household, personal, and business papers. As each of us were of age and left the house, she gave us our file. The file was filled with important childhood papers, pictures, certificates, school report cards, and sports accomplishments she kept that we did not know she was accumulating. There was a small closet for my parents clothes, shoes, etc. It was deep into that closet floor that my dad kept his .22 rifle. It was never loaded, and we all knew not to touch it—but we did get it out a few times and play with it anyway.

Down the hall from my parents room, past the bathroom in the girls' room, was a set of wooden army-surplus bunk beds on the south side of the room and a double bed without a headboard on the other side of the room under two corner windows. I spent most of my childhood and teen years sleeping in one of those three beds at one time or another. There was a four-drawer chest set against the east wall between the closet door and the doorway that led to the front kitchen. Since I was the oldest, I got the top drawer; Sue got the second drawer, and Clarissa got the third drawer. The fourth drawer was used to place baby clothes and other miscellaneous clothing items for whichever toddler was in the crib at the time. That crib was located next to the double bed and was the first thing you saw on your left upon entering the girls' room from the back kitchen.

We did not have any air-conditioning anywhere in the house, so the windows in our rooms were left open at night in the summer, which provided much needed cool air, especially for those of us in beds with two people or more. On some of those hot evenings, we got a small glass of water or a few ice cubes from the refrigerator freezer section, lifted up our pajama top, and dripped a few drops of water or rubbed an ice cube on our stomach, and then blew on the areas where the water drops and ice were. It did help cool us down enough that we could eventually get to sleep fairly quickly and comfortably.

The only fan in the house was a large box fan that was placed outside the bottom half of one of the two screened double French-style doors, only one of which we used to enter and exit from the backyard because the placement of that big fan kept us from using both doors. The fan was placed on cinder blocks so that it covered the lower three and a half feet of the door. In the wintertime, the inside glass door was closed in front of the fan. In the summertime that fan was going almost full time, cooling the den and a small portion of the kitchen. It mostly cooled down the den area, which was the largest room in the house and where most of us gathered to watch TV, play, and do homework. Sometimes we ate our dinner in the den and other times we went to the den to keep warm in the winter, as the fireplace was in there. That fireplace was the only heat available in those back three added-on rooms. In the heat of summer, Dad placed a large wet burlap bag over the back end of the fan that drew cool air into the den for about an hour. He would remoisten the bag and place it back over the back end of the fan. I believe that one of my character traits is that I am resourceful; now I know from whom I got that trait.

Within a few years of moving in, the lock on the back door broke and was never fixed. That back door was *always* unlocked, for over thirty years, before it was fixed by the people who bought the house when it was sold in the early 1990s. I never felt unsafe knowing the back door was never locked. Who in their right mind would ever try to break into a home where fourteen people were living and sleeping? We did not live in a neighborhood anyway where there were burglaries taking place. In the twenty-plus years I lived at the new house, I only remember coming home twice in all those years and finding no one home.

There was another set of army-surplus bunk beds in the den set against the back wall, and a double bed without a headboard or footboard behind the refrigerator. The den was also called the "boys' room" because only my brothers slept in that room throughout the years. The back porch housed the last of the three sets of bunk beds and two more brothers.

One of our morning challenges during the school week was to all get ready and leave for school or work on time. It was difficult with only one bathroom and twelve children who needed to get ready and leave all at about the same time. In 1965, when our youngest was five and attending kindergarten, there were still nine other siblings living in the house with our parents.

Marv, twenty years old at the time, was living in Oxnard with relatives and attending Ventura College, and Mel, at nineteen, was drafted into the Army and was stationed at Fort Dix in New Jersey. That meant that the remaining ten children battled it out each morning at the breakfast table and bathroom competing to get fed and ready for school or work on time. Harry, the fourth-oldest brother, was a junior at St. Don Bosco High School and needed to leave at 6:30 a.m. to get there by 7. John, the second oldest, was working in the shipyards in San Pedro and left on his motorcycle at about the same time as Harry. I and one sister were attending Pius X High School in Downey and left at about 7:40 a.m. to be there by 8. My mom drove us there after she got back from driving Harry to his high school. One younger sister and the younger four brothers were all attending St. Emydius School and usually got themselves off by 8:30 a.m. to be there by 9. Mom got Francine, the youngest, off to kindergarten by 9:45 a.m. Whew!

Having private time and mirror space in the bathroom was the most challenging part of getting ready in the morning. We could stand three-deep in the mirror by graduating height. One could be brushing their teeth, one washing their face, and the other could be combing their hair, all at the same time, and then shift places. Another place in the house where dad put up a mirror to help take pressure off the bathroom morning overcrowding was over the dryer in the front kitchen. Us girls used it a lot to comb and spray our hair each morning. One problem we encountered there was that the laundry never seemed to get folded after it came out of the dryer. Mom would dump the laundry on top of the dryer in front of that mirror. Every school day or Sunday morning, it seemed that just as my sisters and I were using the mirror, several of my brothers would rummage through the pile of clothes to try to pull out a clean pair of underwear or a matching pair of socks. If a brother was running out of get-ready time, but was quick enough to find a set of matching socks that wasn't his (it didn't have his initials written in laundry marker on the toe), they were his for the day, provided he could get the socks and his shoes on quick enough before the real owner noticed.

In my first year attending community college in 1969, I was always having difficulty getting enough time in the bathroom to allow me to leave in time for my first class, which started at 9 a.m. There were times after eating breakfast that I looked at the bathroom line and decided to just throw on some old clothes and drive to school early, where I showered and dressed in the locker room and then went on to class.

My family did eventually come up with a strategy we all agreed upon that got us some quality alone time in the bathroom outside of using it to get ready for school. We normally locked the door whenever we used the bathroom or took a bath or shower. The problem was that no sooner did we settle into taking a bath or shower than someone would come knocking on the door wanting to use the bathroom. This meant getting out of the tub, unlocking the door, getting back in the tub, closing the shower curtain while they were in there, waiting for them to finish, then getting back out of the tub to lock the door again, and then trying to get comfortable enough to finish your shower or bath. This could happen two or three times while trying to shower or bathe.

Our solution to this problem was to walk around and find anyone that was home and ask them, "Do you have to use the bathroom before I take a bath?" Some would say no, and some would go use the bathroom. However, sometimes it took fifteen minutes to find everyone in and around the house to ask everyone and then finally get your bath or shower started. Often, even after going through all that aggravating trouble of asking them, "Do you have to use the bathroom before I take a bath?" someone would inevitably come knocking on the door needing to use it. If we complained to those brothers or sisters for interrupting our bath time, after asking them earlier if they had to use it, they'd say they didn't have to use the bathroom twenty minutes ago when you first asked them, but now, twenty minutes later, they did!

We came up with a way to get into the shower or bath sooner by shortening the time it took to ask everyone, "Do you have to use the bathroom before I take a bath?" We sometimes had to ask all thirteen family members plus any visitors. After asking about the ninth or tenth person, the words got slurred together until eventually the question became, "Iza ba?" If you say, "Do you have to use the bathroom before I take a bath?" over and over again, and faster and faster each time, it does begin to sound like "Iza ba?" Try it. We were able to take our shower or bath at least three or four minutes sooner by shortening those twelve words to two, and you were a little less likely to get interrupted by one of the first family members you asked earlier. An added bonus was that "Iza ba?" could be a code that only the immediate family knew, and other friends or neighbors playing with us did not, which allowed us a comfortable way to ask what could otherwise be a delicate question.

I loved every minute of every day that I spent with my family in our "new house" on San Miguel Avenue in South Gate. Yes, things were crowded, loud, and always busy, but I would not change one minute of those crazy days for anything. I woke up each day filled with excitement and anticipation, figuring how I would navigate another day with thirteen other people, scores of classmates, teachers, and friends, and challenging classroom and play-yard situations; then live to do it all over again the next day. There were nights as I was happily going to sleep that I wished that we would all be together forever, that no one would ever move out or get married.

I especially loved celebrating holidays with my family. It meant being together having fun, eating specially cooked meals by my dad, and creating unforgettable memories. Easter was one of those holidays I really looked forward to celebrating; especially after getting through two hours of the Stations of the Cross in church each Friday morning for two months, not to mention giving up a favorite food or activity for forty days.

Easter mornings started out with most of us getting up early to look for where my parents hid our Easter baskets. It took me a few years as a kid to figure out that the Easter bunny did not exist after I recognized the same straw and plastic baskets were being hidden year after year. When Easter was over, we piled and stored the baskets back up in a shelf up over the refrigerator in the front kitchen. Also, after a while, my parents put our names on our basket because our age and gender determined what and how much candy or toys we got. If we found someone else's basket, we gave it to them and continued looking until we all found our own basket. We were told not to eat any of the goodies in our baskets because we wouldn't want to eat breakfast. We ate the goodies anyway *and* still ate breakfast.

After breakfast, we put on our possibly new Easter clothes for some of us and went to church. If we took too long eating and getting ready for church, it meant having to go to the high mass late Easter morning. The high mass on Easter Sunday was especially designed to celebrate the life, death, and resurrection of Jesus. The high mass usually took nearly two hours compared to the usual hour-long non–high mass. Much of it was spent kneeling on the pull-down padded kneelers. I and probably half the congregation ended up leaning back on the pew edge to relieve our tired knees.

During those Stations-of-the-Cross Fridays, when we did a lot of kneeling, the nuns used to patrol the pews looking for students leaning back on the pew edge just so they could tell us to move forward onto our knees again. Of course, as soon as she moved on to another pew section, students leaned back again; that's what I did.

It may not sound like it, but I am very grateful that I was raised in the Catholic religion and received a Catholic education for twelve years. I probably would not have gone to college or done as well as I did personally and professionally in life if I had gone to a public school. Sorry, public school system. I learned self-discipline and self-reliance from having been raised Catholic. Both served me well in life.

After church on Easter Sunday, we came home, took family pictures, changed into our play clothes, and then ate lunch. The most fun part of Easter Sunday was hiding the two dozen Easter eggs we had fun boiling and dying days earlier. Since there were twelve of us and twelve eggs in a dozen, it meant we each got to color two eggs. We had to dye the eggs either outside on a card table or make sure we dyed them on top of the vinyl kitchen tablecloth that we covered with sheets of newspaper. We had to make sure we didn't spill dye on any furniture or clothes, as it would leave a permanent stain. And heaven knows we didn't want any more stains than we already had on our furniture and clothes!

We could never decide who was going to be the one person who would get to hide the Easter eggs, so we decided that all of us would get a turn at hiding them. We started out with an older child hiding the eggs with a younger child. Those hunting for the eggs stayed up in the front of the house until the hiders called us out to the backyard. Once we collected all the eggs, the next two would hide them, and so on, until the eggs were hidden and rehidden six times. Visitors thought we were nuts! Sometimes, at the end of the day, we hadn't found all the eggs. We often found a rotten egg hidden in the ivy or woodpile months later.

Christmases were great fun and memorable. Several times members of our church showed up at our house a few days before Christmas with gifts of toys and books. They were gratefully and graciously received by my parents, and we appreciated the extra presents. Like Easter, we all got up early on Christmas Day and began opening presents as soon as everyone gathered in the living room. While we were opening presents in the front room of the house, my dad was cooking a turkey and other sides in the back kitchen.

Our routine was to give out one present at a time and wait for that person to open it. All of us would ooh and aah at the present and then open the next one. As I got older, I usually presided over the one-at-a-time handing out of the presents. It took between two and a half and three hours to hand out all of the usually 150-plus presents, given the slow pace at which we went. The only good thing with this time-consuming method of handing out presents was that, by the time we were done, the turkey dinner and all its fixings that dad was making was ready to eat!

If you received a bike for a Christmas present, it was mainly a hand-me-down. Dad went into the garage a few days before Christmas and tried his best to straighten the fenders, fix the chains, and spray-paint some of the old bicycles. Several of us moved up one bike size on Christmas Day!

The presents were housed under the decorated Christmas tree that was placed in front of the mantel on the south side of the living room. We used the same lights, bulbs, and tree decorations

Ray with Christmas presents at the San Miguel house, 1975.

year after year and bought only the long, thin aluminum icicles we threw on the tree at the end of decorating. My dad made sure that we had a water container screwed onto the bottom of the tree and kept it watered. We usually kept the tree up at least four or five days after Christmas was over. The tree did get *very* dry by then, and I remember that we kept the tree lights on all night sometimes. Some of those lights were bubblers that got hot enough, if left on long enough, to start bubbling, and could have ignited the dried tree needles. When I look back at it, I realize how *very* lucky we were over the years that a tree did not catch fire! So many homes have burned and people killed in recent years from Christmas trees catching fire.

Celebrating Halloween every October was fun. On occasion, my parents actually bought a few store-bought Halloween costumes that we wore year after year and passed down until the cheap nylon material tore and we had to throw it away. Most of the time we dressed as bums or hobos, which, much of the time, meant wearing bits and pieces of our own current well-worn play and church clothes. We looked deep into our closets or dresser drawers for old torn tops or bottoms and wore them with a little black shoe polish smeared on our faces and maybe a large pair of our older brother's shoes. Wearing one of our play guns and a holster with a cowboy hat sufficed as a costume. I wore my pajamas as a costume before, and didn't have to change when it came time for bed that evening.

In those days, you could safely walk for miles and late into the evening without fear of assault or getting harmful objects or bad candy in your Halloween bag or pillow case. By the end of the evening, when we all returned home, we emptied our bags out onto the living room floor and bartered with each other to trade our favorite candies. The challenge I had after Halloween was hiding my candy well enough that someone else did not find it and eat it. The challenge for my parents was to find a good hiding place or a way to keep us from eating all the candy they bought for Halloween *before* they could hand it out on Halloween night!

Fortunately for us trick-or-treating Catholics, the day after Halloween, November 1, is a Catholic holy day, All Saints Day, which celebrates all those known saints of the church who have attained heaven. When most kids have to get up early the next day and go to school after a fun-filled previous evening, we were sleeping in and spent much of the day eating and taking inventory of our candy and looking for a place to stash our bounty where no one would find it. However, All Saints Day is a Holy Day of Obligation, meaning all Catholics are required to attend mass on that day. Still, it was not a bad price to pay to get most of the day off after Halloween.

Celebrating birthdays was always fun. We almost always baked a cake for that sibling's birthday and celebrated their birthday after dinner with ice cream and presents. My parents bought a gift or two for us that we always appreciated as we knew that time and money for them was always tight.

One memorable birthday gift my Mother bought for my younger brother Ralph's fifth birthday was what was supposed to be a small plastic airplane. When Ralph went to open the wrapped gift, he found it empty. Mom apparently bought the display box with no airplane in it. I was with her when she saw the airplanes on display at the Sav-On drugstore in town and thought it would make a nice toy for Ralph. She moved the display airplane aside and bought the box under it, not realizing she had just moved the airplane that belonged inside the box she bought. Ralph did not know how to react when he opened the empty box and saw no gift inside. He looked at the empty box for several seconds, then looked at Mom, who by now realized her mistake and was sporting her usual embarrassed look she gave after committing similar previous mishaps. Ralph just set the box aside and opened his next present as he was now used to Mom's innocent silly mistakes. Mom went back to the store and explained what happened. They thankfully gave her the airplane she was supposed to have purchased the day before and happily gave it to Ralph, who gratefully accepted it and ended up really liking the airplane.

There was another embarrassing incident at that same Sav-On drugstore that happened when I accompanied my mom there on another occasion. This time, she was looking for a Gumby toy for Bob's birthday. Gumby was a green clay humanoid cartoon character who had adventures through different environments and times in history. His cartoons ran from 1957 to 1968 but have had several reruns, feature movies, comic books, video games, etc., through 2007. You could buy a six-inch flexible rubber Gumby at the time at any variety or toy store.

So I was following mom around the store as she was looking for where she could find the Gumbys for sale. She couldn't find them but she saw the store manager and flagged him down. I was standing behind her when she asked the manager, "Do you have any zombies here?" He got this puzzled "What did you just ask me" look on his face. He looked at her, looked at me, then looked back at her. Then I looked at him and said, "She means Gumbys.

Do you have any Gumbys here?" Mom threw her head back and gave a little chuckle and said, "Oh, yeah, I mean Gumbys. Do you have any Gumbys here?" He looked down over the rim of his glasses at her and said, "left side, aisle four." My mom was often a day late and a dollar short—sometimes literally!

Birth Order

———◆———

Here is where I would like you to get to better know my eleven siblings, as they, in many ways, have defined and shaped who I am today—good, bad, or otherwise. I love what each of them has brought to my life today and over the years. I have created loving, meaningful, and lasting relationships with them all.

Marv, 1945

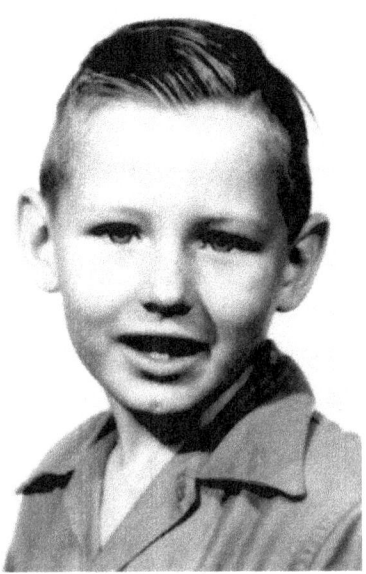

Marv, the first born, was born the year Pepé Le Pew debuted in a Warner Bros. cartoon. Jackie Robinson was chosen to integrate baseball and signed with the Montreal Royals, which was the Dodgers top farm team. The microwave oven was patented. The Detroit Tigers won the World Series, and the then Cleveland Rams were pro football champions.

World War II came to an end on May 8, 1945, in Europe, and on August 14 that same year, the war ended in the Pacific, after involving fifty-seven nations and the deaths of fifty-five million people. Five thousand homes in America had televisions. Life expectancy was 62.9 years. A new home cost $4,625. The average income was $2,390 a year. A new car costs $1,025. A movie ticket was 50 cents, a gallon of gas was 15 cents, and a first-class postage stamp was 3 cents.

As far back as I can remember, Marv always seemed to enjoy the attention and recognition that came with his title of first-born. He often made it known through no uncertain terms that he was number one in the family, and the rest of us better not forget that. He used his executive privilege to frequently ask Mom, even at twelve years old, to cut up his meat for him like she did when he was three. He ended up the tallest in the family at 6'4", which allowed him, even more so, to use his size to intimidate and control. He was good-looking, with baby blue eyes and thick dark-brown hair.

He was good at capturing and maintaining an audience much of the time by being funny and entertaining. I don't remember ever seeing him much in the evenings doing homework, but we did see him mostly in the early evening or late after school when his participation in sports was over for the day or he had finished visiting with his many friends. He always had a good number of friends that he visited or invited over to our house to hang out. He keeps in touch with many of those same friends to this day.

I remember one time at dinner he made us laugh by putting a hot dog horizontally across his mouth in front of his teeth. He closed his lips over the hot dog and when he opened his mouth all we could see was this big hot dog of a smile! He often did similar silly things while standing behind mom when she was scolding us or talking to us about a serious matter. He stopped when she turned around.

It was a family rule that you did not eat or drink anything in the refrigerator that was not yours. We often labeled or announced to everyone those items that we personally stored so no one who ate or drank your stuff could say that they didn't know it was yours. Marv believed he did not have to abide by that rule, so he often helped himself, against our protests, to our refrigerator items when we weren't home or around to catch him in the act of stealing them. My younger brother Bob decided to beat Marv at his own game. Bob had a half-drunk bottle of RC Cola in the refrigerator that he suspected Marv was taking drinks from. Bob was resigned to sacrifice his soda to teach Marv a lesson by putting an absorbent amount of salt in the bottle. The next time Marv drank a big swig of coke from Bob's RC Cola, he promptly ran to the sink and threw up his dinner, followed by about ten minutes of drinking water to get the salty taste out of his mouth. He never drank from Bob's or anyone else's soda again. Lesson learned!

Marv was the first in our family to raise pigeons in the backyard. Dad and he built a large 5-by-15-foot wire cage against the back fence that held up to twenty pigeons at any given time. They were homing pigeons that we enjoyed watching Marv release by opening the cage entry door, then fly for several minutes in a group around the neighborhood, then eventually land back on the entry board, located on top of the cage, where they all dropped back into the main cage.

He and I enrolled in a comedy class at the famous Ice House in Pasadena in 2005. I enrolled because I wanted to add some humor and timing to my class lectures. He enrolled because he had always liked comedy and thought he would do well in the class. It was a ten-week course that met on Sunday mornings at the Ice House, where we each created and honed a five-minute comedy bit that we were to perform at the Ice House for our graduation. There were about twenty of us in the class, and graduation night at the Ice House was a sellout!

I did OK, but Marv was one of the last to perform, as he was one of the best in the class; and you do save the best for last. He had so much fun and was so well received for his performance that he decided to take a second, advanced class and began to perform at different venues, many of which he was invited to perform. His stage name was "Crazy Marvin," and he entered the stage when announced to the song "Crazy" by Gnarls Barkley. He performed for about two years at various comedy clubs like the Coach House, the Ice House, and a couple of the improvs around southern California. He performed at Universal Studios in 2008. He quit performing shortly after that, as he was not making much money at it, and his business was beginning to suffer from all the time taken to perform. One of my favorite jokes of his is the one he tells of the prisoner who is the dead man walking and is asked what song he would like played as he walks to the electric chair. He says, "Anything but Chaka Khan (shock a con). Get it?!"

He was also a very good athlete. He excelled in any sport he played, especially baseball and basketball. He was also very good at bowling. On one occasion, he almost bowled a perfect 300 game. Had he pursued it, he could have been a professional in any of those three sports.

I liked his taste in music. In his mid-teens we could often hear great tunes being played on the radio on a Saturday morning or while he was driving in his car. He liked "Great Balls of Fire" by Jerry Lee Lewis, which came out in 1957. He also liked "Be-Bop-A-Lula" by Gene Vincent and the Blue Caps, which came out in 1956. Other songs he liked and that I enjoyed hearing were Little Richard's famous songs "Tutti Frutti," from 1955, and "Lucille," from 1957.

He married in his early twenties and had two sons. He is divorced now and has two grandsons. He continues to run the family sprinkler installation business with my brother Mel. He enjoys attending family gatherings and outings whenever his busy schedule permits. He is in his seventies but continues to enjoy and play in a senior softball league. He often plays shortstop or in the outfield because he still has a great arm and decent reflexes. He has gone on a few of our family backpacking trips and all the hikes we take during our annual family camping trips. The hard manual labor he performs each day, digging, installing sprinklers, and laying down sod, enables him to stay in remarkably good shape. He maintains his great sense of humor and continues to entertain us any chance he gets.

Mel, 1946

The baby boom officially began in 1946. Birthrates jumped to over 1.4 million in one year with the return of World War II veterans. AT&T announced the first car phone. Alaskans voted in favor of statehood. Vitamin D milk cost 60 cents per gallon. Coffee was 50 cents per pound. Bacon was 47 cents a pound, and eggs were 22 cents per dozen. The Greyhound bus line was encouraging its patrons to take a Greyhound bus "straight to their choicest vacation spots."

I always remember how precise, fastidious, and meticulous to detail Mel was as a child. His school and church clothes were nicely pressed and cleaned. His bed was always made and one of the few you could actually sit on, if he allowed, without getting poked or cut by some object or gadget. We didn't sit on his bed much because his room was the cold and dank back porch that he shared with Harry, and there was nothing of much interest or fun in that room anyway. As far as I remember, he slept on the bottom bunk.

The visual that connects me most with Mel and that room was seeing him at the desk in there for hours at a time completing the four to six hours of homework he and Harry were given each school day from St. Don Bosco High School. I am guessing the reason those two ended up in that small, cold, unforgiving, isolated room was so they would have maximum uninterrupted privacy to study.

He was a good student and a decent athlete. He excelled in the Boy Scouts, where his tenacious, detailed work eventually earned him many coveted badges, one of which was Eagle Scout! He took a shop class at St. Don Bosco High School that came in handy as he single-handedly remodeled the mantel and surrounding wall in the living room at our house in 1975. It was a funky, current at the time, early-1970s pattern that was there until the house was sold in 1985. He is a lot like my dad in that he can fix or repair just about anything. That shop class he took earned him his first job out of high school at a furniture company.

Mel was drafted into the Army shortly after he graduated from St. Don Bosco in 1964. He was nineteen and was stationed at Fort Dix, New Jersey. The Vietnam War was going on at the time, but he did not end up being assigned to combat in Vietnam. After his stint in the Army, he went to college on the GI Bill. He attended East Los Angeles College for two and a half years and then received his bachelor's degree in business at Cal State University, Long Beach. Like my brother Bob, he loved the city of Long Beach. Mel lived in Long Beach from 1990 to about 1996.

After serving in the Army and enrolling in college, Mel began working at a Sears store located in Alhambra, about a twenty-minute drive north from South Gate. It was from Sears that he bought the family our first color TV in 1970. It was also at that Sears store where he met his future wife. They had a lovely outdoor wedding at a park on the Central Coast in Morro Bay, California, in 1992. They have four very active, wonderful children, three boys and one girl. All four of their children are doing quite well, successfully excelling in sports, academics, and professional endeavors.

Mel always encouraged me to pay attention to detail and do things right the first time. He followed Dad's philosophy that no job is worth doing unless you are going to do it right. That is why he continues to have plenty of work to this day, even as he enters his early seventies. His work comes mostly from word of mouth and referrals from satisfied customers. He got his electrician's license in the early 1990s to add lighting to the family sprinkler business. He has indicated that he will probably have to continue working into his late seventies and early eighties to generate funds for his younger two sons, currently in their early teens, to graduate from college.

I enjoy spending time with Mel and his family at their barbecues, birthday parties, and academic celebrations. Mel and I also make it a point to attend an LA Dodgers and an LA Kings game together each baseball and hockey season. He is a great dad, husband, and brother who is hard-working, multitalented, honest, and devoted to his wife and children.

John, 1947

The United States' gross national product begins its historic postwar surge, ushering in an era of economic growth. In the first night game at Fenway Park, the Red Sox win 5–3 over the White Sox. The New York Yankees win the World Series, and Jackie Robinson makes major-league history when he signs with the Brooklyn Dodgers.

Bing Crosby sang his famous "White Christmas." Basic food prices increased by 8 to 10 cents in 1947. The average income increased slightly, and the price of a new house increased from about $4,700 in 1945 to about $5,000.

John was always an aloof mystery to me. I did not know or spend nearly as much personal or quality time with him over the years as I did with my three other older brothers. I often got the feeling that he felt he did not belong and seemed to go out of his way to separate himself from the rest of us, spending time playing by himself, fighting and engaging in combat with imaginary friends and foes. He took over raising pigeons after Marv moved to Ventura in 1965 to go to college.

He was not one of the more studious of the bunch. He never had much interest in school or a college education. He had a devious bad-boy image he worked hard to achieve, as if he needed to unnecessarily prove and defend himself from us and his imaginary demons. He often got into trouble both at school and at home. John's troubles were mostly petty run-ins with his teachers and my parents; talking back, not wanting to do his chores or homework, staying out after curfew, and once in a while, getting into fights at school and at home.

He was almost kicked out of St. Emydius when he was in eighth grade. He did get kicked out of two high schools for fighting and ultimately dropped out of high school between his junior and senior years. My dad put him to work with him during his sophomore year in high school to keep him out of trouble and to give him a little self-earned prestige and money to spend, which gave John a feeling of worth and self-esteem within the family and within his circle of somewhat ruffian friends. John owned, loved, and rode motorcycles from his early teens through his move to Wisconsin in 1974.

He met and married his high school sweetheart in 1968, and they had two sons together and were married for forty-six years. His second son was the 100,000th baby born at St. Francis Hospital, delivered by the same doctor that delivered his dad, my brother John, twenty years earlier! After he married, he worked for several years in the Long Beach shipyards, riding one of his many motorcycles to and from South Gate where he and his wife lived at the time. He moved his family to Appleton, Wisconsin, where he held a job for thirty-seven years at Pierce Manufacturing, making fire engines. He retired in 2011 but unfortunately passed away in January 2015 of esophageal cancer. He smoked much of his teenage and adult years and continued to use chewing tobacco after he quit smoking cigarettes. The cancer was not detected until it was already in its advanced stages. He fought a brave and courageous battle against his cancer, never complaining or revealing the pain and suffering he was experiencing.

Before moving to Appleton, he lived for a short stint in Cambridge, Massachusetts, during the summer of 1968, where he mowed the lawn at an old cemetery. He lived next door to Van

Morrison, who would come over to my brother's place and jam with some of the guys who played in a band. John also loved and was an excellent cribbage player. He once had a perfect 29 hand. He won several local cribbage tournaments. He loved to garden and was generous with his bounty of various vegetables, especially his corn, which many a neighbor and friend enjoyed. His corn was truly the best around. So was he!

In the last year of his life, John and his wife celebrated their forty-sixth wedding anniversary by visiting Niagara Falls, where they took a ride in a helicopter to view the falls. He truly loved his wife and best friend, Janice. He also loved spending time with his family, especially the times he visited and conversed with our Grandmother Lily Mae. Even after he was diagnosed with cancer, he and his wife drove out to California from Wisconsin each of the last several years of his life to attend our annual family campouts. John was aware of how lucky he was to be a part of this loving and caring family. He was a great husband, a wonderful father and grandfather to his two sons and his grandchildren, and was able to see and enjoy his great-grandson, Blake, before he passed in 2015.

Harold, 1949

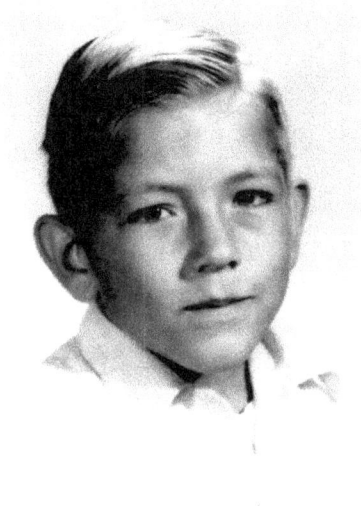

Snowfall is recorded in Lo s Angeles. RCA releases the first 45-rpm single record. *Hopalong Cassidy* became the first network western. Detective drama *Dragnet* first aired on the radio in 1949. Ted Williams and Jackie Robinson were awarded MVP honors for the American League and the National League, respectively. NATO, the North Atlantic Treaty Organization, is formed. The minimum wage is raised from 40 to 75 cents an hour. Volkswagen Beetles are introduced in the United States; two were sold in 1949. Harvard Law School announces it will admit women the following year.

The New York Yankees win the World Series again. Heavyweight champion Joe Louis announces his retirement after reigning for nearly twelve years and defending his title twenty-five times. Average rent is $70 a month, and tuition to Harvard is $600 a year. Gasoline is now 17 cents a gallon, but a postage stamp is still 3 cents.

I believe I am closer to Harry than any of my other siblings. He and I spent and still spend a lot of time together. We were always very competitive athletically; he was always far superior to me academically. So, where I could not compete with him in the classroom, I made up for it on the court and field. Even though he was a year older than I, there was about a year between the ages of twelve and thirteen where I grew taller and bigger than Harry. I could actually run faster and throw farther than him that year! He was a little embarrassed by a younger sister being able to outthrow and outrun him. He made up for it and then some the following year when he turned fifteen and grew two inches and put on about fifteen pounds.

We often walked down to the South Gate Plunge together during the summertime and swam for hours. We eventually shared a paper route, delivering the *South Gate Press* newspaper for a few years. We tossed a football back and forth in the street out in front of our house, moving farther back with each toss, challenging each other to throw farther than the other. We would race down the sidewalk, one on each side of the street, to see who could beat the other the hundred yards to the corner. He usually won those competitions.

Every school year we all took the Iowa basic intelligence tests. There were several of the eight years he took the tests where he scored in the top 99 percent! He continued to excel in his studies throughout high school and eventually earned an academic scholarship to UCLA, where he majored in geography and minored in economics. Students were required to complete a minor as well as a major while in college through the mid-1970s. He loved traveling to various geographic locations in his youth, which led him to become a travel agent in the affluent beach town of Laguna, California. That job allowed him to travel all over the world. He has retired from his job as a travel agent but continues to travel and hike with his wife, Claudia, every chance they get.

At a young age, Harry became fascinated with trains. He must have inherited his strong interest in trains from an uncle who was a conductor for many years for Union Pacific Railroad in Oxnard. Harry used to take a dull kitchen knife and draw an intricate array of railroad lines with complete railroad yards and incoming and outgoing train lines in the dirt over a large area under the big avocado tree in the backyard. He got very upset when any of us walked over his train yard or messed up any part of his detailed work. We couldn't play kickball until he was finished because the top end of his train yard was our approach area when readying to kick.

Before he was married, he often traveled the United States specifically to places where he could park his car and see particular or notable trains traveling over beautiful bridges with scenic backgrounds, or popular trains entering a well-known train yard at a particular time. He told his other train-friendly buddies the specific spots he found to allow them maximum viewing of a train as it passed through that same area they might visit. He eventually wrote a book called *Where to Watch Trains* that listed areas throughout the United States that showed locations and times where train buffs could seek out desirable, appealing views of trains.

I have backpacked with Harry into the High Sierras on several occasions. He met his wife while hiking with the Sierra Club in the mid-1980s. Even though he is retired now, he stays very active hiking, cross-country skiing, and working out weekly at a local fitness center. We are fortunate that Harry continues to use his great travel agent skills by planning much of our yearly family camping trips, suggesting potential camping spots, securing the reservation, and proposing possible ideas for things to do and places to see while camping.

He is one of the smartest, kindest, most low-key individuals I have ever known. I have never seen him angry or upset at anyone or anything. His demeanor is very much like my mother's and her siblings—kind, honest, and optimistic.

Me, 1950

Chuck Cooper broke the NBA color barrier when he was picked by Boston in the second round of the draft. The Federal Communications Commission authorized CBS to begin commercial color TV broadcasts. The New York Yankees won the World Series Championship again. Ben Hogan won the U.S. Open Championship.

The U.S. officially recognizes Vietnam and begins military support of its regime. The U.S. census indicates that there are 150 million people living here. Life expectancy increased from 62.9 years in 1945 to 68.2 years in 1950, an increase of 5.3 years in 5 years.

Suzanne, 1951

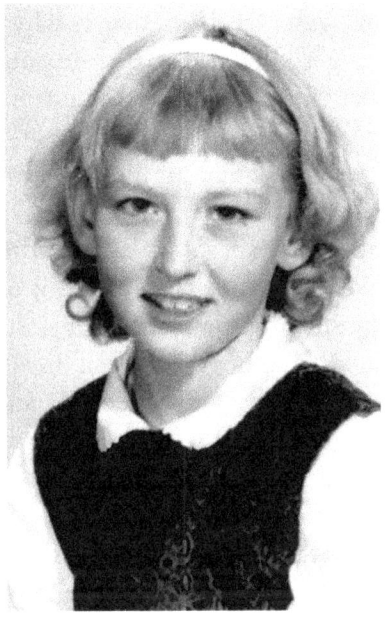

Joe DiMaggio, the "Yankee Clipper," for the third year in a row, signed a $100,000 contract with, of course, the New York Yankees. He also announced his retirement from baseball that same year. Outfielder Willie Mays, at age twenty, joined the then New York Giants. Once again, the New York Yankees won the World Series baseball championships. Ben Hogan was the U.S. Open golf champion again, and the Los Angeles Rams won the pro football championship. That same year, over ten thousand basketball fans gathered at Boston's Square Garden to watch the best of the NBA play in the first All-Star Game.

The sitcom *I Love Lucy*, one of my all-time favorite TV shows, premiered on CBS. One of the bestselling books in 1951 was *From Here to Eternity*. Two very successful movies produced in 1951 were *A Streetcar Named Desire* and one thriller movie I remember watching several times on TV as a young child, *The Day the Earth Stood Still*. *The African Queen* with Humphrey Bogart and Lauren Bacall was produced in 1951 and eventually became one of my all-time favorite movies.

My sister Sue and I have not always been as close as we are now. I believe I always overshadowed her when we were young, never giving her much of a voice or chance to be heard or to beat me at any sport or game. I believe that is why she was a bit shy when she was younger. She followed in my footsteps when she took over my job at the South Gate Laundromat after I started college. She moved out of the house at an early age and lived in the South Gate area for a while until eventually moving to Santa Maria, California, in Santa Barbara County.

She stayed under the radar as a kid, minding her p's and q's, doing well in school and basically staying out of trouble. She is a middle child, where she often saw her older siblings like me get all the glory and attention and her younger siblings sometimes escape discipline. She has always been independent and a little secretive at times, but very good at reading people and staying one step ahead of their thinking, often predicting what their actions and thoughts may be before they do.

Like Harry, she was also very smart and a good athlete—unfortunate that I got sandwiched between two brainiacs! Academic accomplishments came easy to her. She attended a trade college and took a few college courses after high school, and eventually worked her way to the top of her profession, which was running various car dealerships in California. I don't believe she ever meant to run car dealerships for a living when she took a job as a PBX operator at a Ford dealership in Huntington Park a few years out of high school. She currently oversees four dealerships in the Monterey and Santa Cruz area of Northern California as a comptroller. She has an innate ability to thoroughly and successfully execute all aspects of each dealership and the intelligence and hard work ethic to make sure all departments, personnel, and any other entities of the dealerships follow protocol for California and national auto dealership laws and policies.

She lost her husband, Gill, to liver cancer in 2011. It was a devastating loss to her as they knew each other for over forty years. She met him while she and some friends were cruising down Sunset Boulevard in Los Angeles and saw him hitchhiking by himself. They eventually married and moved wherever her job opportunities took them. Gill had a difficult childhood but was a skilled and innovative painter, inventor, and business owner. He operated a gardening service but had the clever original idea to call his business The Yardener. He was eventually a landscape contractor, and since his last name was Powers, he later creatively named his business PowerScapes.

I love everything about my sister Sue: her calm, even-tempered demeanor, her ever-increasing legal intelligence, especially as she navigates the family trusts and subsequent legalities of our family affairs. She is every bit as knowledgeable as our family attorneys about what we need to do to resolve or undertake legal matters. She is always supportive and continually encourages me in a positive way to do what makes me happy. She thankfully slows me down to her pace and demeanor whenever I see or talk to her. Her measured speech and purposeful movements make me want to do the same.

She lives in a rather small community in northern California. I love visiting her and planning fun local activities and other things we both enjoy doing. She is in great physical shape as she stays busy hiking with friends and participating in cardio kickboxing workouts three days a week. I hope to spend more time with her in the days and years to come as she contemplates retiring within the next few years. She is good for me; we are a dynamic pair of siblings!

Clarissa, 1953

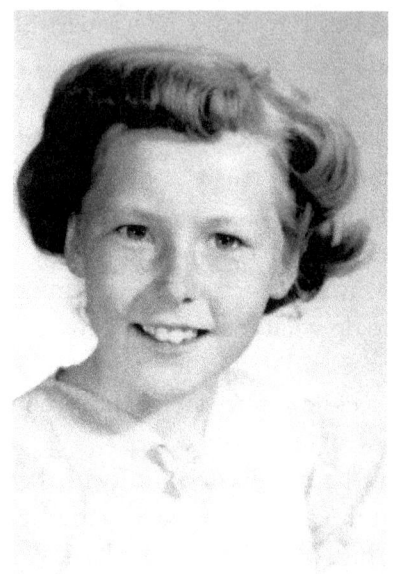

When my second-youngest sister was born in 1953, the Federal Communications Commission ruled that color TV could go on the air. Yeah! The now no longer needed or in print *TV Guide* began publication in 1953. In January of 1953, Little Ricky was born on my favorite television show, *I Love Lucy*.

John F. Kennedy and Jacqueline Bouvier got married. *The Old Man and the Sea* by Ernest Hemingway won the Pulitzer Prize. The price of a new house went up to an average of $9,525 in 1953, an increase of nearly $3,000 since the cost was $6,650 in 1947, just six years earlier. Food prices were steadily increasing since the late 1940s, especially the price of vitamin D milk and coffee. The price of a stamp at 3 cents and a gallon of gasoline at 15 cents in 1947 remained relatively the same. *Shane* with Alan Ladd was a popular movie made in 1953.

I believe my sister Clarissa was the forgotten child; often lost in the shuffle of the chaos and mayhem that often persisted in the house. She was truly a middle child who I believe felt that she did not have a special place in the family, so her friends and peer groups became important to her. For several years, she spent as much time at her friends' houses as she could. I don't blame her. I am sure she got more attention and nurturing there and avoided more conflict than at home.

Clarissa has always been slight in stature and got hurt easily when playing or climbing around with other siblings, who were all bigger and rougher than she. She held her own most of the time. Like many of the rest of us, she was a good athlete and did well in school. When she and I and Sue all played on our high school basketball team together, Clarissa was left-handed, with a great eye for the basket, so she played on the offensive end of the court. She also left home at a fairly young age and eventually ended up in Santa Maria, graduating from Hancock College with a degree in accounting.

She is currently married and retired from her position as a highly successful and sought-after auditor at Vandenberg Air Force Base. She is an excellent tennis player and has taken up golf since her retirement. I enjoy visiting her and spending time with her and her lovely new home that she has smartly redecorated and remodeled, much of it herself, in the past few years. I love Clarissa as much as I love my sister Sue. In the past, we have enjoyed driving to and browsing through local antiques stores on the Central Coast. I hope to spend more quality time with her in the future.

Robert, 1954

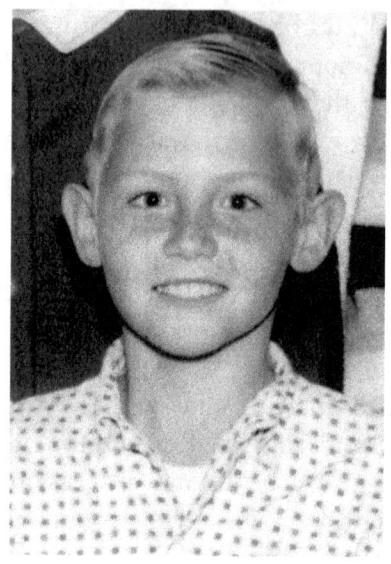

The year my younger brother Bob was born was the year that children in Pittsburgh became the first group to receive Salk's polio vaccine. Disney aired the first episode of one of our family favorites, the *Davy Crockett* TV series. RCA introduced the first color TV sets; the cost: $1,000! Oprah Winfrey and comedian Jerry Seinfeld were born in 1954.

Bob's family nickname is "Dubert." He has always moved, talked and walked at a slow pace. I liken him to a turtle. I am always the rabbit when I am around him. I get impatient waiting for him to finish what he is doing or saying or needing to get done. He took an early interest in gardening and landscaping and ended up attending Los Angeles Pierce Community College, majoring in ornamental horticulture. In 1983 he joined the family business with three of my other brothers, who took over the sprinkler company in 1977 when my dad died.

He eventually left the family sprinkler business and moved to Morro Bay, California, on the Central Coast, and attended Cal Poly, San Luis Obispo, where he received a bachelors in landscape architecture. After graduation he moved and started his own landscape architecture business in Long Beach, where he currently lives with his spouse, Donald, whom he met while living in Morro Bay. Donald is a retired professor from Hancock Community College of Santa Maria, California, and moved with Bob to Long Beach a few years after retiring. Donald suffers from a disease called Huntington's disease. He has inherited an abnormal gene from a parent that results in cognitive decline. Donald is one of the kindest, gentlest, most intelligent, and artistically talented human beings I have ever met. Bob has put his business on hold and has dedicated himself to taking care of Donald full-time. They have a beautiful marriage and a loving relationship.

Since 1998 Bob and I have backpacked nearly every summer together for a week or so in the west side of the High Sierra Nevada Mountains. The hikes have been challenging and awe-inspiring, as we have traversed some of the most beautiful terrain in California and the United States. We get to see what only a handful of people ever get to see. Since we are both in our sixties now, we have begun to plan less strenuous and physically demanding hikes. Like me, he looks forward to and cherishes our hikes each summer and the quality time spent together on them. I like that I slow down when I am around him, which is good for me. I look forward to many more years of backpacking with Bob in the summers to come.

Michael, 1955

Ray Croc opened his first McDonald's fast-food place in 1955 in Des Plaines, Illinois. President Eisenhower increased the minimum wage to $1 an hour. Rosa Parks was arrested for refusing to give up her seat on a public bus in Montgomery, Alabama. *Captain Kangaroo* and *The Mickey Mouse Club* made their debut. Three of the top TV shows in 1955 were CBS's *What's My Line?*, *I Love Lucy*, and one of my ever-popular favorites, *The Ed Sullivan Show*.

Life expectancy rose to 69.6 years in 1955, a little more than six and a half years more than ten years earlier, in 1945, when life expectancy was 62.9 years, when my oldest brother Marv was born. A new house in 1945 cost $6,300, and in 1955 a new house cost $10,950. The average American income in 1945 was $2,000, and in 1955 it more than doubled to an average of $4,137.

Like many of us in the family, Mike did not receive much parental nurturing or effective, positive guidance as a young child. My mother was sick off and on after Mike was born. By 1955, when Mike was born, she had already had eight full-term pregnancies and two miscarriages. Mike was essentially raised by his brothers and sisters, which isn't saying much, given our own lack of effective relationship skills with each other.

I remember Mike as being very headstrong and obstinate from a young age. It was difficult to get him to mind or obey anyone. He was highly intelligent and kept pretty much to himself over the years. He was quiet but often displayed a quick, violent temper that would come out of nowhere. He started smoking pot and drinking at a young age as well as smoking cigarettes off and on, which never helped his already volatile personality. His relationships with women never lasted very long, as they tired quickly of his drinking and subsequent difficult behavior that followed.

He never went to college, but he did join the family sprinkler installation business along with Marv, Mel, and Bob in the late 1970s. He had worked off and on with dad in his early teens. He was very good at repairing and replacing broken or outdated sprinklers. His drinking and drugging took an early toll on his body and mind, so that by the time he was in his early fifties, he had lost his driver's license, his work van, and his sprinkler repair business. He lived on the streets of Pasadena for the last six years of his life. He passed away in his hotel room of a massive heart attack two months before his fifty-eighth birthday.

I did my best to help him as much as I could in his later years, but to no avail. He was sent to Alcoholics Anonymous on several occasions by the courts but he never gave AA a chance to work because he said he did not believe in God, and he wrongfully though AA advocated that you have to have a God to be successful in the AA fellowship. He passed away the day before my sixty-third birthday. At the time of his death, I had given up on him and hadn't seen him in several weeks. I know I did everything I could to help him, but his death was nonetheless a shock to me. He is buried at All Soul's Cemetery in Long Beach in a crypt not far from where both my parents are buried. By no coincidence, there is a sprinkler next to Mike's burial site that sprays water on his crypt three times a week!

Ralph, 1957

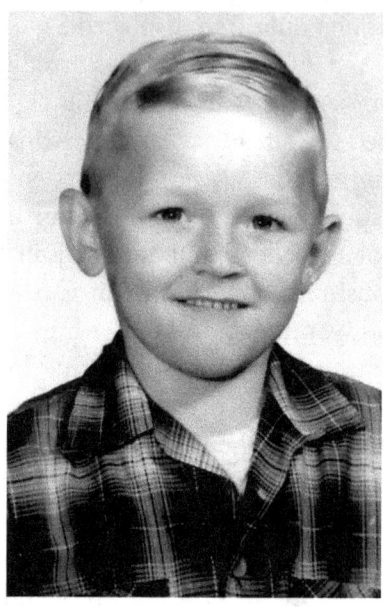

Troops were sent to Little Rock, Arkansas, to protect African American students integrating a previously all-white school. Dr. Seuss published his famous The *Cat in the Hat* book, which became a classic in children's literature. The popular TV shows in 1957 were CBS's *The Danny Thomas Show*, NBC's *Howdy Doody*, and NBC's *You Bet Your Life*.

In 1957, the Wham-O Company produced its first Frisbees. I did not know this, but Frisbees were patterned after a pie pan from the Frisbee Baking Company of Connecticut. A movie ticket in 1957 now cost $1, up from 50 cents twelve years earlier, in 1945.

"Ralphie" has always been a pleasant, easygoing, likeable person with a wry sense of humor and a hearty appetite. He looks the most like our grandfather on our dad's, side which means he has a round face and a flat head in the back. Sorry, Ralph. He was quiet and never spoke much, probably because no one would acknowledge him, or he couldn't get a word in edgewise anyway, even if he attempted to say something. He always seemed to have this half smile on his face, which I read to mean that he was either telling us that he was fine and OK or he was up to no good.

He was bed partners with Harry until he wet the bed often enough that Harry moved, at the first chance he got, onto the back porch with Mel, when John moved out of the back porch. Ralph eventually moved in with Mel on the back porch when Harry moved out of the house. Ralph always seemed to enjoy and have a lot of fun during our summer family camping trips to Soledad Canyon Campground, Carpinteria State Beach, or anywhere else we camped. I remember him telling me a few years ago how difficult it was riding in the car or pickup truck packed with six to ten kids, with the car or truck overheating or with dangerously worn tires. He remembers someone ultimately getting sick in the car, in our hot vehicle with little ventilation. He said that getting out of the car at the destination was a gift in itself!

Ralph joined the Air Force in 1978 and married his high school sweetheart, Cindy, in 1979. Like Mel's family, Ralph and Cindy had four children: three boys and a girl. He left the Air Force in 2000 and currently works for a transportation company in Oakland. I enjoy being around Ralph. He and his family attend our yearly summer camping events. He owns a pop-up trailer camper that he hauls behind his car. I wish I could see him and his family, with his amazing twin grandsons, more often, but he lives in Northern California and I live in Southern California. At least I get to see him once a year.

What I still love and enjoy most about Ralph is his sense of humor. He has an innate ability to make us laugh with his impromptu off-the-cuff remarks and comments. He delivers his humor with a soft voice and a natural comedic style. I believe we all developed a sense of humor to help us cope and make light of the challenges that developed in our large family. Ralph has always been good at giving us a reason to smile and laugh regardless of the situation.

Raymond, 1959

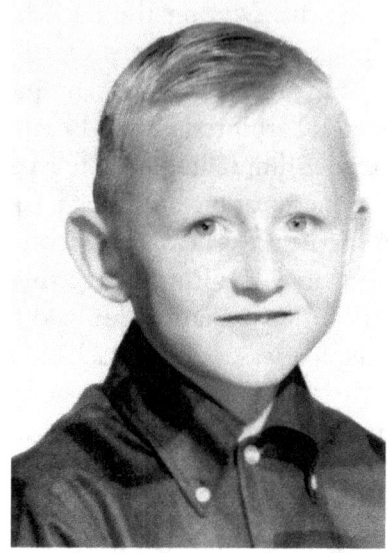

The Ford Motor Company won its battle to call one of its new cars Falcon. Ford registered the name twenty minutes before Chrysler could. My second car was a 1961 Ford Falcon station wagon that my brother Marv gave me in 1966. I drove it for several years during my late high school and early college days. Pantyhose and Barbie dolls were introduced to U.S. consumers. In January 1959, Alaska became the forty-ninth state. In November 1959, Hawaii became the fiftieth state.

The top three TV shows that aired in 1959 that became family favorites over the years were *Father Knows Best, 77 Sunset Strip,* and one of my longtime favorites, *The Price Is Right.*

At 6'3", Ray is one of the tallest of my eight brothers. He was also one of the most stubborn of my four younger brothers. It took every ounce of my energy and creative thought to get him to make his bed or get dressed for school in the morning. One time I had to literally pry him off one of the bunk-bed posts, where he had wrapped his arms and legs, trying to get him to brush his teeth before going to bed! To get Ray away from the disarray going on in the house, Dad often took him to work. He remembers his child labor days, starting at four years old, when he was on a job site with Dad, occasionally turning valves off and on for Dad for 5 cents a day. Eventually he got 25 cents a day, then eventually a buck a day working with Dad. Ray was a good athlete through the eighth grade, successfully competing in basketball, baseball, and track and field.

Working with Dad through high school did allow Ray to transition to a labor-union job with a landscaping company that Harry had defected to a few years earlier. Ray wanted to go into radio announcing and started by attending Cerritos College in Norwalk, California. He knew he had a better chance at a radio job if he moved away from the Los Angeles area. He moved up to Morro Bay on the Central Coast of California and attended Cuesta College, where he completed his AA degree in telecommunications/speech. He then went on to eventually work at and receive a degree at Cal Poly, San Luis Obispo, in business administration. Over the past seventeen years, at Cal Poly, San Luis Obispo, he has gained experience in public relations, marketing, fund-raising, and major event production specifically for the College of Architectural and Environmental Design.

Upon arriving in San Luis Obispo County, Ray worked in Morro Bay at KBAI AM radio, going on to be the news and then the program director. Work after that included creative services at an ad agency, and in the early days of the internet, marketing coordinator for The Grid, which was bought by OneMain.com, followed by Earthlink. Before the dot-com bubble burst, he switched over to work at Cal Poly.

Ray has a *very* impressive resume that, besides his employment accolades, boasts many community achievements and awards and acknowledgments given to him for his valuable contributions to the Morro Bay Harbor Festival, the Morro Bay Beautiful Foundation, the Morro Bay Chamber of Commerce, and the Mid-State Fair. In 2003 he was the co-creator of the ongoing Morro Bay Citywide Yard Sale Weekend. He continues to promote environmentally and business-friendly events that enhance the growth and relations of his community.

He and I have a great relationship. I have not pried him off a bedpost in years! I know he has a great deal of respect for me and I appreciate that about him. He listens to me and often seeks advice and suggestions. He has gone backpacking with my brother Bob and I a few times and, as the eleventh of twelve children, he is good at adapting himself to all situations, as he did on his first rather challenging backpacking adventure. He is great at managing others and gets highly successful results on the various projects in which he is involved with his superb negotiating skills.

He is rather humble, given how much he has achieved and how much he has contributed to his community. In addition to working full-time at Cal Poly, San Luis Obispo, he manages several rental homes for our family as well. His hectic schedule has now slowed down a little since he completed his bachelor's degree in 2016. I am hoping he can start joining Bob and I more often on our summer backpacking trips.

Frances, 1960

Sixteen years after our oldest brother Marv was born in 1945, much had changed by the time our youngest sister, Frances, was born in 1960. The first animated prime-time series, *The Flintstones*, premiered. One of our family favorites, CBS's *The Andy Griffith Show*, ABC's *The Real McCoys*, and *Rawhide* on CBS were popular TV shows in 1960.

In 1945 a new house cost $4,625. Fifteen years later, in1960, a new house cost $12,675. The average income went from $2,390 in 1946 to $5,199 in 1960. A movie ticket doubled from 50 cents in 1945 to $1 in 1960. The price of a gallon of gas only increased by 10 cents. It cost 15 cents per gallon in 1945, and only increased to 25 cents per gallon in1960. Those were the days! A first-class postage stamp went up only 1 cent from 3 cents a stamp in 1945 to 4 cents a stamp in 1960.

Frances, the youngest of the twelve, was a beautiful baby and got a lot of attention as that girl born after the youngest four boys. A lot was determined for her. Throughout her early childhood, she did not have much choice or say in most matters. Like several other of her young siblings, much of her upbringing was done partially by me or partially by other siblings. Mom did most of the bulk of her care, but Mom was still ailing from her painful excessive uterine bleeding and cramping and was not always up to caring for her. At three years old, Fran soon found her own voice and began making her own decisions, like what to wear, choosing her own place to sit at dinner, and fixing her own bowl of cereal.

Fran and our four youngest brothers went to South Gate Junior High School, now called South Gate Middle School, after attending St. Emydius. The last four siblings did not attend a Catholic high school like many of the rest of us did. Fran was a sophomore in high school when dad passed away. His death affected our mother deeply, and during her anguish, Fran promised she would take care of her. Fran eventually moved up to Vandenberg Village and moved in with mom in 1997 so she could attend Pacifica College in Santa Barbara to receive her doctorate in marriage and family counseling. Frances did end up taking care of our mother for the last several years of her life, making sure Mom got to her doctor's appointments, fixing healthy meals for her, and making sure her meds were taken properly.

Frances was a good athlete in high school, especially in volleyball. Her coach was an East LA College volleyball teammate of mine, Margaret Galvan, who eventually interviewed at and received a teaching and coaching position at ELAC and became the Kinesiology Department chair. Fran, then, as she is now, is a real head turner. She is very attractive, thin, 5'11", with long blond hair and green eyes. She looks like Cameron Diaz!

She has done a lot of volunteer work for nonprofit organizations. She volunteered several years at the West Hollywood Gay and Lesbian Center and was a volunteer chaplain at a hospital when she lived in Portland, Oregon, a few years ago. She has moved to a lovely community on the Central Coast of California, where she works and takes walks on the beach. She is still as beautiful now as she was as a child.

As I am sure my parents were, I am proud of my brothers and sisters and the wonderful, caring individuals we have become to each other. I am sure they would be proud of the lovely families we have created and the contributions we have all made to our communities.

We have all accomplished so much despite the unforeseen, sometimes chaotic and unstable upbringing we received. We were all well educated and have led highly successful professional lives in our respective fields. We get along with each other no matter what and never raise our voices toward each other nor show anger or animosity no matter what the situation or discussion may be. We *always* make our family decisions or choices based on what's in the best interest of everyone involved. We always ask ourselves, before making family decisions, What would Mom have wanted? What would she do in this family situation? It has been a complete and total honor and privilege to be a part of the Ladd clan. I would not change a minute of my life I have spent with my wonderful parents and caring brothers and sisters.

All of the national and world news, TV shows, facts, and statistics described above, along with famous births, year timelines, and other facts I have listed from the years we were born, were provided by Seek Publishing's *Remember When* booklets. After I bought and consulted the information within each Seek Publishing booklet, I then gave all my brothers and sisters their own respective birth-year book.

Family Vacations and Day Trips

My dad always took my four older brothers out camping to Yosemite, Sequoia National Park, the Mojave Desert, and a few other beautiful California areas of interest. His favorite place to take them was to Soledad Canyon Campground, near the city of Acton, located out in the direction of Lancaster and Palmdale, northeast of Los Angeles. My brothers came home excited and full of fun stories and camping experiences from each trip. My two younger sisters and I started getting more and more upset every time they returned home. We wanted to know why we never got to go on camping trips. We bugged our dad enough that one summer he reluctantly took my two sisters and I one weekend to the famous Soledad Canyon Campground.

I was eight, and this was my first camping trip. I and my sisters loved every minute of the weekend trip. We arrived at our campsite late Friday evening because we left to drive the fifty-five miles after dad came home from work. We drove in our 1950 two-door Plymouth station wagon. We got there after dark, and since we had already eaten before we left, we found a site, used the restroom, and went to sleep. Clarissa, the youngest and smallest of us three girls at the time, slept across the front seat in a sleeping bag, and Sue and I slept on either side of dad in the back of the car in sleeping bags. The second seat folded down to make a long, comfortable, convenient six-foot bed. The back of the car had a tailgate that dropped level to the back floor. Above the tailgate was the back window that could be lifted and locked into place or could remain closed while the tailgate was down. A major drawback about this car was that it was only a two-door!

After crawling onto the second seat upon entering from either of the two front car doors, someone in the second seat would often forget and leave their foot in the crease at the bottom of the back of the front seat when it was being pulled back into place. The front seat inadvertently crushed a few toes and blackened some toenails while it was being placed back into its closed position.

My sisters and I were still in our pajamas and my dad was

Ray with our 1950 two-door Plymouth station wagon, 1963.

still asleep when we got up early on Saturday morning at Soledad Campground and began to explore the camping area. My sister found a large squirrel scrounging for food at the back end of a three-foot-long ground-level rock-and-metal stove in one of the campsites. I believe we were the only ones camping that weekend in the campground. She reached in and pulled the squirrel out by its tail! It was trying to curl itself up toward her arm to bite her when Dad came out of the back end of the car and screamed at her, "Let go of that squirrel before it bites you! It will give you rabies." She was so startled by his yelling at her that she dropped the squirrel. It scrambled off quickly with the same startled, frightened look on its face as Sue had on hers. It was a cool way to start our weekend.

What was the most fun and the most memorable part of the trip for me was my dad letting me drive the car for about ten minutes on a deserted road near the campground with my two envious sisters sitting in the backseat. It was a column stick shift. I thought I did pretty well for my first-time driving. I was able to shift into third gear and got up to about twenty miles an hour. I was so pleasantly surprised that my dad offered me an opportunity to drive our family car that day, and I have never forgotten the experience. It was rare to be singled out by a parent and invited to have one-on-one quality time with them. That first initial driving lesson on a stick shift was helpful, especially when years later I took my driving test in my first car, which was a stick shift.

We spent the rest of the day and evening on that Saturday running around the campground and playing in the creek nearby. Dad cooked us a dinner of hamburgers and canned beans followed by a campfire in the fire ring in our campsite. The reasons we mostly stayed at Soledad Campground were, one, it was free; two, it only took about an hour and a half to get there from South Gate; and three, my dad's brother, Roger, and his wife, Maxine, and our grandmother lived in a mobile home park in Acton, about a fifteen-minute drive north from the campground. We often visited them while we were camping. We could also resupply with food, etc., while in Acton as it had a small grocery store that remains today not far from where our relatives' mobile homes were located.

We got up early Sunday morning. Breakfast was special because for the first time we got to eat out of a few of those small individual cereal boxes, where you cut into the front of the box and pour in milk. What was also special was that a lot of the choices were cereals that were sweet, like Frosted Flakes, Trix, and Cocoa Puffs, that we did not ordinarily get at home. The milk was powdered milk that was mixed with water, but it tasted OK. We broke camp shortly after breakfast and headed home. We arrived back in South Gate at about 1 p.m. That was the first camping trip I took with my dad, and it went off without a hitch. There were many camping adventures to come that would be fun and memorable but would have their fair share of challenges and unforeseen mishaps.

The most memorable summer vacation ever was the one we took to Yosemite National Park in early July of 1959. I was nine and will never forget how much fun and adventure I experienced from before we even left the house to our tired but happy arrival back home. Dad had a camper shell that fit over the back of our black 1949 Dodge pickup truck. The shell had been stored for years in an area just outside the back door of the house. It sat about four feet above the ground on a set of steel poles. My dad backed the truck up under the shell, and with the help of my brothers, slowly lifted it up off the storage poles and onto the truck bed. It had been so long since the shell was last used that my dad had a very difficult time attaching the shell to the bed of the truck. We were scheduled to leave early the next morning. He worked through most of the night and finally had it ready to go about midmorning.

Nine of us, along with my dad and his mother, went on the Yosemite camping trip. My mother stayed home with Ralph and Ray, the two youngest brothers. Ray was about six months old and was still being breast-fed, and Ralph would have been about two. I am sure my mom was grateful for the downtime she was given for two weeks that summer, but they were all glad to see us when we returned.

Once the camper was ready to go, we were told to put our travel bags (our clothes) in the back of the camper. Our travel bag was a large brown paper shopping bag with our clothes in it and our name on it. No way could we afford ten or so pieces of luggage, let alone find room for that much luggage in the camper and still get all of us and our camping equipment in there as well. We placed our bag under the double bed my dad took from the den and fixed into place across the width of the back end of the camper closest to the front cab of the truck. Four of us slept *across* that double bed; me, my two younger sisters Sue and Clarissa, and Bob, the oldest of the four younger brothers. We slept head to toe across the width of the bed, sharing two blankets placed over the four of us. My dad and younger brother Mike slept in a single bed he fixed into place about three feet above the double bed and level with the rear truck window. My grandmother slept in a sleeping bag on the only space left available, which was on the floor of the camper. She slept just inside the back door of the camper, perpendicular to our beds. Any other space left in the camper was used to store our food, ice chest, and other supplies. My four older brothers slept in a tent just outside the camper. The seemingly cramped and crowded quarters were not much different than what we were used to experiencing at home!

Yosemite is about 350 miles from South Gate, and in 1959 it would typically take about seven or eight hours to drive there in the type and style of cars that were on the road in those days. Highway 41 is the main highway that leads east to Yosemite from the city of Fresno and Highway 99, which we took north from Los Angeles. I remember that Highway 41 eventually became a winding single-lane road, and there were a lot of cars going in our direction that day, as it was the week of the Fourth of July. Three people were sitting in the front seat of the truck, which included a sibling, my dad, and Grandmother. The other eight were crowded into the back of the camper on the two beds and any available floor space. We kept ourselves occupied by either trying to sleep or by playing games or playing with some small toys we brought.

About halfway up Highway 41, the truck understandably began to overheat, what with eleven people and two weeks of food and supplies in there, and a steady forty-mile climb. When the car started to overheat, and Dad was pulling the truck onto the shoulder, even from the back of the camper I heard him clearly say his typical swear phrase, "Damn it to hell." After we pulled over, I remember watching all these cars and trucks passing us on their way up to Yosemite, which meant to me that we had been going so slow up the mountain that we had been holding up a long string of cars until we pulled over. We were well off the side of the road and started eating peanut butter sandwiches that my grandmother fixed for us. We drank soda in paper cups and ate from a large bag of potato chips. By the time we finished eating lunch, the truck had cooled down, and we were on our way again. We arrived in the late afternoon, found ourselves a nice big campsite, and settled in for one of our best vacations ever!

Most of the days were filled with hiking, swimming in the small gentle side streams of the Merced River on our rafts, and enjoying dinners cooked over our two-burner propane stove. I remember seeing a *lot* of bears rummaging through the many large trash bins all set in a particular area that campers throughout a large portion of the campground brought and dumped their individual trash. I was scared for the people who wanted to take pictures of the bears and who got dangerously close to do so. I remember one man got so close to a bear while trying to take its picture that, as the small crowd gasped, the bear took a swing at him. He moved safely out of the way at the last second.

We had several nightly family campfires that were a lot of fun where we roasted marshmallows and recounted the day's events. The one memorable sight that is no longer enjoyed by Yosemite Valley campers that we were fortunate to have experienced while there was the Fourth of July Yosemite Fire Falls.

Camp Curry in Yosemite Valley, where our campsite was located, was where people gathered for the nightly campfire program. At 9 p.m., the crowd would grow silent. A man from the campfire program below would call out to the top of Glacier Point, a couple thousand feet above the valley, "Let the fire fall," and a faint reply of acknowledgment could be heard from the top of the mountain. Then a great bonfire of red fir bark would be pushed evenly over the edge of the cliff, appearing to onlookers below as a glowing waterfall of sparks and fire. That tradition was carried out every year around the Fourth of July for eighty-eight years. The last Fire Fall was in 1968. We were fortunate to have witnessed the Fire Fall when we were there in 1959. The Fire Fall I witnessed that evening made a lasting impression on me, and I considered it the highlight of the camping trip. We did drive up to Glacier Point on one of our day trips while we were there. It was a beautiful, scenic drive with awesome, impressive overlooks at the top of the point.

One other event that stands out to me from that unforgettable Yosemite vacation was a day trip we took to the Indian Caves in Yosemite Valley. We were casually walking from one cave area to another, looking at the interesting artifacts and remains, when my brother Melvin, then thirteen, began to talk to us about his knowledge of the artifacts and the Indian history. As the ten of us followed him from one area to another, we began to draw a bigger and bigger crowd along with us, who now thought Mel was a tour guide! I will always remember the look on Mel's face when he realized he was speaking to more than just his immediate family. We all turned around at about the same time to discover the small crowd standing behind us. The crowd was a little disappointed when we started laughing and they realized he wasn't a guide from the Forest Service. At about that same time, we were at the end of the caves, and walked back to the truck chuckling about the incident. If we had noticed the crowd gathering sooner, one of us could have charged them a fee and made a little money off "Mel's Tours."

I camped in Yosemite Valley that year as a nine-year-old. I have visited the valley many times since as either a camper or as a backpacker in more recent years. Out of all the many times I have visited Yosemite Valley, that first trip with my family will always be my most memorable and enjoyable summer vacation trip ever. My favorite family photo is the one that my grandmother took of my dad and us nine siblings sitting in birth order, oldest to youngest, next to dad on a smooth, two-foot-high rock wall while we were there in 1959.

The ride home was uneventful and quiet. We were worn out from two long fun-filled weeks of experiencing the beautiful scenery and wilderness that gave me, at that young age, a lifetime of awe and respect for nature and a desire to return again and again. I realized, after that initial trip and subsequent trips in nature, that it was now my responsibility to become the next generation of caretakers and protectors of any state and national forest I visited. We did take pictures at the famous entrance to the valley as we left. One of them was a sweeping picturesque view of Yosemite Valley that included Half Dome, Yosemite Falls, and El Capitan.

The first thing my dad and grandmother did when we got home was to make sure we all brought in our luggage (shopping bag) and then returned to the truck to help bring in and put away the other supplies and equipment we brought. That became the routine thereafter whenever we returned home from any camping trip. We all helped pack, load, and unload the car or truck.

Every summer, starting in 1961, our family began spending a week or two camping somewhere in Southern California. My mom began taking us on our camping trips, as summers were the time of year in which my dad stood to make the most money, putting in lawn sprinklers and utilizing his three oldest sons to help him. We usually had ten of us on those summer trips, which was my mom and the youngest nine, from Harry, who was twelve in 1962, down to Frances, the youngest, who was two when we went on our first trip with our mother. Most of the time she drove us in the 1950 Plymouth station wagon.

Many of our summer trips were spent at Soledad Canyon Campground. The campground is no longer there, but it was located about twenty miles northeast of the San Fernando Valley. We got there by driving north through the San Fernando Valley on the 101 freeway, which at that time ended at Cahuenga Avenue, which, after turning north, led us to old Sierra Highway, which led us north to Soledad Canyon Road, which in turn led to the campground. Highway 14, the current Antelope Valley Freeway, was not built yet. Often, for a day or two, we were the only ones in the ten or so total campsites in the campground. This gave us the run of the place, which we absolutely took advantage of, yelling, running everywhere, in and out of the other campsites, in and around the campground, until some other families showed up. There were a lot of bats that came out and began flying around at about sunset. We had fun throwing objects in the air, like a folded newspaper, and then watching the blind bats dive at them.

Several of us slept in the back of the car or truck, and the rest slept in a tent. It could get pretty cold at night; the sleeping bags we had were not very warm, and we had no padding underneath us when we slept. I woke up a few times shivering in my sleeping bag and in need of going to the bathroom. It was a bit harrowing to walk the fifty yards or so to the outhouse by myself in the pitch black of the night without a flashlight. I got lost one night coming back from the bathroom. It took me several agonizing moments to find my way back to the tent, only because I happened to walk right into a fallen tree trunk whose prickly bark I recognized by touch from the day's play, and luckily found my way back. Otherwise, in about two more seconds, at about 2:30 a.m., I was ready to start yelling for help!

Acton is where my Uncle Roger, his wife, Maxine, and my grandmother lived in their mobile homes. They moved there from Tustin in the early 1960s when my uncle began working as a cement layer during the construction of the 14 freeway.

Acton was a small mining city, established in the late 1880s, that supplied miners with equipment and supplies and hauled out their gold, copper, and titanium from the local hills and creeks down to San Pedro to be shipped north to the Sacramento area. The Southern Pacific Railroad eventually came through the canyon and began hauling out the miner's finds, which horses and wagons had hauled out previously. The railroad ran along the west side of the canyon against the base of the mountains. Many freight trains came through daily. There was a double track where the railroad came by the campground, and sometimes the train would come to a stop on a side rail to let another train coming from the opposite direction pass. Sometimes hobos and freight riders would jump from their boxcar when it was stopped and run over to our campsite to ask for food or money. They never got much of either, as food and money were scarce for us while there. One time I remember Mom giving a few carrots to a thin shirtless guy who came running off a train. He looked like he hadn't eaten in some time.

From our campsite we often climbed the mountains on the other side of the railroad tracks. There were a few occasions when we sent a tired younger sibling back to the campsite while the rest of continued to hike. On one occasion that sibling just made it back across the tracks when a train came racing through. Whew!

There was a lovely freshwater creek that ran through the east side of the campground in which we spent many hours cooling off, making small dams for swimming, walking up and down it, and capturing drinking water from it until a pump was installed many years later at one end of the campground. We would get bored hiking the same old mountains near the tracks, so we often crossed Soledad Canyon Road and hiked up the small valley and mountains over there. Those mountains are where I saw my first scorpion hiding under a rock just off the trail.

Once about six or seven of us walked south along Soledad Canyon Road for about two miles and then came back. We ranged in age from about fourteen to four. We never considered how dangerous some of our wanderings were until we looked back years later at what we had done. As long as we ate breakfast first, we were allowed to pretty much go anywhere and do anything, as long as we returned later in the day to eat lunch. The campground and surrounding area were a long, fairly remote, and wide-open canyon with plenty of areas to explore to keep us occupied most of the time trip after trip. My mom probably would have been upset and worried if she knew where we went and what we did on those adventurous day trips. She trusted the judgement of the older two or three and knew we would not purposely put all of us in danger. We did put ourselves in danger at times; we just didn't do it on purpose!

On one particular trip, we had just packed up and were one of the last families to leave the campground on a pleasant late Sunday morning. About fifteen minutes down the road, a voice from the very back of the car yelled out, "Hey, where's Ralph?" The car suddenly went silent and quickly slowed down as our eyes focused on the rearview, mirror where all we could see were Mom's huge distraught eyes desperately searching the car for some sign of Ralph. You could see a part of her was hoping we were just kidding. Ralph, five at the time, was not in the car! Mom, tense and frantic, quickly turned the car around and drove back to the campground. There was Ralph, calmly sitting at our campsite picnic table, believe it or not with a half smile on his face. He casually got into the car, and my now semi-composed mom asked him why he was smiling. He replied by saying, "I knew you would have to come back for me eventually." Nobody noticed he hadn't gotten into the car because he said he was off playing in the creek, and after returning to our campsite, discovered we had left without him. Mom made sure she never left anyone behind again, at least not at Soledad Canyon Campground.

The most memorable but scary Soledad Canyon camping trip was the one where my brother Ray fell out of the back of the truck and onto a busy highway when we went into Acton to go to the grocery store. There were six of us in the back of the Dodge pickup truck. The truck tailgate had metal hooks that held up and latched it into the back end of the truck. The hooks had become loose, and the tailgate dropped open just as Mom took off across an intersection. The truck jerked when she shifted from first to second gear. Ray was sitting next to me against the tailgate. I had my left arm around him when he suddenly fell out onto the highway. I quickly crawled to the left front of the truck bed and yelled, "Mom, stop! Ray fell out!" She pulled over, and I jumped out of the back end and ran back to where Ray was now standing up in the middle of the right lane, about thirty feet back, crying and holding his left side. Fortunately, and thankfully, the cautious woman driving behind us, who pulled over and got out to help, said, "I thought something like one of you falling out might happen, so I purposely kept my distance behind you." Thank goodness she was so alert to the potential danger and avoided what could have been a terrible outcome.

We got Ray back into the truck, where he lay across my lap, away from the tailgate, of course. My mom had to drive the rest of the kids all the way back to the campground and drop most of us and our groceries off, leaving thirteen-year-old Harry in charge of six siblings as Mom and I drove away to take Ray to a nearby hospital. He lay across my lap for the hour and a half it took from the time the accident happened until we got him to the emergency room. I was getting tired of lying in the same spot in the same position with him, but every time I moved he would cry out in such pain that I stopped moving. Turns out that fortunately he only had bruised ribs and a few scratches on his left side. Needless to say, none of us ever sat up against the tailgate while driving again.

In 1963, when I was thirteen, our summer camping vacation that year was spent down south of Los Angeles at La Costa State Beach near Del Mar, California. We got the car all packed up and were ready to pile in and go when we realized that we had all grown such that there was no longer enough room for the ten of us to fit in the car with all the camping supplies and equipment. Dad had already left for work for the day with a couple of my older brothers, so mom went to the local U-Haul place, rented and drove home a small five-by-six-foot wood slat–framed trailer. We were now able to get all our supplies into the trailer and all of us into the car.

We finally got underway and drove south to La Costa. We got there in about an hour and a half. I was sitting in the middle of the front seat next to my mom. We exited the 5 freeway and were on our way to the campground, driving on an elevated two-lane street parallel to a street on the beach below. My mom decided to give us a scenic tour of the beach before going to our campground, so she turned right from the road we were on and went down a fairly steep hill to the road below. I looked at my sister, sitting to my right, with a perplexed, half-worried look on my face as to why Mom was taking us and this fully loaded car and trailer down this steep, road knowing we would have to go back up it to get to the campground.

Turns out my concerns were warranted. After our little scenic jaunt along the beachfront, Mom turned left to go back up to the street that would take us to our campground. She got about ten feet from the top of the hill when, after several attempts, the loaded car and trailer couldn't make it over the top. I looked up at Mom and she had this pained, terrified look on her face and nearly began to cry. By this time a small crowd had formed along the curb and sidewalk. She decided to give it one more try to get the car et al over the hill. The car was a stick shift, so she told me, "Put your left foot right here, and take it off when I tell you to." She was telling me to put my foot on the brake. She put her right foot on the gas and her left foot on the clutch. She gave it a lot of gas and slowly brought up the clutch. She told me to slowly take my foot off the brake, but the car still wouldn't move, no matter how much gas she gave it. We could now begin to smell the clutch starting to burn out.

At this point, the car was stuck, and nine pairs of worried and anxious eyes were staring out at the ever-growing crowd of people, who by now were giving suggestions to my mom and each other as to how to get the car up over the hill. One suggestion was to unhitch the trailer. How would that help? After several agonizing moments, finally, a nine- or ten-year-old boy on his bike across the street yelled out, "Hey, lady—why don't you just get all the kids out of the car?" So we all piled out onto the curb, Mom put the car in gear and got up and over the hill easily. We all piled back in, and we were on our merry way to the campground. All this crazy excitement already, and we hadn't even gotten to the campground yet!

Thankfully the rest of the trip had only one small mishap. It turns out the campsites were set on two sloping levels above the beach. Our campsite was on the second level, which meant having to climb down from our campsite to an established path that led past the lower level of campsites and then on to the beach. On one of our runs down to the beach, we got to the bottom of our tier and were ready to walk down to the bottom of the tier below when Ralph called down to us, "Wait for me!" When we looked up, he was sitting on the edge of the dirt on top of the road above. I yelled up to him to "Come on!" We turned and started to walk down to the beach when all of a sudden Ralph came whizzing by us, tumbling as he went. Fortunately, the angle of the slopes was not that severe. He landed sitting upright several feet below us. We looked at him to ask if he was all right, and he had that same silly half smile on his face that he had at Soledad Canyon Campground when we left him behind. He had slipped and fallen about thirty feet, but as usual, he was none the worse for wear. He picked himself up and promptly walked on down to the beach with the rest of us, where he dipped into the water briefly to wash off the dirt he picked up on his swim trunks when he fell. What an easygoing trouper he always was. It was that demeanor that usually got him the Good Camper Award that Mom gave out at the end of each camping trip. It was her psychological attempt to hopefully get us all to behave while camping if we knew there was a possible reward in it for one of us. The reward was usually a toy or a puzzle.

We did go back to La Costa State Beach again the following summer. The trip was uneventful compared to the first time we went. We were excited that this time, while we were there, the Del Mar Fair was going on a few miles away to the south, and we were going to get to go. We all piled into the car and arrived at the fair in the late morning. It turns out there is an entry fee for each person, and Mom did not have enough money to get us all in, so we did not end up going. What was amazing about that scene that I remember most was that Mom was more disappointed than we were that she couldn't afford to get us in. Upon hearing the bad news from mom and seeing the sad, anguished, apologetic look on her face, we all just turned around, locked arms at our elbows, casually and happily made a nine-person human chain, and skipped back to the car. We knew it was not her fault; there was nothing she could do about it or foresee it. She walked quietly behind us to the car with her head up and a slight grin on her face.

All our other summer vacations were fun and went well, with just a few bee stings, mosquito bites, and scratches. I remember the last family camping trip we took where Mom drove was in the summer of 1967, when I was seventeen. The only thing that stands out to me on that last trip was the fact that we kids did all the planning, from where we would go, the dates we would leave and return, to loading up the car with all the food and camping supplies. Once the car was all loaded and we kids were ready to go, we woke Mom up. She got dressed, ate breakfast, and we were on our way.

I can still vividly envision those times I woke up in the back of our Dodge pickup truck on a cool morning after setting up camp at Soledad Canyon Campground the night before and seeing a big, bright, beautiful blue sky with the gentle movement of shimmering green aspen leaves freely flowing in a slight breeze. The other fantastic bonus scenes at the campground were the times we were there when there was a full moon or no moon at all. A full moon at night meant the campground was lit up well enough to easily see our hands in front of our faces and actually see with the naked eye a few of the many craters on the moon. The only other times I experienced that kind of brightness and surface definition on full moon nights while family camping was at Leo Carrillo State Beach in Ventura, when we camped there a few summers. On those nights when there was no moon at Soledad Canyon Campground, we were treated to a most magnificent view of the Milky Way. It seemed to stretch endlessly across the sky. There were parts of it that actually were milky, where I could not clearly see the stars in a given section. Leo Carrillo State Beach offered that same beautiful, clear view of the Milky Way. It has been many decades since I have come anywhere close to seeing a clear, luminous full moon and Milky Way like I experienced as a child and young teen while camping.

As many times as I have been backpacking in the mountains and remote wilderness areas over the past thirty-five years, I have not witnessed anything quite like what I saw on those special nights and evenings at Soledad Canyon. I believe there is just too much smog, smoke, and lights surrounding our wilderness parks and forests today to create what I had the privilege of seeing so many years ago.

By the time I turned eighteen, many of us older campers, who always went before, were now preoccupied with work and school and other activities and were no longer interested in going camping, so in 1968 the family quit going on summer camping trips. However, when I was nineteen, in 1969, my five younger brothers and youngest sister talked me into taking them back to Soledad Canyon Campground one more time. The five of them at the time ranged in age from nine to fourteen. We went during their holiday break in December, and it was *very* cold at the campground. We had difficulty staying warm, especially at night. At the time, I was a part owner with one of my brothers of a large old stick-shift delivery truck that resembled today's large UPS delivery trucks. He and I converted it into a two-bed camper that I took to Soledad that winter. The large vehicle made it pleasant traveling for the six of us, with our equipment, food, and all, and the spacious truck floor served us well when sleeping. We were able to fit comfortably on the two beds and the truck floor, staying reasonably warm with our bodies fairly close together.

There was one frightening incident I miraculously avoided one of the nights we stayed there. I placed the small barbecue we had used earlier in the evening to cook some hamburgers on top of a four-foot-high chest of drawers permanently attached to the far back corner of the truck. I thought it was a good way to keep us warm until the charcoals burned themselves out. Something told me to keep the louvered window slats over the barbecue and chest of drawers in that same corner slightly open, even though it meant some cold air would be coming in. At the time, I was totally unaware that leaving those coals burning in a closed area would give off carbon monoxide, which would have probably killed us all! Those coals did keep us warm until we fell asleep. I had carelessly but inadvertently saved our lives that night by choosing to keep those louvered windows open. I truly believe I was guided by divine intervention that night. One thing that helped is that we were all mostly sleeping on or close to the floor of the truck, and some of the heat from the coals was rising out the windows rather that floating down where we all were. I thankfully dodged a bullet that night. Like mother, like daughter, I guess!

On that same trip, we had a fun day ride over to Vasquez Rocks, located about ten miles from the campground. Bob, at fourteen, the oldest of the five siblings I took on that trip, successfully guided us everywhere we went, from getting us to the campground from South Gate to guiding us to Vasquez Rocks and back to the campground. He learned at an early age how to read maps and was instrumental in planning and getting us where we needed to go. He continues to plan, in great detail, our yearly summer backpacking trips.

Vasquez Rocks are located in the Agua Dulce area off the 14 freeway and are one of the movie industry's most recognizable film locations. The rocks were named after a notorious bandit named Tiburcio Vásquez, who used the craggy rocks as his hideout. He was eventually captured, tried, and convicted in San Jose for the murders of three men he and his gang killed while robbing a general store near present-day Hollister in Northern California. He was hanged in March 1875. Hollywood studios have used Vasquez Rocks as a backdrop for movies, television, and various commercials since 1931 (Moviesites.org).

Outside of braving the cold while we were there, the six of us had a wonderful time together at our last-ever camping vacation at Soledad Canyon Campground. A large portion of the 14 freeway, the Antelope Valley Freeway, was completed in 1963. That last trip was the first time I had driven on the 14 freeway to and from the campground from South Gate.

On a whim, not too long ago, I drove out the Antelope Valley Freeway, exited at Soledad Canyon Road, and drove the seven or so miles to where Soledad Canyon Campground once existed. It is no longer a campground but a private movie ranch. I walked past the property sign to the area where we once camped. The creek was still running through the area, the entry road to the former campground was somewhat in the same location as before, and those lovely mountains on the other side of the railroad tracks that we climbed so often still had a visible trail I could see that still led to the top. As I returned to my car and began to drive away from my spontaneous nostalgic return to a favorite childhood vacation spot, I suddenly heard the familiar sound of a freight train in the distance, struggling in low gear to come up the steep canyon and through the former campground. I was brought back to those early summer evenings when we heard a similar train as we were settling down at our campsite table to a dinner of hot dogs and beans after a long exhausting day of fun and adventure. Nothing can replace those cherished, unforgettable, sometimes harrowing yet carefree and treasured vacations days I happily spent with my beloved family. I reluctantly drove away from my favorite childhood vacation spot and soon found myself driving south down the busy 14 freeway, headed back to Los Angeles.

As a family, we continue to spend a few days each summer camping somewhere in California. We reside all over California, from Sacramento in Northern California to Santa Ana in Southern California. We alternate camping one summer in Northern California and the next summer in Southern California to even the travel time and distance for everyone. The ideal and most popular area we also camp at is on the Central Coast, like Morro Bay or Jalama Beach in Santa Barbara County. We have *not* had any misadventures or calamities on the now eight or so summers we have been camping again as an extended family. We do, however, certainly and thoroughly enjoy ourselves on our camping trips as much as we did as children. The only thing that has changed is that now we make and pay for our reservations six months in advance, for twenty people, instead of the party of ten that, without charge, just used to show up and set up camp wherever we could find a picnic bench and a fire pit.

Some of our day trips we took as a family were as exciting and thrilling as our camping trips. Most of the day trips I am talking about were ones we took to visit relatives, museums, zoos, etc. Over the years, Dad drove us on some of our day trips, mostly the ones where he drove us to visit his mother in Tustin or Acton on Sundays. Grandma usually had some lemonade or fresh-squeezed juice for us. As she talked to Dad, we would head outside and walk through her vegetable garden or around the mobile home park where she lived. When she passed away in 1984, my sister Clarissa bought her mobile home, which had been moved back to Tustin from Acton, and lived in it for several years until she sold it and moved up north.

Mom drove us on our day trips, especially on those trips we took to visit her family in Ventura County. Dad's trips were uneventful; he was a good driver and always knew where he was going. Mom's trips, on the other hand, were quite unpredictable, with some unexpected outcomes, like the time we were driving in the rain on our way back to the freeway after visiting my mom's sister, Margaret, in Ventura. She had the usual younger nine kids in the car with her when we were stopped at a signal. The brakes of the car behind us locked up in the light rain, and the driver rear-ended us going about ten miles an hour. None of us in the car knew he was about to inevitably hit us, except my mom. She said she saw him coming in the rearview mirror, and saw from a distance that he was having trouble stopping, and knew he was going to hit us. She said afterward that she did not want to warn us of the impending impact, as she thought we would tense up, and that to warn us would cause us more physical damage. I want to think that she was right in not telling us he was coming. She also said she could see the whites of his eyes just before he was about to hit a car full of people. His eyes got even bigger when he approached a fully loaded car full of kids.

My mom chose to stay in the car and not look to see if there was any damage, which I think was also a smart thing to do given the conditions. She showed an overriding need to stay in the car and protect her kids. He was very apologetic and indicated that the trailer hitch on the back of our car prevented any damage to the car or bumper. He asked if we were all OK. A few of us bumped heads and a few others fell forward at impact into some other siblings, but we had experienced similar, if not worse, contact while routinely playing with each other in the back of the car. Since I was sitting in the very back, I could see that his car had a small dent in the front bumper where he hit our trailer hitch.

We then went on our merry way without exchanging license numbers or insurance information with the driver. I am sure he was relieved when we left. I could just see him trying to explain to his insurance company why he wanted them to pay for ten neck braces for inflicting whiplash on a car full of children. As soon as we got back to South Gate, we all got out and looked at the back of the car. As he indicated, there was no visible damage to our car, at least nothing any different than the many existing scratches and small dents. With as many day trips as we took over twenty years, we fortunately never again experienced a traffic accident like that one.

In 1962, while returning from a visit with my mom's brother Lewis and his wife, Ethel, in Camarillo, we did get a flat tire at the bottom of the Conejo Grade on the 101 freeway. Again, there were the usual ten of us in the car, and to make matters worse, it was raining. We attempted to change the tire ourselves but had no luck. We were parked on the shoulder just feet from the busy car- and truck-filled freeway. My mom got us out of the car and moved us over against a barbed-wire fence that was about twenty feet from the car and the freeway. She sent Harry and Sue, who were thirteen and eleven at the time, to walk up to the next off-ramp and find a pay phone, and tell the operator where we were, and find and call either her brother Tom or Lewis Gill and ask them to come help us change the tire. Camarillo Springs Road was the next off-ramp, about a quarter of a mile away from where we broke down, which was at the bottom of the Conejo Grade. There was an entrance to a county park about another quarter of a mile from the end of the off-ramp, where they found a pay phone and called the operator.

Mom had me stay behind and help her keep an eye on the seven other kids. About twenty-five minutes later, just as Sue and Harry were returning to the car, this guy stopped behind our car and approached my mom. He said his name was Louis Gill. Turns out there were two Lewis Gills in Ventura County. He changed the tire quickly for us, and we were soon on our way up the grade and back to South Gate. He said to my mom when he initially got there that "I was puzzled as to why I would get a call from a telephone operator indicating my wife and kids wanted me to fix a flat tire when I knew they were out of town." We were grateful he decided to come anyway. He did say he knew our Uncle Lewis, but was glad he was available to help us.

Just as we were picking up speed and merging back onto the freeway, our Uncle Lewis slowly drove by us, honking his horn. We found out later that he too had gotten a call from the operator after she called the other Louis Gill. Everything thankfully worked out in the end, as was usually the case. We were always very fortunate that these incidents, for the most part, had happy endings, and after all was said and done, we were none the worse for wear!

A day trip we were excited about taking when I was eleven was to the petting zoo at the Lynwood city park. Mom got us all dressed up to go, but when we got there, she discovered that she did not have enough money to pay for all of us to get in. She had enough money for herself and seven siblings to enter and enjoy the animals. So, Harry and I, the two oldest, were sent across the street to the park to play until everyone was done at the petting zoo. We tried to keep ourselves busy and occupied, but it seemed like forever before they all came running across the street excited about what they saw and did. I know my mom always felt bad when unknown-beforehand entry fees caused these unforeseen things to happen, but we just did our best to adjust and be understanding of our family's constantly fluctuating financial situation.

One fun place she could take us that did not require a lot of money was to Knott's Berry Farm in Buena Park. At that time, in the 1950s, there were minimal parking fees, and she could get us into the main part of the farm for free. This was before they began selling ticket books like Disneyland. It cost to go on the rides, which, at times, we could afford to ride. We rode the free merry-go-round and the train around the farm and could go into many of the shops and free sideshows.

One sideshow was a large, dark room that about fifty people were shuffled into and stood while watching a bust of Christ turn into a glowing lifelike figure that would rise and disappear into the ceiling. Once it was over, we were all shuffled back out to the main street again. On one occasion, when we exited, there was a small crowd that had gathered just outside the exhibit. They all had concerned, bewildered looks on their faces and appeared to be circled around a small crying child. We made our way to the center of the crowd to discover that this time it was my eight-year-old sister Sue who was inadvertently left outside the sideshow while the rest of us were inside. She stopped crying when she saw us but was very upset. She perked up when mom promised to buy her an ice cream cone. Fortunately, in those days, there was not much worry about having something bad happen to a lost, or in our case, carelessly forgotten child.

We used to have a lot of fun day trips to parks with lakes. There was a park we went to when I was eleven. Seven of us decided to walk all the way around the lake while my mom stayed back at our picnic area with the younger two siblings. This lake had a small dam at one end. The only way to get to the other side of the dam was to cross it at its base, just above the water line; otherwise we would have to walk all the way back around the lake to get back to Mom. The wall of the dam was slanted at about a 25-degree angle and was made of rocks cemented together. We felt we could all make it, so we started walking across just above the water line. We got about halfway across the fifty-foot-long dam face when we saw a group of about twelve wide-eyed adults on the other side of the dam with frantic looks on their faces. They were *very* concerned about seeing seven young children, ranging in age from four to twelve, walking across a rocky, somewhat slippery dam. They were more afraid than we were at the thought of watching one of us falling or slipping into the water. Little did they know that this kind of dangerous adventure to them was a typical normal adventure for us. We all made it safely across to the other side, walking right by all those shocked and concerned adults, who were still shaken by what they had just witnessed. It was just a short walk after that to get back to a none-the-wiser mother and two eager siblings, who were happy to see us. Looking back at all the risky situations we placed ourselves in, we were very fortunate that we did not have any real mishaps, serious injuries, or lasting physical and possibly emotional consequences.

It was second nature for us to take risks. We trusted and depended on each other for help and support during those risky times in our lives when we needed each other the most, something we continue to do to this day. It helped that our parents trusted us (or at least hoped they could trust us) to make wise choices when we were out and about without them. We got bored easily doing what was safe and normal on our vacations, day trips, and in and around our neighborhood. We all liked a challenge and challenging each other. It was a way for us to find out what our limits and boundaries were and what we were willing to do to find out. I believe our living out-of-the-box thinking and actions in our youth better prepared us for life's challenges and risks. After surviving all those harrowing childhood experiences, the rest of my life ever since has been a piece of cake!

I consider myself very fortunate to have had so many opportunities at such a young age to share and enjoy so many adventures, exploits, and escapades with all my brothers and sisters. I know each of us would say that the most enjoyable times of our lives then and now were those spent with family. I believe the early family challenges and positions of responsibility I held from age ten developed in me a desire to be assertive, confident, and successful in everything I did in life.

Age Ten and Beyond

*I*n 1960, when I was ten and my brother Harry was eleven, we started delivering the *South Gate Press* to earn some money. I didn't think about it much at the time, but I was probably one of the few girls in the LA area delivering newspapers to earn money. The paper was only delivered on Thursday and Sunday mornings. Our route was the three blocks east of us that ran north to south from Tweedy Boulevard to Abbott Road. On Thursday mornings, Harry got up at 5 and folded and packed the papers into our delivery bag. I would get up at 6 and place the bag on the front of my bike and deliver. On Sunday mornings I folded and packed the papers and he delivered. We decided he would deliver on Sundays because the paper was bigger and heavier and he had more strength to ride a heavily loaded bike. When my mom found out that I was delivering the papers by myself on Thursdays, she became concerned for my safety as a girl and made Harry deliver on Thursdays and Sundays, and I folded and packed each time after that. We probably could have both folded and both delivered, but I think we only had one bike between us at the time.

We either went together to collect from our customers each month or we each took turns alternating collecting. After we collected from our customers, we had to take the bus or get a parent to take us over to the neighboring city of Huntington Park to the *South Gate Press* office to turn in our money and get what we were owed for the month for delivering. We usually made a total of about $7 to $10 a month for our efforts, which we split. My problem was that on those months when I collected from our customers, I often spent some of the money at the Foster Freeze on Malison and Tweedy Boulevard before I got home. One month I spent more than I made. After that, we either collected together and Harry kept track of the money, or Harry collected by himself. We delivered for about two years before I moved on to mowing some of my older neighbor's lawns and babysitting to earn money. Harry continued for several more months to deliver the *South Gate Press* by himself.

I mowed the front and back lawns of my neighbor, Mr. Baldwin, who lived across the street. I also mowed for Mrs. Lang, who lived next door. It was great having money to buy candy and ice cream or birthday or holiday gifts for my family. They each paid me one dollar a week to edge and mow. Mr. and Mrs. Baldwin lived in a house that looked like a small castle. Part of the backyard was shaded by a few small trees. He had a large beautiful carp pool and fountain located against a fence behind the house. Mr. Baldwin could be gruff and demanding at times, insisting each week that I mow his lawn in a certain pattern and direction. He usually stayed outside with me to make sure I mowed it to his liking. He was of average build, about 5'9", with dark balding hair, a deeply wrinkled face, and always wore dark pants and a white T-shirt. I liked that he had an electric mower, which made mowing his lawn a breeze.

Mrs. Lang was a small, soft-spoken woman with graying hair and an energetic, playful golden retriever named Skipper who had the run of her backyard. She had one of the few streetlights on the street on her lawn, on the street side of her sidewalk. Her husband had passed away just before we moved in. Her daughter, Nadine, a teenager at the time, died of polio a few years after we moved in. Nadine was an attractive, friendly girl with long beautiful brown hair. I remember how sad Mrs. Lang was for many years following her death. It seemed she was never the same again. One of the few times I ever saw my mother cry was when Mrs. Lang called to tell her Nadine had passed. I remember my mom took over a casserole she had cooked for the houseguests who had attended Nadine's funeral. Why I mention the casserole is because the dish it was

GLAD TO BE A LADD

taken over there in came back to us clean as a whistle. I had never seen it so clean as the way she returned it to us!

When I was thirteen, I began babysitting for some of my neighbors' kids and cleaning a few houses for neighbors when I wasn't competing in sports. It was in the summer of 1964 when I was fourteen and had just graduated from St. Emydius that one of our church friends, Mrs. Cyrs, called my mom to ask if I would be interested in working with her at the South Gate Laundromat, owned by another church friend, Mr. Tom O'Farrell. I remember when my mom hung up the phone after talking to Mrs. Cyrs, she came into the living room, where I was still in my pajamas at mid-morning, playing with my younger sister, and shyly asked me if I was interested. I said yes, and started working there the following Monday. I had to apply for a Work Permit, which I got. I promptly spent the next four years working at the South Gate Laundromat six days a week through the summer and on Saturdays during the school year.

It was a laundromat at that time where customers brought in their dirty clothes and dry cleaning. If they brought the dirty clothes in by 10 a.m., we would have them washed, dried, folded, and ready for pickup by 3 p.m. Each order of clothes was weighed and charged by the pound and separated by whites and colored clothes into big blue mesh net bags that were closed at the top by interweaving a large safety pin across the open end of the bag. Each pin had a number on it that corresponded to a customer's order. There was a large washing machine that could wash fifteen or so of these large mesh net bags at once. When finished, the customers bags were opened and emptied into several individual dryers. The clothes were then folded and placed back into the customer's box in which they came.

If our customers brought in sheets, those were washed and fed through an eight-foot-long hot iron with rollers designed for sheets, pillow cases, and tablecloths. After washing, drying, and folding all the clothes for the day, Mr. O'Farrell would warm up the iron. Mrs. Cyrs and I stood at either end of the long hot roller and ironed and folded everyone's sheets. Mr. O'Farrell would wrap the folded sheets in a strip of thin light-blue paper and write the customer's last name on it and place them with the rest of the customer's order. All dry cleaning was sent out daily and usually returned within two days. Some people just brought in dry cleaning, and some just brought in dirty clothes and sheets.

Mrs. Cyrs was a small round Italian woman with three children, one of whose name I forget but who played on the school's girls' basketball team with me. Mrs. Cyrs had curly shoulder-length hair and was diligent in initially teaching me the ropes of the laundromat and looking after my safety. We worked well together for nearly five years. She was still working there when I left the job and started college in 1969. My two younger sisters, Sue and Clarissa, each worked there for a while after I quit. I began working at a Winchell's Donut House near the college.

Mr. O'Farrell was a tall, thin, loud Irishman with a full head of thick white hair and who constantly smoked big long cigars. His son Tim was an altar boy and a year older than me. He was shy by comparison to his dad. Mr. O'Farrell was an important member of our church's congregation. At Sunday mass, along with other church members, he went from pew to pew, front to back, collecting donations by extending a long, thin, wooden-handle with a basket on the end of it down each pew. He helped the priest during Holy Communion and was a member of our church choir.

In the laundromat, he would stand several feet in front of me with his back to me with a cup of detergent in his hand, ready to dump it into the large washing machine in front of him as I was folding clothes behind him. I will never forget the odd movements he did with his butt as he stood there. He would squeeze the muscles in his butt cheeks together making them rise and fall each time he squeezed. I didn't know whether I should laugh or be embarrassed by his actions, or even why I am mentioning this!

The laundromat was a small, narrow shop that had a front entrance accessible to customers from Tweedy Boulevard and a back entrance for customers accessible from the large parking lot behind the laundromat, the Better Foods Store, and the Five and Dime Store. The minimum wage in 1964 that I earned was $1.25 an hour, and when I quit in the summer of 1969 to attend college, the minimum wage was a whopping $1.60 an hour. I made enough money to buy gas for my car and pay my own tuition for my senior year at Pius X Catholic High School in 1967–1968, which was, as I remember, about $100.

I will always have a special place in my heart for Mrs. Cyrs and Tom O'Farrell for entrusting and supporting me in successfully navigating me through my first job. That first job enabled me to develop a valuable work ethic that I have maintained for a lifetime. I did not take for granted the importance of their guidance and trust nor the money I generated that brought me a level of financial independence and self-reliance at a young age. I was not the least bit hesitant to take this job at fourteen years of age. I had already accumulated four years of positions and jobs of responsibility at home, in the neighborhood, and at school that prepared me for bigger and better positions and jobs to come. I believe in that law of the universe that you attract what you put out there.

In 1964 I had another opportunity, unrelated to working. I was picked to appear on *The Three Stooges Show* with guest host Don Lamond. I wrote in several months earlier to request to appear on the live hour-long TV show, which quizzed two invited child guests about various facts and information. The questions were asked live between the airing of Three Stooges episodes and commercials. I was thrilled when I got a phone call one afternoon to appear the following week. My mom picked me up early from school the day of the show, and together we drove down to the Channel 11 television studio lot. My best friend, Nancy O'Connor, was invited by the studio to come with me in case they needed her to fill in if the other contestant did not show.

The Three Stooges were a vaudeville comedy act of the mid-twentieth century. They were best known for the ninety-four short subject films they made at Columbia Pictures from 1934 to 1946. Many of these are still in syndication today. Screen Gems syndicated the shorts to television, whereupon the Three Stooges became one of the most popular comedy acts of the early 1960s (Wikipedia).

I competed against a boy. Over the hour, we were asked five questions each, and whoever got the most right won some prizes. The last question I was asked, which I successfully answered at the last second and which put me over the top to win all the prizes that day, was: "Where is the Vatican located?" Now, as a Catholic, if I had gotten that question wrong, I would have been excommunicated and probably not allowed to return to school, not to mention the ridicule I would have suffered at the mercy of my brothers and sisters, the nuns, and my school friends. Two prizes I remember winning were a pogo stick and Super Skates. To top things off, my mom drove Nancy and me over to Olvera Street after the taping to walk around and eat a late-afternoon Mexican dinner. I was in seventh heaven! What a great experience that was. It showed me that I was a confident risk taker at a young age and had the courage and the willingness to experience life above and beyond the ordinary person.

I got a lot of mileage out of the pogo stick and the Super Skates. Also, my popularity at school increased, as several students the next day said they saw me on the show. My appearance took place near the end of eighth grade, and I now found myself preparing for high school and looking forward to continuing my education and furthering my sports career there.

I attended Pius X Catholic High School in the adjoining city of Downey, about a fifteen-minute drive from home. I carpooled with longtime St. Emydius girlfriends for the first year and a half. There were five of us close friends who were in the carpool. We all lived within two miles of each other in Lynwood and South Gate. Our mothers took turns once a week driving us to school. It worked out well the first year, until I started playing on the sports teams and they did not. I would drive in the carpool each morning to school with them but I would take a city bus home after practice each day. The money I had earned at the laundromat that summer gave me enough bus money to enable me to pay the 25 cents it took to take the bus home each school day. I got my driver's license and owned my first car in April 1966, as a sophomore, and started driving myself and my freshman sister, Sue, to school.

I adjusted easily to high school life mainly because most of my friends from St. Emydius were in my freshman class and so were many of the girls from other local Catholic elementary schools that I had competed against in seventh and eighth grade. Our teachers at Pius X were nuns and lay teachers, with priests teaching our religion classes. I enjoyed going from one class to another and having six teachers instead of one. I especially enjoyed my freshman homeroom class that I attended right after lunch.

The campus was constructed in 1953 and is part of the Los Angeles Catholic Archdiocese. It offered a quality education to girls and boys for grades nine through twelve. Monsignor George J. Parnassus was the principal when I attended Pius X High School, from the fall semester 1964 through the spring semester 1968. It was a school that experimented with unconventional educational methods.

Saint Pius X was born Giuseppe Melchiorre Sarto in 1835 in Riese, Italy. He possessed the saintly virtues of piety, charity, deep humility, pastoral zeal, and simplicity, and spent most of his life in the service of God. His help toward the poor was well known; he gave away much of his own clothing and food to the needy. He became Pope Pius X in 1903 and worked tirelessly to find practical solutions for social problems. He died in 1914 at the age of seventy-nine. Shortly after his death, people began making pilgrimages to his tomb, where accounts of miraculous cures and favors were said to have occurred. In 1954 he was canonized a saint of God.

Before entering Pius X, everyone took an entrance exam to determine their level of intellectual aptitude. Students were placed in academic classes with others who tested at their intellectual level. If a student tested at the highest level, the student was placed in what was called the Honors Group. These students were considered the smartest students in their grade. The next smartest level was called Group I, then there was Group II, Group III, and lastly, Group IV. It amazed me that they would group us into these intelligence levels knowing there would be a stigma attached to each group, especially poor Group IV. I was placed in Group II, the middle of the five groups. I got mostly B's and C's in Group II, which told me I was of average intelligence in the average intelligence group. Just where I wanted to be: not too smart, not too dumb. I was in the one group that wasn't looked upon by others as being either too smart or not smart enough.

Surprisingly I never heard a student, teacher, or parent ever complain about us being pigeonholed and labeled by our level of intelligence. I guess if we didn't question the beliefs and mores of our religion, then we didn't question the intentions of our educational institutions either. This method of teaching was used for many years but was abandoned when the school became an all-girls

Catholic high school years later and was renamed St. Mathias.

My sister Sue was placed in Group I, which didn't make me feel that great since she was younger and considered smarter than me. I rarely saw her study, but she still made good grades in Group I. Our teachers designed our classes around our level of intelligence. In support of this revolutionary concept of modern teaching, students were encouraged and able to move up or down a level depending on how they performed from year to year.

The girls in each of the three lower classes, the juniors, sophomores, and freshmen, wore a different color skirt. The boys wore the same color shirt for three years. This was to distinguish one class year from another. I wore a green-and-black print skirt with a white blouse for three years. Sue's skirt was red and black, and Clarissa's was mustard and black. When you became a senior, you had free dress! There were about 250 students in each of the four grade levels, totaling nearly 1,000 students in the entire student body.

The teams on which I competed were very successful throughout the four years I attended Pius X. We ended up having six or seven really good athletes on our teams whom I had competed against previously in grade school. They were the best on their teams from the surrounding feeder Catholic elementary schools. They all decided to continue their athletic competition, and like me, they played on all three sports offered at Pius X: volleyball in the fall, basketball in the winter, and softball in the spring.

I excelled in basketball more than any other sport in which I competed. In my freshman year, our girls' team competed in Long Beach at St. Anthony's annual basketball tournament, with sixteen of the biggest and best Catholic schools in Southern California. Public schools did not offer any girls' interscholastic competitive athletic teams at that time. Our team won the prestigious tournament against a very good St. Anthony's team. I was voted to the first team all stars, on which very few freshman players were ever voted.

We wore our PE clothes, which consisted of red shorts and white blouses and with what was called a pinnie that we placed over our heads and tied on each side of our waist. The pinnie had a number on the front and back. The nuns from our school who showed up to cheer us on at that championship game were appalled and embarrassed that we were playing in front of a packed gym of spectators wearing our worn-out PE clothes and the team we were competing against had nice purple-and-white uniforms. The next year the school purchased beautiful new uniforms we used for many years for volleyball and basketball.

The boy's teams, on the other hand, had a different set of uniforms for each sport. They also practiced and played their basketball games in the gym. We practiced and played our basketball and volleyball games on the blacktop outside, rain or shine, through my sophomore year. Once we started winning more than the boys' teams, we got to play our volleyball and basketball games indoors. The school also started to rent buses for the girls' away games, something they had already been doing for the boys for years prior. This was in the mid- to late 1960s, when the women's movement was just beginning to establish itself and women were starting to gain strides in social and economic equality. I credit the nuns at Pius X at the time for speaking up and getting the girls' teams our equal due in uniforms, transportation, and recognition.

When I was a freshman at Pius X, my mom used to drop my friends and me off at school on Friday nights to watch the boys' basketball team play. There was one particular player that year who caught my eye. He played head and shoulders above anyone else on the court. He was a senior born in Lynwood who went on to play his collegiate basketball at Loyola Marymount and then played in the NBA from 1968 to 1974. He finished his basketball career as an NBA coach from 1977 to 2014. He was a three-time NBA All-Star Game head coach, in 1991, 2001, and 2003 (Wikipedia). His name was Rick Adelman. I never got to meet him, but I did watch him play after high school, and I was certainly impressed by his superior playing and coaching ability whenever I saw him on TV. He inspired me to play at the same high level of excellence as he did.

It was during my junior year in high school in 1966 that we were finally allowed a continuous dribble in girls' basketball. We were no longer limited to just three dribbles. As a rover, having unlimited dribbling really opened the court for me and allowed more opportunities for full-court driving and scoring. I averaged about 25 points a game throughout high school.

It was in 1968 in my senior year when our girls' basketball team won what was equivalent to today's CIF (California Interscholastic Federation). The public schools in 1968 still did not have organized competitive athletic teams to the degree that the Catholic schools did. On the team with me were my two younger sisters, Sue and Clarissa. Sue was a junior and Clarissa was a freshman. Sue was a starting guard on one end of the court, playing defense with those long arms of hers, and Clarissa was on the other end, playing offense with her highly accurate left-handed offensive shooting. They both contributed immensely to the success of my senior season and that last high school game I ever played.

In the fall of 2018 I attended our fiftieth-year Pius X High School reunion in Seal Beach, California. I had a lot of fun seeing my classmates and elementary school friends who attended Pius X after going to St. Emydius. Debbie Miller and Judy Lake were instrumental in organizing the event, and they did a great job. They also were my classmates throughout the eight years at St. Emydius.

One of my high school teammates was Maggie Le Duc, who was a senior when I was a freshman. She attended California State University, Long Beach, after graduating from Pius X. In my senior year at Pius X, she invited me to be a ball girl for the U.S. Women's Olympic Volleyball Team, whose tryouts were taking place at Long Beach State. Players were vying for a position on the 1968 U.S. Women's Olympic team. The Olympic Games that year were held in Mexico City. It was a once-in-a-lifetime opportunity to see up-close and personal some of the greatest women volleyball players in the world. Unfortunately, the United States did not medal that year, and placed eighth in the world, but I thank Maggie for getting me that ball girl gig.

Maggie was my high school sports mentor, friend, and avid advocate of my basketball and volleyball skills. She was an experienced and knowledgeable player who often taught us the basics and was as encouraging and enthusiastic as our coach. She was about 5'8", a little heavy in the hips and midsection, with a full head of brown hair fixed in a pageboy-style cut that turned under just below her ears. She was pigeon-toed and shot with her left foot forward, which should have been counterproductive for a right-handed shooter. It was most pronounced when she shot free throws. Despite her awkward stance, she was the best player and free-throw shooter on the team. She possessed a great sense of humor and was forever optimistic about everything.

Maggie was playing on an outside women's basketball Amateur Athletic Union (AAU) team sponsored by a chemical company named Animil. The team owner, Wayne Salmon, like many other company owners at the time, coached as well as sponsored the team. At nineteen, in the summer of 1969, Maggie invited me to one of their summer workouts, and the coach liked my playing ability well enough to put me on the team. The team traveled throughout California and the western United States competing against other AAU teams. I was not a starter, but I was one of the first players off the bench in many of our games. The team comprised women ranging in age from the then sixteen-year-old future Olympian, collegiate national champion, and women's basketball Hall of Famer Ann Meyers Drysdale to a thirty-five-year-old player named Lauri Lindahl, who was a physical education teacher from Long Beach Poly High School. Ann's sister, Patty Meyers, also played on the AAU team. Patty was a member of the 1970 Women's National Championship Basketball team when she played at Cal State Fullerton.

What I like most about Ann Meyers Drysdale is that she did then and remains now a very humble, modest, and unpretentious person. She did a great job of broadcasting the women's basketball competition at the 2016 summer Olympics in Rio de Janeiro recently. She is without a doubt one of the greatest female basketball players and athletes of all time. It would be difficult to list her innumerable athletic accomplishments, honors, Hall of Fame induction, broadcasting career, and her marriage to famed Dodgers pitcher Don Drysdale, but here are just a few of her firsts that I would like to acknowledge:

- made NBA history when she signed a $50,000 no-cut contract with the Indiana Pacers
- first four-time All-American at UCLA
- first quadruple-double in NCAA history, Division I
- first husband and wife to be inducted into their respective halls of fame

I have been honored to have known Ann as a teammate, at times opponent, and more recently as an invited guest speaker at East Los Angeles College during our March Women's History Month events. You can Google Ann to see all that she has accomplished both personally and professionally. I am sure you will be as impressed and in awe of her as I have been. My claim to fame with Ann is that I am one of the few players in this world who ever blocked one of Ann's famous jump shots!

It was about 1980 when I, one of my former teammates at ELAC, Sally Sue, and two other players entered the first annual Southern California Foot Locker 3-on-3 basketball contest. Our team ended up in the finals playing against, of all people, the then-single Ann Meyers and her 3-on-3 team. We competed in that finals game at the Forum in Inglewood, before a Lakers-versus-Phoenix Suns game. It was a fun championship game, but her team beat us hands-down. We all got to stay to watch the game from some really great courtside seats.

Playing on the same court at the Forum that my idol, Jerry West, played on was quite thrilling. I drove to the Forum box office while in high school and bought, with my hard-earned laundromat money, two of the few remaining playoff tickets to the seventh game of the 1969 championship series against Boston. The seventh game was the only game that still had tickets left for sale, so I was thrilled when the series went to a seventh game. I went with my mom, and we sat directly behind Helen Dell and her organ! It was a great game from beginning to end, despite Helen's distracting organ playing in front of us. The Boston Celtics unfortunately won that seventh and final game 108–106.

One of the AAU teams we played against in 1969 was the Wayland Baptist College Flying Queens. They flew from one playing venue to another in their own private airplane. They had been offering full athletic scholarships to their female athletes since the early 1950s, preceding the education amendment Title IX by more than twenty years. They hold the record for the most consecutive wins in women's and men's collegiate history with 131 games between 1953 and 1958. They won ten AAU national championships. Their women's college basketball program and coach Harley Redin were enshrined in the Naismith Memorial

Basketball Hall of Fame Class of 2016.

Another AAU team we competed against was the Nashville Business College, which won eight national AAU championships in a row and sported notably the best woman basketball player of all time, Nera White. She was selected to the All-American Team fifteen years in a row (Tennnessean.com). Unfortunately, she retired from basketball in 1969, the year I joined the Anamil team, so I never got to see her play.

We also played against the All-American Red Heads in an exhibition game in 1970. They were the female equivalent of the Harlem Globetrotters. They barnstormed throughout the United States from 1936 to 1986. Most of their early games were played against men, playing the men's rules, with a 70 percent win rate (Americacomesalive.com). One of their players, named Karen, left the team and joined our Anamil team for a couple of years. She was a terrific left-handed shooter.

These corporate-sponsored teams offered women their only national playing opportunity in the 1950s and into the 1960s, before the first National Women's Collegiate Invitational Tournament was founded in 1969 by the owner of the Flying Queens. Women's AAU national basketball championships were played in Gallup, New Mexico, until the early 1970s, when women were offered athletic scholarships and preferred to play for colleges. The Animil team I played on competed in one of the last AAU national tournaments in 1969. We finished fifth overall in the nation that year.

One memorable game we played that year was a team from Colorado that boasted a 6'10" player named Gwen Bachman. It just so happened that we had a player, Mary Mitchell, who was 6'8". We ended up playing that Colorado team in the second round of that national AAU tournament. It was amazing and unprecedented at the time to see two exceptionally tall players play against each other. We won the game, but my story about these two unique women started in the restroom before the game. Mary and I went into the restroom, and as we entered, our attention was immediately drawn to a woman's head sticking up over the top of one of the stalls. I knew it had to be Gwen Bachman. She looked at Mary before she sat down, and Mary looked at her, and then Mary and I looked at each other.

The most incredible and extraordinary part of the encounter was when Mary and I looked over at something that caught our eyes on one of the sinks. There we saw what had to be Gwen's shoes, which were so big that they lay completely across the entire sink from edge to edge! They had to be at least a size 14, or 15, or more. Gwen was also probably forty pounds heavier than Mary. Those shoes were a sight I will never forget. Mary, despite the pregame incident, held her own against Gwen in the game. They did not play that many minutes against each other, as Gwen was a starter and Mary was not. After college Mary went on to become a highly successful nurse. We went on to win that national tournament game against Colorado and finished in fifth place.

The only other shoes larger than those that I ever saw were at Los Angeles Southwest Community College, years later, when I was there attending our athletic conference athletic directors' meeting. We were moving from a classroom through the gym, going to lunch on campus, when I passed by what is called the towel cage, where athletes drop their dirty towels into a large white laundry bag, and where athletic shoes and supplies are stored between workouts. This unusually large pair of shoes caught my eye as I passed by. They were sitting on a shelf toward the back of the cage. The Athletic Director at LA Southwest, Henry, happened to pass by at the same time and saw me gawking at these shoes. He said they belonged to Shaquille O'Neal and were a size 22 shoe! The Lakers at that time were using the LA Southwest College gym for their off-season workouts, and the shoes were left there to be used by Shaquille at the Lakers' next practice. The college was not that far from the Forum, so it was a convenient place to play and practice in the off-season.

Maggie and I did not see much of each other after the AAU team we played on disbanded in 1970, until I saw her in 1983 at an athletic directors' meeting. She was the women's volleyball coach and Athletic Director at Santa Monica City College, and at the time I was the women's basketball coach and Athletic Director at East Los Angeles Community College. A few years later she left athletics at Santa Monica College and started a Women's Center on campus, one of the first established in the nation at a community college. Maggie was always the innovator and a visionary for others. I have not seen her since.

When I graduated from Pius X in June 1968, my plan was to attend Compton College and begin pursuing a degree in nursing. I started in that fall 1968 semester taking one class in chemistry. It was a very difficult subject for me, and I ended up dropping the class midway through the semester. That was the end of my attempt at pursuing a nursing career. I could only take one class at Compton College because I did not live within the college district. In the fall semester of 1969, I began attending a college within my district, East Los Angeles Community College. Little did I know that my decision to attend ELAC would lead to forming lifelong relationships with my ELAC teammates, and a future teaching, coaching, and administrative position at the college over a more than thirty-five-year career.

I participated on the women's basketball, volleyball, softball, and badminton teams while I attended ELAC. It was the best two and a half years of my life! ELAC was and is currently a predominantly Hispanic community and student body, but our teams were *very* diverse. My first year on the basketball team was the most diverse team in which I had ever played. There was Vicki Opanui, who was Hawaiian and taught us a motivational word we said when we broke from a huddle. The word was *imua,* which in Hawaiian means "first," "front," "ahead," "forward," or "number one." Tina Chow was Chinese; Judy Kakauuchi was Japanese. Then there was Aida Benitez and Margaret Galvan, topped off with Kathy Greenwood, Becky McKenzie, and myself. We also had two Jewish teammates, Barbara Zacky and Marilyn Cohen.

The women I met would literally give me the shirts off their backs. Anytime I needed anything, they were always there to help or support me in any way needed. We continue to do so to this day, seeing each other through breakups, deaths in the family, reunions, and other events. We still get together on occasion to celebrate summers or holidays or other special occasions. I have been fortunate and blessed indeed with having chosen East Los Angeles College to attend for my first two and a half years of college.

The Women's Physical Education Department at East Los Angeles College offered female athletes membership in a sorority called Delta Pi Gamma, also known as the Women's Recreation Association (WRA). We elected officers and held regular meetings in what was called the WRA room, located in the back of the Women's Gym building. Some of our activities included participating in campus Associated Student Union (ASU)–sponsored events with other clubs. We held bake sales in the student quad area during lunch to raise club monies to host other events. We had lots of fun, and were very organized in whatever we did, and always operated by majority consensus. I enjoyed my participation in Delta Pi Gamma and was honored to hold officer positions in the sorority. I will never forget how much I enjoyed the camaraderie and the wonderful campus and community work we did. Fourteen of us got together at ELAC in the spring of 2018 to begin planning the college's seventy-fifth anniversary with a reunion of female athletes who had participated at ELAC from 1953 through 1973. If you are one of those athletes reading this book, you can contact the ASU office at ELAC and give them your contact information and participate in the seventy-fifth anniversary the college will be celebrating in 2020.

It was during my first year at ELAC that I encountered a lifestyle that I didn't know existed. I was unaware that women could fall in love with other women. Up until then, I had only once, as an early teenager, questioned the odd clothes and behavior of a woman I saw standing outside a liquor store in South Gate. She was wearing all men's clothing, had her hair combed back, a cigarette in her mouth, and her short-sleeved shirt had the sleeves rolled up. She was leaning against a wall with one leg bent at the knee with the bottom of that shoe against the wall. Her looks and demeanor stood out to me but I really didn't give it a second thought. It wasn't until while I was playing on the basketball team at ELAC in my freshman year that I had a teammate whom I liked a lot approach me to let me know she liked me. I became a little bewildered and confused as to what she really meant. My first thought went back to that woman standing against the wall at the liquor store. I was less confused about her but more confused now about myself. It didn't make sense because the teammate who approached me, and I at the time, did not look anything like that woman at the liquor store.

It wasn't too long after that encounter that my teammate and I began dating. At first, I was a little hesitant to enter that lifestyle because I was afraid of what people would think. I knew I couldn't tell my parents or anyone else in my family, as I believed they would not understand, just as I was having trouble understanding my own new feelings and actions. I also thought back and remembered that I really liked one of my high school coaches but never went beyond those personal thoughts because I knew nothing about the gay lifestyle then and had no conscious intention to pursue those feelings. All I knew at the time in high school is that I had those unexplained feelings, and now here, three years later, I was experiencing those same feelings again.

The relationship did not last long, as I found out within a few months of being together that she was dating and "bringing out" a few other previously nongay-at-the-time teammates at the same time she was dating me. We were all just out of high school, and I guess she believed it was her responsibility to show us the lifestyle she believed we were destined to live. But after that first relationship, I wondered why I hadn't realized and acted upon my gay tendencies before, because I was always comfortable with women and realized I had never had any special or intimate feelings or desires for boys or men. I just did not know there was such a behavior where liking and loving someone of the same sex existed. Several athletes came out in those first few semesters and athletic seasons at ELAC. Most were happy with their new lifestyle but a few were confused and had difficulty coping with their feelings.

Soon after that first brief encounter with my teammate, I found myself attracted to a 5'3" beautiful, quirky Hispanic student with dark brown eyes named Margo. She was attending ELAC with a friend who tried out for the college softball team. She was very open with her sexuality and had dated several women before me. She was one of the most unique, unusual, rare souls I have ever met. She had been a well-liked cheerleader at El Rancho High School in Pico Rivera and was a lot of fun to be around. She had a great sense of humor but an odd sense of logic.

She had a different mind-set from most people and did not seem to think and behave in the same ways as your average person. That was one of her many notable idiosyncrasies that attracted me to her. Margo absolutely hated peas, but she absolutely loved macaroni and cheese. She could eat mac and cheese all day long. Margo told me that one time a friend of hers made a heaping plateful of hot and delicious macaroni and cheese for her, but when she set the plate down in front of her, Margo could see that her friend had placed one lone pea at the very top of her mac and cheese. Margo looked at the pea and almost threw up. Her prankster friend took off the pea, but Margo still refused to eat the mac and cheese. I believe that Margo still loves and regularly eats macaroni and cheese.

Margo owned and loved this beautiful little yellow canary that she would let out of its cage at home and let fly around the living room. She would raise her index finger and whistle, and the canary would either land on her finger or fly back into its cage. She decided to get the canary outside for a change and took it down the street to the local park for some fresh air. She let the canary out of its cage as she did at home, thinking it would come back when she whistled or put up her index finger. She was unfortunately mistaken. She whistled and whistled for an hour but the canary remained high up in the magnolia trees in the park. Margo was very upset but could not seem to grasp why the canary would act so obediently at home and not the same in the outdoors.

While we were both attending ELAC, Margo got a part-time job near the campus as a gas station attendant, where she collected money from customers before they pumped their gas. There was not a protective glass enclosure in the station office separating the clerk from the customer as there is now. Customers walked into the office, gave her cash for their gas, and then pumped it themselves. I usually sat in the office with her when she worked. One early evening when I was sitting in the office with her, three young teenagers suddenly entered and began to overtake us and destroy the office. One young man ran behind me and the chair I was sitting on and put his belt around my neck and began tightening it and said, "This is a hold-up, give us all your money!" One other young man inexplicably picked up several oil cans from the display case and was violently throwing them all over the office and out the front door, breaking a lot of them open getting oil everywhere. The third young man had a long stick in his hand, threatening

Margo and telling her to give him the cash in her desk drawer.

I suddenly got a rush of adrenaline and stood up and grabbed the belt off my neck and out of the hands of the kid who was choking me from behind. Margo said later she heard me say as I was standing up, "Take that off of me!" The young man throwing the oil cans everywhere suddenly stopped when he saw my super-human strength toward his friend with the belt, and stopped and ran outside the office, followed by his belt-wielding friend. By now Margo was emptying the cash drawer as much as she could get into both of her cupped hands and started to hand the cash over to the third robber, when he suddenly took the stick and struck her across the palms of both hands, sending much of the cash and coins flying around the office. He quickly picked up as much cash as he could, and just as quickly exited the office and joined his friends, who were about a half a block away, fleeing down the street.

Margo sustained a bruise across the palms of her hands, and I had a clearly visible red mark around my neck for a few days, but we were fine and remained amazingly calm during and after the incident. Margo immediately called the station owner to let him know that the gas station had been robbed, and after he asked if she was OK, he wanted to know how much money she thought they had taken, which may have been about $35 or $40. Needless to say, Margo wisely quit working there shortly after the robbery happened.

We were together for about a year or so, but we split up when I started to attend Cal State Fullerton. I really enjoyed being around Margo. There was never a dull moment during our time together. She was a very good softball player and a pool shark. She could run the table sometimes at the local pool hall that we frequented with other friends and teammates. I have fond memories of Margo. We still keep in touch with each other.

My dad had given me a 1961 Ford Falcon station wagon that I drove to school. I believe he got it in return for work he had done for a customer who could not pay in cash. The car did not have a gas gauge that worked, so I never knew when the car was getting near empty, nor at times did I have the money to put gas in it if it was near empty. Twice I ran out of gas near school and was able to walk the rest of the way to school. I would call my dad or brother or get a teammate after practice to drive me back to my car, bringing a borrowed gallon can of gas with me.

That car also overheated at times. Fortunately, it almost always overheated near school, where I could walk the short distance to class or just nurse it slowly the rest of the way and park it in a safe place and let it cool until I got out of school. When I could get it home, my dad soldered the holes in the radiator, and that got me back on the streets for a while. It had a passenger-side wind wing that had a broken latch. If the shotgun passenger did not know this about the small latched window, it commonly fell out onto the street if they opened it before I could warn them. I just pulled over and had them go retrieve it, bring it back to the car, and relatch it, and we would be on our way again.

The battery was going bad, and I couldn't afford to buy a new one. At school, I purposely parked facing downhill on one of the hillsides above the north side of campus. After school I got in the car, turned the key slightly to the right in the "on" position, and put it in Neutral. I then took off the emergency brake and started rolling away from the curb in Neutral, and then put the gear shift into Drive, which started the car, and off I drove. I couldn't do that everywhere I went for long, so I was able to talk my dad into buying and installing a used battery for me. I often asked my friends to leave the glass soda bottles they drank in my car, which I took to a grocery store and received 3 cents a bottle, which I used to buy gas.

My teammates and I often went to the nearby International House of Pancakes after practice or a home game and ordered their all-you-can-eat spaghetti dinner. I didn't always have money to buy the spaghetti dinner special, so a few of them bought the dinner for themselves and then ordered seconds and thirds that I ate. The waitresses were usually students at the college who knew and understood what we were doing and didn't mind us ordering the all-you-can-eat dinner for others. That IHOP is still located across the street from the college; it's just not in the same nearby location it was back in 1971.

In my second year at ELAC I got a job at the Winchell's Donut House, located a block away from the college. I worked on Friday and Saturday nights from 4 p.m. to midnight making and cooking a variety of the cake doughnuts as I waited on customers at the window. Another worker made the raised doughnuts. By now I had given up my job at the laundromat. It closed in about 1973, a few years after I transferred from ELAC to Fullerton. I liked the Winchell's job because the money was helpful in getting me through college. However, it was difficult seeing my friends dropping by for a dozen free doughnuts from me that they enjoyed at the drive-in when I wasn't going with them.

After attending strict, rigid, iron-fisted Catholic schools for twelve years, ELAC was a welcome sanctuary where I no longer had to raise my hand before answering my instructor in class or stand to give an answer. I also had to get used to not having to pray at the beginning and end of each and every phase of a school day.

For spring semester 2019, *Hispanic Outlook* magazine ranked East Los Angeles College the sixth-best two-year college in the nation and the best two-year college in California to grant community college degrees and certificates to Hispanic students. ELAC's diversity of offerings is one of its greatest strengths. It also has a child-care center that provides on-campus child care for student parents. It also provides and offers a lot of learning assistance and academic support for its students, as it did for me forty-seven years earlier.

In the academic year 2015–2016, ELAC enrolled 57,400 students. ELAC offers courses at dozens of local high schools, at community centers, online, and at the South Gate Educational Center. It is one of the largest community colleges in the United States. It has the largest enrollment of the nine colleges in the Los Angeles Community College District. It houses the Vincent Price Art Museum. Actor Edward James Olmos, LA County supervisor Gloria Molina, and former mayor Antonio Villaraigosa are former students. Ben Davidson of Oakland Raiders football fame attended ELAC, and so did Lynn Cain, who played for the then Los Angeles Rams. Lynn coached the ELAC Huskies football team from 2007 through the 2011 season.

I loved every minute I spent at East Los Angeles College as a student and athlete, and I was thrilled when I was given the opportunity to come back and teach and coach at ELAC just a few short years later. By the way, Jaime Escalante was the famous math instructor at nearby Garfield High School, our largest feeder school, whom the movie *Stand and Deliver* was about. His role in the movie was played by none other than ELAC alumnus Edward James Olmos. ELAC now proudly administers the one and only Jaime Escalante Math Program.

My coaches and instructors at the college were gold. It was at the suggestion of my basketball and badminton coach, Mary Farnell, that I changed my major from nursing to physical education. Until she suggested it, I had never thought about actually getting paid for having fun teaching physical activity classes and coaching. I attended ELAC in the fall semester of 1969, and transferred to California State University, Fullerton, in the spring semester of 1972, the same semester that Title IX became law. I had three colleges that I was interested in attending after ELAC. One was Cal State Los Angeles, and the other, besides Fullerton, was Cal State Long Beach. I was first committed to attending Long Beach because it was close to home and I knew a few players I had played with and against for many years who were already attending. My high school friend Maggie Le Duc had attended Long Beach. I was also familiar with the coach at Long Beach, Fran Schaafsma. At the last minute, in mid-December 1971, I chose to play for Billie Moore at Fullerton, even though it was farther from home and meant living with my grandmother.

Besides coaching the women's basketball team at Cal State University, Fullerton, Billie Moore was a state basketball official who officiated some of our basketball games and was familiar with my playing ability. Before Title IX, an interested coach could not talk directly to a player to recruit her but had to go through her coach. At the time my coach was Flora Brussa, an internationally known field hockey player who was instrumental in establishing ELAC as the men's and women's field hockey venue for the 1984 Los Angeles Summer Olympics. During my second season at ELAC in the fall of 1971, she told me that Billie was interested in having me play for her. It was at this time that women were now playing five-on-five full-court basketball. I am glad I chose Fullerton, as I had a wonderful experience playing and furthering my education there and creating and maintaining wonderful lasting friendships.

Flora Brussa was also my softball coach during my sophomore season at ELAC. As the Athletic Director at the college at the time, she asked me on several occasions to shadow her while she carried out her duties, as she believed I would probably become an athletic director someday. Never in my wildest dreams did I believe that I would not only eventually become an athletic director, but I would take her place when she stepped down from the position in the early 1980s after battling breast cancer.

Flora was the California State Athletic Director in 1980, representing over ninety community colleges throughout the state. During the 1970 fall semester at ELAC, my teammates and I found out that coach Brussa was called to Washington, D.C., to write an important document. We did not know what that document was, but we were very proud that she was chosen to write it. We found out when her flight was returning to LAX from D.C. and several of us met her as she deplaned. She was thrilled to see us, and we were honored to greet her on what soon would become a momentous occasion. What we later learned, in the spring of 1972, when Title IX legislation was enacted, was that she was called to Washington in 1971 to help author one of the most important pieces of educational legislation of all time, Title IX, which ensures equality in all aspects of education, including athletics.

I remember during the closing ceremonies of the 1992 Olympics, held in Barcelona, Spain, my favorite sports announcer, Bob Costas, said to the listening audience, twenty years after it was first enacted, "This is the first generation of U.S. women's Olympic athletes to benefit from Title IX." For the first time, our United States Women won more medals than our men, even though there were nearly two hundred more U.S. men competing than women in 1992.

One of my teammates at Fullerton was Linda Sharp, who eventually coached the University of Southern California to two national championships in 1983 and 1984 and coached famed player and sports announcer Cheryl Miller. She also coached the WNBA's Los Angeles Sparks one season and the Phoenix Mercury for half of the 2002 WNBA season. She coached the 1987 U.S. World University Games Team, and compiled a 138–85 record in eight seasons at Southwest Texas State University. Like Billie Moore and Ann Meyers Drysdale, who were inducted in years previous, Linda was inducted into the Women's Basketball Hall of Fame in 2001.

She was honored recently at halftime at the 2017 national championship women's basketball game in Dallas with a national championship ring for winning the 1984 NCAA Division I national championship. At that 2017 championship game, the South Carolina Gamecocks beat the Mississippi State Bulldogs by a score of 67–55 (Wikipedia).

When Linda was in her first few years of coaching at USC, she asked me if I wanted to help her at her home games. At that time, her teams in the late 1980s played in what was called "The Dungeon" at USC: the original old dilapidated gymnasium that was so small there was little room for spectators, let alone out-of-bounds space to inbound the ball for the teams playing. The men were playing at the Los Angeles Sports Arena at the time. At one particular game in 1990, I was running the clock for her when it stopped working. There was now no visible time on the scoreboard for anyone to see, so I had to use a stopwatch for the remainder of the game. It was difficult because a stopwatch runs forward in seconds and minutes, and a scoreboard runs backward from the two twenty-minute halves that were played in women's basketball at that time. My challenge was to let the game announcer know at a time-out or a foul how much time was left so the players and referees could know. I am telling you this because the announcer at that game, who I kept having to give the time to, was former NBA player and one of the top all-time NBA coaches Pat Riley, who was on hiatus from coaching. He was so understanding and patient to bear with me as I tried to keep constant and quick track of how much time had gone forward on my stopwatch, and keep trying to accurately subtract that from what I could calculate was the time left in the quarter, to come up with the correct time remaining.

Shortly after that, I stopped running the clock and started taking team stats instead. It was the first and only time I had ever met Pat Riley. He was then and is now the consummate professional, with illustrious and highly successful NBA playing, coaching, and franchise executive careers.

Linda and I played against each other when she was at Fullerton College and I was playing at ELAC. She had an unorthodox shot but was a great player in her own right on both offense and defense. She was also a terrific left-handed softball pitcher. She and I and just about every woman basketball player or athlete I ever knew in any sport in my playing days had very little, if any, formal coaching. We were the last group of the self-taught, self-made athletes until Title IX was enacted in 1972, in which schools and colleges were mandated to provide equal opportunities for girls and women athletes.

I met and watched several other great self-made athletes play in the early 1970s while I attended Fullerton College in Orange County. The athletes I watched were softball players who made names for themselves throughout the years participating on AAU and professional teams, like the highly successful Orange Lionettes softball team. I watched the famous Shirley Topley pitch and play first base, and Nancy Ito catch while they played for the Lionettes. Nancy later taught a few adjunct physical education classes at ELAC at the same time I was teaching and coaching there. Joan Joyce was another great softball pitcher and batting champion for the Lionettes and the Connecticut Brakettes teams and a highly successful softball and golf coach, currently at Florida Atlantic University. She was also a national basketball referee who officiated one of our Fullerton games in the 1972 national tournament. Joan holds a slew of softball sports records that have yet to be broken. She also played on the Ladies Professional Golf Association (LPGA) for seventeen years, another great self-made athlete.

I played with Nancy Dunkle, a Fullerton alumna and member of the 1976 U.S. Olympic basketball team. I got to know Mickey Davis, who played in the outfield for the Lionettes and is in the Softball Hall of Fame. She eventually became the Athletic Director at Long Beach City College. Long Beach City College and ELAC competed in the same athletic conference. As the Athletic Director at ELAC, she and I attended several of our conference's athletic directors' meetings. Like many other retirees from their sports and coaching, like Billie Moore, she is a very good golfer.

I am fortunate to have witnessed the accomplishments of these great women athletes, coaches, athletic directors, Hall of

Famers, etc. during my playing, coaching, and teaching days. I never attained their high level of success and fame, but it was a privilege and an honor to have at least been on the fringes of that fame with many of them. You probably have never heard of or read about many of these women and their many accomplishments. They were the forerunners and pioneers in their respective sports and professions who never received their well-earned and deserved recognition, support, or compensation for all their hard work and efforts in paving the way for what our female athletes of today enjoy. Google any one of the women mentioned and you will be delightfully surprised to read their bios and athletic and professional accomplishments.

In my first year playing for Fullerton, our team went undefeated in conference and non-conference play. Billie Moore was able to get us invited to the 1972 National Invitational Tournament at Southern Illinois College. We placed third in the nation by easily beating Mississippi State in the consolation game. We lost to Westchester College of Connecticut in the semifinals by two points. Immaculata College, with their nationally known player at the time, Teresa Shank, won the national title over Westchester 50–45. Our overall win-loss record that year was 26–1, with Westchester being our only loss.

I thought we got a bad call by an official late in that game against Westchester. We were tied with about a minute and a half left in the game, and the referee called a three-second lane violation on our team, but never indicated who it was, as she had done on every previous three-second call in the game. They went down to the other end and scored, and ended up winning by two. It was a devastating loss because we—especially me—were looking forward to playing the number-one ranked team, Immaculata, in the championship game. I was looking forward to guarding Teresa Shank in that game.

That 1972 national invitational tournament was the last invitational ever played and sponsored by the National Association of Girls and Women's Sports (NAGWS). In the following year, colleges now had to qualify for the national tournament instead of being invited. In 1973 we went into the California state qualifying tournament undefeated but unfortunately lost to the University of

California, Riverside, by two points in the last few seconds of the state qualifying tournament game. UCR won the state title and went on to represent California in 1973 in Queens, New York, where the tournament was played that year. We had to be satisfied with another 26–1 season, with our only loss being to Riverside.

Based on my performance in the 1972 national tournament in Illinois, along with fifty-nine other women from around the Unites States, including two of my teammates from Fullerton, I was invited to try out for the U.S. World University Games basketball team that was to compete in Moscow, Russia, in 1974. The tryouts were held in Council Bluffs, Iowa, at Parsons College in the summer of 1973. Even though I gave it my best shot and enjoyed every minute of the tryouts, I did not make the team. While at the trials, I remember a sign over the door to the entrance to our practice gym that I will always remember, which read: "Through these doors walk the greatest women basketball players in the United States."

My coach, Billie Moore, was one of the assistant coaches for that 1974 World Games team. She was chosen as the head coach for the United States' first-ever Women's *Olympic* basketball team, which would compete for the first time in the 1976 Olympics in Montreal, Canada. She coached the U.S. team to a silver medal. Billie established herself as a more-than-qualified Olympic coach by winning two national women's basketball championships: one while coaching during her first year at Fullerton in 1971, and another championship while coaching Ann Meyers and Denise Curry at UCLA in 1978. That 1978 tournament was run under the newly organized American Intercollegiate Athletics for Women (AIAW).

One of the players who tried out for that 1974 U.S. World University Games team, at age twenty-two, was Pat Head. She was a standout at Cheatham County High School in Ashland City, Tennessee. She was the all-time leading scorer at the University of Tennessee at Martin. She had just been newly hired at the University of Tennessee when she not only made the 1974 U.S. World Games Team but was eventually the cocaptain of the first U.S. Olympic Team in 1976, and later coached the 1984 U.S. women's Olympic basketball team to a gold medal.

After the 1976 Olympics, she returned to coaching at the University of Tennessee, where, over thirty-eight seasons, she coached her teams to eight NCAA national championships and thirty-two combined Southeastern Conference titles, to become the winningest coach in NCAA Division I history. What is also remarkable is that Coach Summitt had a 100 percent graduation rate for all Lady Vols who completed their eligibility at Tennessee (Wikipedia).

I remember the first time I saw Pat at the trials. She was being escorted into the gym by two individuals through a side door not used by the other athletes. I could tell then she was someone special, as she took the court and started warming up. I did not know anything about her athletic prowess before the trials, but I got to know her during the trials as the proven winner, champion, master motivator, and role model she was then and eventually became to her athletes. No wonder she was so well loved and respected throughout the years by all. I certainly admired what a forthright and ethical person she was at the trials and remained so through the years. I remember hearing not long ago that Pat credited Billie Moore with encouraging her to getting into coaching.

I was devastated to hear in 2011 that Pat was diagnosed with early onset Alzheimer's. What a tragic shame to have her life cut short by such a cruel and unforgiving disease. It was in November 2011 that she announced the formation of her foundation, the Pat Summitt Foundation Fund, with the proceeds going toward cutting-edge research for Alzheimer's. She was larger than life when I first met her, and she was larger than life as I followed her throughout her life and illustrious coaching career. She is in the elite company of legends with her numerous titles and awards, too many to list. I feel blessed that I got to be in her presence for that brief moment in time at the 1974 U.S. World University Games trials.

Teaching and Coaching

I graduated from Cal State Fullerton in June 1974. My first teaching job was at Los Altos Intermediate School in Camarillo, California, in Ventura County, where my mother's family resided. I was required to declare and complete a major and a minor while in college. I graduated with a major in physical education and a minor in English. My teaching assignment at Los Altos was teaching three English classes and three physical education classes. I taught seventh and eighth graders. I replaced a woman who went on maternity leave for the year.

    I was offered and accepted the position just a few weeks before the semester started and had to prepare to move to the Camarillo area on short notice in the late summer of 1974. Fortunately for me, my aunt and uncle who lived in Camarillo, not far from the school, were taking off to Europe for a month and offered me to stay in their beautiful home. I accepted their offer and used that month to get my classes started and look for a place to rent. I ended up renting a one-bedroom fully furnished apartment in Ventura near the cities of Santa Paula and Somis for $300 a month. It was about a twenty-five-minute drive to school on beautiful old one-lane back-country roads through the rustic city of Somis and along railroad tracks and through old established ranches and farms. A lot of the route was familiar from my childhood travels with family through these same areas. I loved that daily drive to school and back. Living away from the school afforded me some privacy, away from my students, whom I ran into often while shopping or eating when I was living in Camarillo at my aunt and uncle's house.

My students were twelve, thirteen, and fourteen years old with a *wide* range of emotional and physical levels of maturity. It took me nearly the entire school year to get used to their varied levels of intelligence, ability to listen and retain material, and their unpredictable behavior patterns. As a first-year teacher, it took all my effort and energy each day just to get my students to sit down and listen or get them out to the physical education teaching area on time and dressed properly.

I was not prepared, during my college senior-year student-teaching experience at Santa Ana Valley High School, for the erratic and unpredictable behaviors of my current young intermediate school teenagers. The principal at Los Altos visited my class one time. He watched me struggle to establish and maintain control of my seventh-grade English class. He did not seem pleased with what he saw when he left without saying a word. When the woman returned from her pregnancy leave, she took back her previous position, for which I was hired. I did not make much of an impression in my first year of teaching, but it was a great learning experience.

Within that first year of teaching at the Los Altos campus, the woman with whom I taught physical education knew several women physical educators and coaches at many of the local high schools in Thousand Oaks, Ventura, Newbury Park, Camarillo, Oxnard, and Simi Valley. I got to know them all through her. We all played on various city recreational volleyball, basketball, and slow-pitch softball teams during that 1974–1975 school year. We also gathered at many of their homes for birthdays and special occasions. It was through one of these women, who was the Girls Physical Education Department chair and Athletic Director at Simi Valley High School, that I was asked to interview for a physical education and coaching position there for their fall 1975 semester. I was hired as a full time physical education teacher and the volleyball coach. Another teacher was already committed to coaching the girls' basketball team one more season when I was hired, but would relinquish the job to me the following 1976 season. I ended up coaching against many of those high school coaches and physical educators I had met while teaching at Los Altos Intermediate School.

I was hired by California Lutheran College in Thousand Oaks to coach the women's basketball team during their 1975–1976 season since I was not coaching basketball at Simi Valley High School that year. It was a terrific experience. The women were very receptive to my coaching style and worked hard to perform their best. The team did well, winning most of our games that year. My coaching techniques were basically what I had learned from Billie Moore while playing for her. I had not yet attended any basketball coaching clinics.

I remembered the Cal Lutheran campus from the summer of 1973 when I had been invited by Billie Moore, along with many other women, to help her conduct her girls' basketball summer camp there. It was a wonderful learning experience that did help me to coach that first season with the Cal Lutheran women's basketball team.

On the Cal Lutheran campus at the same time as the girls' basketball camp that summer was the NFL Dallas Cowboys summer workout football camp. Just as the girls' camp was walking to the cafeteria for lunch, I remember watching Ed "Too Tall" Jones in full uniform walking from one part of his workout area to another. He was an imposing figure at 6'8". I can imagine how he intimidated his opponents with his size and stature on the football field. The Cowboys ate lunch after the girls were done. I was flabbergasted when I watched the girls' leftover food dishes being removed from the food line and being replaced by *huge* plates of food that were much more numerous and varied. I could not believe what remarkably large appetites the players all had and how much each player was capable of consuming. A few of the players sat down with four plates of various foods on the table in front of them; one plate of meat, a plate of nothing but salad items, one plate of various vegetables, fruits, and breads, and one whole plate for some of them that was nothing but desserts!

My first year of coaching the Simi Valley High School girls' basketball team in 1976 was a wonderful experience. I was pleasantly surprised how many girls tried out for the varsity and JV teams and the amount of experience and athletic ability they possessed. There were over fifty girls who tried out for the two twelve-person squads. The team did well during my first season, winning most of our games. The students were wonderful. They were attentive and worked hard to do well in school and athletics. At the time, many of the students were from long-established local families who owned businesses in the area. Since it was a small isolated valley, most everyone knew each other, as they had all grown up together from a young age, attending the same schools and churches.

Simi is a Chumash Indian word that means the "little white wind clouds" that are so often seen when the wind blows in the valley. Indians living on the coast twenty miles away would never venture into Simi Valley when they saw those white wind clouds in the sky over Simi. When I was teaching at Simi Valley High School, there were times when there were sustained winds that blew constantly for days on end. We could not teach any outside classes because of the high winds. This meant keeping all classes offered at any given hour of the school day in the gym. Some played half-court basketball or volleyball while most of the rest of the students sat on the bleachers and talked or tried to stay active by participating in mass exercises held on the other half of the gym floor. After a few days of being indoors without much to do, a few of the students would eventually go stir-crazy or get cabin fever and venture outside to play softball or soccer in the wind. I saw one student kick a wind-driven soccer ball that flew seventy-five yards in the air and nearly the same distance downfield. Thankfully those white wind clouds did not appear that often.

Simi Valley is situated in the southeast corner of Ventura County and is located thirty miles from downtown Los Angeles. It is surrounded by the Santa Susana Mountains and considered a bedroom community. The Ronald Reagan Library is located in Simi Valley and is where former President Ronald Reagan and his wife, Nancy, are buried. It is considered the fifth-happiest and the seventh-safest city in the United States.

There was one extremely focused and intense girls' basketball player who was my starting guard during the 1977 season, when she was a junior. At times while competing she had these unusually fixed and intently engaging eyes and behavior that suggested to me she was very involved in and took her role as playmaker and team leader *very* seriously. When her eyes were wide open and fixed, all I could see were her huge pupils and the whites of her eyes. She was a very smart, talented player who was dependable and great on both offense and defense. She constantly encouraged and motivated her teammates during games and practices and was a good student as well. I didn't really think much of her behavior other than she was just an unusually passionate and exceptionally zealous and fervent basketball player.

I kept in touch with her and a few former Simi Valley athletes after I was hired at East Los Angeles College in the 1978 spring semester. I started to coach the girls' basketball team at Simi Valley High in that 1977–1978 season but relinquished the team to the boys' JV coach early in the season when I began teaching at ELAC. That zealous point guard and a good friend and teammate of hers were invited and attended my fiftieth birthday celebration at my house in April 2000.

That extraordinarily ardent and exceptionally passionate player was Stephanie Lazarus, the former Los Angeles Police Department officer accused and convicted in 2009 of murdering her ex-boyfriend's wife, Sherri Rasmussen, in 1986. She is currently serving a twenty-seven-year-to-life sentence in state prison. I was saddened, disappointed, and surprised when I first heard about her cold-case arrest and then reluctantly watched the unfortunate and tragic series of events and outcomes unfold on television, knowing this was someone I once knew and that a number of lives were tragically affected forever.

My first day of teaching at East Los Angeles College was on Monday, January 3, 1978. I had a fist full of keys that belonged to my former coach and mentor, Mary Farnell, the woman I replaced. She passed away suddenly in the middle of the fall 1977 semester. My first class was in the gym, and as I came around the corner to let my large, patiently waiting volleyball class into the gym, I suddenly realized I had no idea which of the more than twenty keys in my hands was the one that would open the gym door. At the risk of looking stupid in front of my first class, I was hoping and praying I would not have to go through too many keys to get to the one that would open the door. They were looking over my shoulder as I randomly picked a key, and to my pleasant surprise, it opened the door! I knew then that, like that key, I and East Los Angeles College, from day one, were meant to be a perfect fit. And after forty-one wonderful and successful years of teaching there, I was right.

The women who were my coaches, mentors, and instructors while I attended ELAC in the late 1960s and early 1970s were a hard act to follow. They were, each in their own right, visionaries and trendsetters in their disciplines who worked diligently and tirelessly to bring equality to the Women's Physical Education and Athletic Departments at ELAC during their teaching and coaching days. Several of them were tremendously talented national and international athletes in their respective sports.

One woman in particular that I mentioned earlier was Flora Brussa, the great international field hockey player. Flora was instrumental in bringing our campus and those other colleges in our athletic conference into Title IX compliance. She made my job easier when I took over the Athletic Director's position from her in 1983. Like her, I administered both the women's and men's athletic teams for many years. I was thankful that Flora took me under her wing when I was an athlete at ELAC and showed me the ropes of the position.

Flora was Greek and an identical twin. Both had similar personalities. You knew when Flora entered a room. She had an unforgettable personality. She was high energy, commanded your attention, and had a strong loud voice and laugh that could be heard from a distance. She was highly professional, very diplomatic, and an accomplished, well-respected athletic administrator. Her cancer went into remission for several years but came back a few years after she retired in 1989, and unfortunately she passed away in 1992 from the breast cancer. She was an unforgettable part of my past that made an indelible lasting impression on me personally and professionally and affected and guided my athletic career as a coach and athletic administrator. What a privilege and an honor it was to have known one of the contributing authors of Title IX and one of the most unabashed accomplished feminists of her time.

Another one of my highly professional instructors was Gloria Quintana, whose glove is bronzed in the Softball Hall of Fame as one of the greatest shortstops to play the game. Before she retired, she took up and became an accomplished equestrian rider and won a national senior division tennis championship in 1989. She coached our women's tennis team to a conference title one year as a last-minute substitute coach. Like me, she came from a large family, with ten brothers and sisters. She was tall, thin, and always stayed in great physical shape.

As a student, I took a tennis class from her during my third semester at ELAC. In that class, I learned that, when teaching others, I would get more accomplished with my students by using as few basic words as possible. I believe I learned to play tennis so well and so quickly in her class because of her hands-on, simple, basic-talk teaching style. She moved to Las Cruces, New Mexico, after retiring in 1989. She continued to play tennis at the national senior circuit level until she contracted Legionnaire's disease from an air conditioner at a hotel she was staying in while on tour playing tennis. She did recover but was not the same tennis player she once was. The last I heard was that she continued to live in Las Cruces. Unfortunately, she passed away in the late 1990s.

Another gifted athlete in her time was Betty Reeves, who was ELAC's first women's Athletic Director in the early 1960s and held that position when I was an athlete at ELAC in the late 1960s. She was one of the first women ever hired to teach in the Women's Physical Education Department at East Los Angeles College. In her early twenties, she competed in the national synchronized swimming championship in the singles division in the early 1950s. She coached our men's and women's swimming and volleyball teams, including coed volleyball. She also had a three handicap in golf and taught golf classes at ELAC. She secured our college women's volleyball team, which I played on in the fall of 1970, a place in the U.S. National Volleyball Tournament that was held at Long Beach State College that year. She was a state and national volleyball official and taught a volleyball officiating class at ELAC that I took. I was able to later make enough money to facilitate my educational costs by officiating local intermediate and high school volleyball matches.

Mary Farnell was the most memorable coach and teacher, whose strict old-school ways and mores I will never forget. We had to dress in all-white clothes when playing on the badminton or tennis teams. We had to attend her physical education major lecture classes dressed professionally and not in activity attire. I didn't then, but I do now, appreciate that she held us accountable and responsible for our actions at all times and made us pay the consequences when we broke one of her rules. She was a small woman raised in the Mormon religion. When she developed uterine cancer in 1975, she did not seek traditional medical treatment and died a difficult death in 1977. It is her keys that I use to this day to open my office, gym, equipment rooms, etc. I was humbled to replace such a revered and iconic figure.

It was a real honor and a privilege in late 1977 to have been chosen by a hiring panel of my former mentors to join their elite group of highly professional and tremendously talented forerunners and pacesetters of women's sports and athletics. I always felt tremendously inspired and supported by them as I worked through my rookie year and beyond in the department. Like me, as an athlete, these women were self-made administrators and coaches, depending on their own early instincts to successfully guide their teams and staff without much guidance from the past or others.

The first team I coached at ELAC was the 1978 Women's Basketball team. It was a very talented group of players, several of whom had played on the team that had won the conference title the year before. The team did well that first year, placing high in the conference but losing our first conference play-off game. I coached the Women's Volleyball team the next fall semester in 1978. I also taught various physical education activity classes in addition to coaching.

While still at Simi Valley High School, I had met a woman at a summer physical education clinic at the Cal Poly, San Luis Obispo, campus in 1976. She and I were immediately attracted to each other and soon moved into an apartment together in Thousand Oaks. It turned out that she was the coach from a rival team in the same athletic conference in which Simi Valley High School competed. We coached against each other in basketball and volleyball starting in that 1976 fall season after we had met that summer. It wasn't easy coming home after one of our teams had just beaten the other's.

I initially drove in 1978 the hour's drive from Thousand Oaks to my new teaching job at ELAC. I was teaching and coaching full time at ELAC and working on my master's degree two nights a week at California State College, Los Angeles, located just a few minutes from ELAC. I started to stay a few nights a week at my mother's house in South Gate, as the lengthy drive and busy hectic schedule became a bit too much for me; getting home to Thousand Oaks late at night just to get up very early the next morning to make that drive to get to my first class at ELAC. This began to put a strain on our relationship.

We both saw the handwriting on the wall. We broke up, or at least I left her, and moved back in with my mother and two brothers in the fall of 1979. She and I kept in touch for a while, but I have not heard from her in many years. I wished things could have worked out differently for both of us. She was a pleasant person to be around and had a great sense of humor. She was also a very good coach, especially in softball. She was a very successful softball pitcher when she played the game in her youth and on local adult teams. She was a very ardent, savvy, and astute football aficionado who wanted to coach the JV football team where she taught. I wish she would have had an opportunity to coach the team because I believe she would have been a terrific, successful football coach.

January 3, 1978, when I opened the gym door and led my first ever college physical education activity class students to a seat on the bleachers for their orientation, was the beginning of a more than forty-year love affair with nearly every single student or athlete who has ever entered any of my health or activity classes or played on any of my athletic teams. ELAC's students are the world's best! Many of them are from low-income families and communities and are most often the first in their family to pursue a college education. They are always truly grateful for any support or assistance they are given. They are focused and dedicated to bettering themselves and committed to giving back to their communities.

I love that the majority of the 23,000-plus students and athletes I have experienced in my classes over the past forty years have been willing to listen to suggestions to make positive change and have benefitted from their choices to change those actions and behaviors in their lives that were not working. The suggestions to which I am referring were those presented in the health classes I taught for thirty-three years. I taught over 250 health classes with an average class size of about forty-five students.

I believe if there is any activity or educational course that can encourage and develop life lessons and the whole individual, it is those courses taught in physical education and health. It is in these classes in which the students, if they choose, learn teamwork, leadership, and social skills, and the capacity to value collaboration and cooperation and successfully incorporate both into their lives. I am fortunate indeed to have had the opportunity to be an integral part of building and encouraging the development of positive societal values in my students. I would like to think that I was instrumental in fostering their social, physical, emotional, and spiritual growth.

Over the years I have taught courses in General Health and in Women's Health. A health and a physical education activity class are graduation requirements. If a student enrolled in a health and an activity class and passed those courses, it would satisfy their requirement for graduation. I have taught a wide variety of activities courses, ranging from rhythmic gymnastics to badminton. Other courses I have taught are tennis, volleyball, basketball, speed walking, soccer, step aerobics, spinning, weight training, body conditioning, swimming, and handball. I currently teach two Adaptive Kinesiology classes at ELAC designed for students with special needs. I enjoyed teaching this wide range of activity classes, but the one I enjoyed teaching the most was a course called Backpacking Skills.

My students in this class were mostly inner-city individuals who had never experienced hiking in the nearby mountains and had little contact with nature. I emphasized to them that "Nature is life's classroom!" In this Backpacking Skills class, I encouraged my students to develop a love and respect for nature, just as they would develop a love and respect for life. The skills and concepts involved in hiking and backpacking are similar in nature, if you will, to the skills and concepts developed in life. Lifelong skills that students can utilize in their lives daily and forever are taught in this class.

The coursework included discussions on pertinent equipment and hiking essentials, first-aid, route finding (compass work), knot tying, edible plants, and some basic survival skills. The class was offered once a week on Friday mornings from 9 a.m. to 12 noon. Once a month, instead of meeting in the classroom, students drove about twenty miles north of campus, up to the trails in the Angeles National Forest in the San Gabriel Mountains. Each of the first three hikes was five or six miles round-trip, and each included a test on a topic previously discussed in class. The final in the class was for the students to put together a comprehensive backpacking unit and spend a night together in the wilderness, utilizing and incorporating all that they had learned in class.

One of the first classroom discussions we had just before our first hike was on assembling and bringing the ten essentials to each hike. We also brought a sack lunch to each day hike to be eaten at our destination. I taught them that it does not matter if they are hiking or backpacking for three hours, three days, three weeks, or three months, they *must* always have these ten essentials with them. Just as in life, we need to have developed and have available on any of our life's journeys essential, effective, learned ways of surviving and navigating in the world.

These essentials include bringing a topo map of the hiking area, a compass, water, extra food and clothing, sunglasses, matches, a first-aid kit, and a fire starter. What they didn't know, what I did not tell them during class time, is that when we finished eating our lunch at the hike destination, I would be asking them each to show me their ten essentials. Those who did not bring them all were the ones with the most surprised and astonished looks on their faces. They all got that the essentials are important to have assembled and ready to use, if needed, just as it is important in life to develop essential basic life skills and have them at the ready. It means the student is properly prepared for each hike if something unforeseen were to happen, just as they would need to be properly prepared in life for any unforeseen situations. After that hike, they didn't know whether or not I would be checking their essentials on subsequent hikes, so they were usually inclined to make sure they had all ten all the time after that.

Each hike is steeper to climb than the last, just as each stage of life is more arduous and challenging than the last. I let them know this at the start of the course and emphasized that they should work on building their endurance by walking or running a couple days a week outside of class. I discussed basic first-aid in class specific to hiking, like treating bee stings and snake, mosquito, and tick bites. I did not test them on their first-aid learned in class, but I had them each bring a basic first-aid kit with them on each hike.

Sometimes students would ask why everyone has to bring all ten essentials when they could be shared with their friends or classmates. My answer is, hiking groups often get separated or equipment gets lost or ruined, and those essentials are key to surviving emergency situations. Each person needs to have their own, especially if someone you know is the one who lost their equipment somehow and needs your essentials to get by. Just as in life, each person needs to assemble and create their own necessary and crucial basic skills to rely upon instead of relying on others to fulfill their essential needs.

The first hike would be classified as easy. We hiked up the beautiful Arroyo Seco, which means "dry creek," trail that starts just north of the Rose Bowl and the Jet Propulsion Laboratory in Pasadena. We hiked about two and a half miles to Gould Mesa Campground. Along the way we stopped and talked about the edible plants that the Hahamongna Indians used for supplementing their diets and medicinal needs, just as a person would stop along life's path and discuss and utilize available means to similar living. It was at Gould Mesa Campground, located about two and a half miles up the trail, that we ate lunch and I checked for their ten essentials.

The next class field trip was a six-mile round-trip, relatively easy to moderate hike up a beautiful trail called Sunset Ridge, where I tested the students at our destination on common knots used for backpacking and first-aid. Those knots include the bowline, half-hitch, and square knots, which can be lifesaving and instrumental in the care of life's common unforeseen circumstances and situations. We practiced in class the knots being tested before our hike. Our destination at the top of the ridge had a few benches that made for easy testing and a beautiful view of the west end of the San Gabriel Mountains while testing and eating lunch before heading back down the trail.

Before our third hike, to Echo Mountain above Pasadena, we practice basic route-finding essentials in class with topo maps and compasses provided by the college. The maps were of the San Gabriel Mountains and valley. Echo Mountain is three miles up the Sam Merrell trail and boasts a breathtaking view, when it is clear, of downtown Los Angeles and Catalina Island, twenty-three miles off the coast of San Pedro; about fifty miles from Echo Mountain. Students ate lunch and then were tested individually with a compass in hand to find the correct location on the map of a local destination I gave them. That location I asked them to find on the map could be physically seen from Echo Mountain, and once they took the compass off the map and stood up, they *should be* correctly facing the destination I gave them, if they performed all the steps correctly. It is imperative and important early on to create our own moral and social compass to successfully guide us in the proper and appropriate direction to achieve our life's destinations and goals.

Listening carefully and following instructions is the key to successfully navigating and passing this class and doing well in life. The majority of students who have taken my backpacking skills class have not had any hiking or backpacking experience, so paying close attention for first-time hikers is vital. What I find is that many students depend on their friends in the class or classmates to pay attention for them and depend on their knowledge to get them through the hikes and classwork. They are followers in life, and probably do the same in other areas of their lives.

When we went on our Echo Mountain hike, we took a group picture at the trailhead with Echo Mountain visible in the background. I loved to watch the varied reactions of the students when, after taking our class picture, I asked them to turn around and point out where Echo Mountain was located above us. Some students who did not believe in themselves almost immediately got wide-eyed and worried, and questioned whether they would make it to the top because it looked overwhelming to them and not possible to achieve, even before they tried. Others got excited and anxious to lead the rest of the class up the trail on what they considered a new and challenging adventure. I remember one student leader said, when I pointed out Echo Mountain behind them; "Wow!

That's Echo Mountain up there?" "Come on; let's go; follow me!" Other students who had difficulty taking risks began to ask questions like, "What if I didn't bring enough water?" or "What if I fall or get hurt?" These varied behaviors and reactions indicated to me the wide range of environmental and social experiences the students have had and shows me that the way they show up on the trail and in the classroom is the way they show up in life. Nature *is* life's classroom!

With the advent of the cell phone and GPS devices, compasses and topo maps are rarely seen on the trail or bought in sports stores anymore. They can now be uploaded to cell phones with solar plates that hang on backpacks while hiking that powers their GPS devices and cell phones as they hike. The last time I tested students with the map and compass was in 2015, when I took a large group of Los Angeles Unified School District gifted high schoolers to Echo Mountain.

The fourth and last hike was our overnight in the San Gabriel Mountains above the Santa Anita Race Track in Arcadia. We drove up Santa Anita Avenue until it ends at Chantry Flats and then headed up the Santa Anita Canyon to Camp Hoegee. This was where the students put together their comprehensive backpacking unit with the ten essentials and those items discussed in class necessary to comfortably stay one night. The campground is next to a creek that we used for cooking and cleaning dishes. We did not clean our dishes in the creek; rather, the water was brought up to our campsites to be used to wash or cook. It is a loop trail: we hiked up and out of the canyon on Saturday morning on the Old Winter Creek Trail, back to Chantry Flats.

The overnight bonded the students together as they shared food, utensils, and tents, collected firewood together, took off in small groups for a day hike, or stayed around to play cards or take a nap in their tents. The class does allow the students to learn to appreciate each other and work together as a team to ensure a fun, successful adventure, as any group or organization would do in life. The class also develops leadership skills. Students learn how important it is in this class and in life to "Be prepared!"

A few months ago, I was walking through campus when I heard someone call to me and wave from an outdoor third-floor stairway of our new campus Technology Building. I forget his name, but he told me he got to know one of the female students in one of the last backpacking skills classes I taught. They started dating and eventually married. He showed me pictures of her and their new baby girl. I was thrilled that they had met in my class! All my activity classes that I have taught have always been fun and exciting to teach. The students get so much out of their classes because they are in college and taking these courses because they want to, not because they have to.

I have had several unforeseen incidents over the twenty-two years I taught this class where first-aid and rescue was needed. I taught the class only in the spring semester each school year. The fall semester was usually too hot and rainy to offer the class. About eight hundred students have taken my Backpacking Skills class over the years. It helped that I already had some camping and backpacking experience before teaching this class. These incidents were few and far between compared to the large number of students who attended these hikes and overnights over the years.

Most of the incidents involved minor scrapes and bruises, some mosquito bites, a few sprained ankles, and a few cases of poison oak. One incident did involve a large overweight male student (about three hundred pounds) who wandered away from the group and climbed onto a fifteen-foot-high cement dam, which he was not supposed to have done, and fell about eight feet onto his back. He was complaining of back pain, and his blood pressure was up. Fortunately, a student paramedic in my class had brought his blood pressure device and his first-aid kit. This happened before there were cell phones, so I sent a student back to Chantry Flats, where rescuers were called. They brought up a three-wheeled cloth-lined basket to carefully bring him down to the Chantry Flats ranger station. He was transported from there to Huntington Memorial Hospital in Pasadena, where he was released after a few hours under observation. Fortunately, he was fine after a few days of recovery and was able to finish and pass the class.

Late in the evening of one overnight at Camp Hoegee in 1994, a student who was diabetic started to go into a diabetic shock because he had not taken his insulin earlier that day. He was nearly unconscious and unable to tell us where his insulin was located. We had to wake up his friend and tent mate to ask where his insulin was. Before we woke him up, I looked around with another student and found a small blue zippered bag that we noticed this student hung around his neck on all the hikes, so we figured that was where he kept his insulin. We opened it up, and to our surprise there was a small handgun in there!

His friend came out of his tent and showed us where he kept the insulin. He administered it, and the student was fine after several long, agonizing minutes. The student who assisted me was a cadet on our campus police at the college. He kept the gun in his possession, and I told him to give it back to the student when we all arrived back at Chantry Flats. The thirty-year-old student said that he had had a very rough life and had carried a gun for a number of years for protection. I understood, but had to scold him for not telling me he had it with him. It was after that incident that I had to add to my class rules, no guns or weapons in class or on the class outings!

The worst incident happened in 2011 on my last class overnight to Hoegee. It was Saturday morning, and everything had gone well the day and night before. It was about 10 a.m. when the last of the students started up the Winter Creek Trail to the ridge above that would take them back to the parking lot at Chantry Flats. I was sitting on the top of a picnic bench enjoying the peace and quiet for a few minutes, absorbing the smells, sights, and sounds of birds, the creek below me, and the voices of the students hiking uphill to the ridge behind me. I was just about to put my backpack on and hike out behind everyone when I heard a pounding, thumping noise to my right that sounded like something or someone falling down from the ridge above. I was frantically thinking to myself as I ran over to see what it was, "Please don't let this be one of my students; please don't let this be one of my students!" I ran about thirty feet over and twenty feet up the hill to see a young man in his bicycle-riding gear tumbling head over heels over and over down the hill. He came to a sudden stop about twenty feet from me. He stopped in an upright, sitting position facing downhill. He was screaming in pain when I got to him, and staring straight ahead for several seconds in shock from his fall. He had fallen nearly 125 feet before he stopped.

One of the first things he asked about was, "Can you see my bike anywhere above us?" He was also yelling for his friend who was riding with him. His friend was nowhere in sight. What we didn't know is that his friend rode on down on the trail they were on and stopped at an emergency call box a few hundred feet below the campground to call for help.

The young man and I were about thirty feet above the campground. Before help arrived, he kept wanting to move down the mountain to the campground so his buddy could easily find him. He was in tremendous pain and yelled every time he moved. We were about fifteen feet from the campground floor when his buddy and another man from a nearby canyon home came running up to assist him the rest of the way down to the campground floor. He was covered from head to toe in bruises, cuts, and dirt. I'll never forget seeing the small rock that was lodged in the front of his helmet. Thank goodness he had that helmet on, or I believe things would have been much worse.

I left him in the good hands of his friend and went back to the picnic bench I was sitting on, and put my backpack on and began walking up the trail to the ridge above from where he fell. It took about ten minutes for me to climb up to the part of the trail where he had fallen. By then I could see a sheriff's helicopter flying up the canyon toward the campground. It began to hover over the only open area in the thick tree canopy large enough where they could airlift him up and out to a nearby hospital. I took pictures of him and his helicopter rescue, had them developed, and took them over to Huntington Memorial Hospital to the emergency room, where I figured he was taken, and did find his family there waiting for him. I gave his family my phone number and the pictures, and he called me a week later to thank me for helping him. He ended up with two broken ribs, a cracked pelvis, and a severely bruised shoulder.

I was exiting the Arroyo Seco trail with another class in 1998. We were near the end of our hike when a young man on a bicycle, coming up the Arroyo, was showing off to his friend by doing a wheelie. As he lowered his bike back down to the road, his foot slipped off the pedal right in front of me and slammed it onto the concrete, dislocating his foot. As he lay on his stomach in excruciating pain, with his knees bent and his feet in the air, the bottom of his dislocated foot was at about a 45-degree angle from his ankle. Where he fell was within a half mile of the trailhead, where the trail was wide, smooth, and at a slight incline, so it was easy for a fire engine and a paramedic vehicle to enter the wide trail and render him first aid about twenty minutes after he fell. I and another student sat with him until help arrived. The young man was extremely disappointed with himself, not only because he fell doing something stupid, but because he was supposed to start a new job on Monday delivering Arrowhead water!

One more incident occurred while I was hiking near Lake Tahoe while on a break from a three-day California state Athletic Director's meeting in 1992. I was hiking along a popular well-established trail when I met eyes with and said hi to a man walking toward me in the opposite direction on the same trail. I did not think much about the encounter until I was walking out on that same trail about an hour and a half later. I was finished with my hiking and was exiting the area when I heard a voice calling to me from a steep area about twenty feet below the trail. I leaned over the trail and saw that same man's hand waving back and forth and asking me to help him. I slowly and carefully walked down the steep embankment and grabbed his hand and pulled him back up onto the trail. He was so thankful that I had come along and "saved my life," he kept repeating over and over. At one point he said I was "an angel" sent to save him. I hadn't thought much about the earlier encounter he and I had when our eyes briefly met, but I am just glad I was walking along that trail when he needed me later that day.

There was a recent troubling ill-fated encounter I had while hiking down Eaton Canyon in Pasadena with my two dogs in 2016. For the hour and a half hike I had been taking that afternoon, I had been making eye contact and saying hi to all the hikers I met coming at me in the opposite direction. There was only one person who did not make eye contact with me and appeared rather sad. She was a young woman who kept her head down in a closed body position, with her arms folded, and was walking close to the shrubs on her side of the trail. I thought it was unusual for a hiker not to smile or make eye contact and say hi, but I didn't give her demeanor another thought until I was home watching TV in the early evening that same day and her face appeared on the 5 o'clock news. She went up to the steep falls at the top of the canyon and committed suicide by jumping to her death. I only wish now I had read her look of despair and paid more urgent attention to her closed body position and maybe had engaged her in a conversation that may have possibly led to a different, less tragic outcome.

I do believe I have attracted more than my share of encounters with others, sometimes perfect strangers, for a reason. Thankfully, most of the encounters have had positive, in some cases, life-saving results. I am grateful that I was often in the right place at the right time when these encounters occurred. I hope if I am ever in need of a guardian angel, one will appear and help me through a difficult situation, as I have been blessed to have done. I think a person with a fairly high level of spirituality, which I believe I possess, would make a helpful guardian angel to others. A spiritual person seems to be able to attract and *sense* the existing and potential behaviors or actions of others and render them beneficial help to hopefully save them from themselves or others in a positive way. I base this on what I have attracted and sensed over the years that has created the positive results in the stories and situations I have mentioned. I have attracted a lot of good fortune and good luck over the years, for which I am eternally grateful.

I was fortunate and blessed to have been given the opportunity, with one of my sisters-in-law, to be part of the audience during Ellen DeGeneres's tenth season of twelve days of giveaways in early December 2013. We had attended the first show of her tenth season earlier in the year, when Pink was her opening guest. We were actually part of her overflow audience, just outside the studio. Before her first commercial break, the studio audience went crazy when Ellen announced that they would be coming back for one of her twelve days of giveaways in December. As part of those individuals that did not make it into the main studio that season's opening day, we were happy for the audience going to a giveaway show, but we were all pretty bummed that we weren't. At the first commercial break, Ellen and Pink came walking back to the overflow crowd and stood looking at all of us screaming at them as they stood at the top of the stairs leading into the studio. Just before the end of the show, Ellen announced that the overflow crowd would also be going to a twelve days of giveaways. We all went nuts!

We received a *lot* of gifts the day we attended our giveaway day. We were all told to drive our cars to the back of the studio lot to pick up all our gifts, which included two really cool three-wheeled bikes, a bunch of wonderful small kitchen appliances, like a toaster, coffeemaker, drinking glasses, etc. The gift I loved the most was two $500 gift certificates from J. C. Penney. I used one to buy various things for around the house and for gifts for the holidays, and was again fortunate and blessed to be able to give the other one to the East Los Angeles Women's Center, who bought a couch for the room where they do much of their counseling.

I was paid in October of 2015 by a Hollywood studio to use my house to tape part of the opening episode of the second season of *Aquarius,* the series with David Duchovny about the murders in the late 1960s committed by Charles Manson and his followers. I was just sitting in my living room one afternoon when someone from a Hollywood studio knocked on the door and said my house looked like a beach house that would be typically found at Venice Beach, where one of Manson's groupies would be living, and David Duchovny, as an LAPD officer, was going to be investigating him in the episode.

I was recently dealt a royal flush in Las Vegas on a video poker machine that netted me $1,200. I am especially blessed to have been placed in what I believe is the position to speak and do for those who cannot speak or do for themselves in this world. I was given the gift of helping guard and protect the emotional and mental lives and well-being of my students through my classroom teaching and campus and community work.

I believe I have had some of the finest, well-mannered, hard-working students you'll find anywhere in our American college educational system. They are extremely proud to be the first in their families to attend college. Many are full-time students, taking twelve or more units and also working either part- or full-time. Several have children and are single parents. Typically, 60 percent of our student body are females. The average age of our students is twenty-seven. The average combined total yearly family income is about $38,000.

East Los Angeles College is one of the nine community colleges that make up the largest community college district in the world, the Los Angeles Community College District (LACCD). East Los Angeles College has the largest student population of the nine campuses, at about 46,000 students per semester.

The five semesters that I attended ELAC were the best two and a half years of my life. I thoroughly enjoyed the genuine care and concern the faculty and students displayed toward one another. I never felt like I was just another student known by my Social Security number. Current students tell me the same positive things about their experiences at the college with faculty, staff, and other students.

I was thrilled when I was given an opportunity to interview for a full-time position at ELAC in December of 1977. I was even more thrilled when I was offered the position and would be teaching at my alma mater and have a chance to give back and treat my students in the same caring manner I was treated.

I played my first two years of college basketball at East Los Angeles Community College. It is located, of course, east of downtown Los Angeles in the city of Monterey Park. What a thrill it was to have attended ELAC from September 1969 through January 1972 and then come back six years later to teach there.

I was thoroughly enjoying my coaching and teaching position at ELAC when the recession in 1982–1983, during Ronald Reagan's administration, resulted in our district searching for ways to cut the budget. I and many other newly hired instructors were laid off in June 1984. I was hired back a few months later and began teaching at one of our sister schools, Los Angeles City College, where a gentleman in the Men's Physical Education Department took a disability retirement. I replaced him because I was next on the rehire list. I was fortunate to receive that position two days before the fall 1984 semester started.

I had been the Athletic Director at East Los Angeles College in the spring semester in 1984 when I was laid off, then reassigned to teach physical education activity and health classes at Los Angeles City College. After two years of teaching at Los Angeles City College, I asked for and was granted a transfer back to East Los Angeles College. When I transferred back to ELAC I became the

Athletic Director again in 1987 and held that position until 2005.

It was also in early 1984 that I broke up with someone I had been seeing for about four years. That breakup and the transfer to a college where I wasn't the happiest led to a lowered level of self-esteem that I had never experienced before. This was devastating to me, as I was someone who had always had life under control; who was usually the captain or one of the contributing players on many of the teams and sports I played on for twenty-five years. I got just about every job for which I had interviewed. Going from an admired, successful, needed faculty member and coach to the possibility of no job at all in 1984 was difficult to handle.

This was the first time in my life that I needed support in getting through a series of personal and professional challenges. I did not know how to go about getting that support I desperately needed. Who supports the supporter? Who takes care of the caretaker? Instead of asking for traditional support from the College District's Employee Assistance Program, or seeing a therapist, or perhaps reading self-help books, I chose to turn to alcohol to drown my sorrows, to numb my emotional pain, to cope with the sudden loss of control in my life. My drinking did begin to affect my teaching and personal relationships. It did nothing to resolve my feelings of inadequacy and self-doubt.

Before I was laid off in June 1984, when I was a few years into my teaching and coaching position at ELAC, I met a pleasant, vivacious athletic staff member with a great smile, and at first it developed into a friendly relationship. We soon began to date, and she and her daughter from a previous marriage eventually moved in with me in 1986. We had a lot of fun together traveling, entertaining family and friends, and spending quality time with her daughter.

As usual I was controlling the relationship, dictating how things were to be done around the house and within the relationship, and my drinking was still out of control. As an alcoholic, I just wasn't present for her and her wonderful daughter. She put up with my drinking for several years, until one afternoon in 1988. She came home from work, and I met her at the back door, and she gave me a look that she had given me many times before. It was a look of disgust and frustration, rolling her eyes and shaking her head. For whatever reason, which I cannot explain to this day, after that look she gave me, I quit drinking cold turkey.

The relationship did not improve much even after I stopped drinking. The damage had been done. I may have stopped drinking, but I did not address the issues that led to my drinking. I quit on my own and did not go to an alcoholic treatment program. Had I gone to an alcohol treatment program when I first stopped drinking in 1988, I believe I would have addressed some of my personal issues, and she and I would probably be together to this day.

I was still in emotional pain and unaware of how much that pain was affecting me and my relationships with my students and others in my life. I continued to be inflexible, stubborn, and obstinate with a "my way or the highway" attitude. Well, she eventually took the highway and left me. I begged her to stay, but in 1993 she wisely stood her ground and left. She was also instrumental in developing in me a love and respect for animals, especially dogs. She brought into our lives a beautiful collie named Topper who was a gentle giant with a lovely demeanor. Growing up, we could never have pets because we would have been competing for food and floor space! She also taught me what to forgive and forget looks like because she tolerated a lot from me during the years we were together, and she was able to find it in her heart to forgive me for the way I treated her, and still accept me as a friend in her life. I remain friends and close to her and her daughter and three grandchildren, with whom I still spend time and continue to consider my own.

I am also still coming to terms with knowing that I was treating my brothers and sisters and probably all my friends and some colleagues and former teammates with my insensitive, controlling behavior. I am only grateful that I did eventually see the error of my ways and have curbed that behavior considerably. I realize now that I have been, for so many years of my life, all about being right no matter what and playing life with an "I win, you lose, I'm right, you're wrong" attitude. I have been my own worst enemy and have sabotaged my relationships at every turn. That is something I am not proud of, but again, I am grateful that I finally found the willingness to notice when I display that ineffective behavior and chose to change it to create more effective, meaningful relationships that I continue to work on and develop in my life today.

TEACHING AND COACHING

I am also sorry to many of the athletic teams I coached and probably a lot of my early students I taught, whom I owe apologies to for not giving them my best at coaching and teaching during my first several years at the college. I did not keep up on the latest offensive and defensive strategies by attending coaching clinics and seminars and therefore did not challenge these athletes nor prepare them for their opponents properly. I kept teaching the way I learned to play and was coached, which was largely self-taught and unstructured play. I was successful in coaching the first couple of years as many of my early players were also self-taught or did not receive much formal coaching. My success diminished significantly when I started getting well-coached players at Simi Valley High School and eventually at East Los Angeles College.

I had fair warning of my mediocre at best teaching style and techniques when I received less than satisfactory evaluations during my student teaching at Santa Ana Valley High School during my senior year at California State University, Fullerton. My master teacher from CSUF and my master teacher contact at Santa Ana Valley High School, who both observed my student teaching, indicated that it would be best for me to start at a middle school, that I was not a high school–quality teacher. That is why I only got calls to interview at junior high schools. My first job was at an intermediate school.

I did not coach in 1984 when I started teaching at Los Angeles City College after being laid off at ELAC. When I was transferred back to ELAC a few years later, I became the Athletic Director again. It was about 2005 that I wanted to spend more time with my domestic partner, and the school happened to be experiencing some budget cuts and could only afford to pay one Athletic Director, so it was easy to step down at that time. The remaining Athletic Director has done a tremendous job in hiring highly qualified, experienced, extremely professional coaches and support staff. Some of his successes over the years, and a few of mine, include:

- In 2015 Laura Aceves twice became an All-American in cross-country for ELAC and an All-American three times in track and field, twice in the steeplechase and once in the ten thousand meters. When asked about her greatest

achievement as a Husky (our mascot), she said it was her ELAC education.
- Sylvia Mosqueda won the 1984 cross-country state title, setting a record that stood for thirty years. In 1985, she won three state titles in track and field in the five-thousand-, fifteen-hundred-, and eight-hundred-meter runs. She tried out for the 1988 Olympic team marathon and four other subsequent Olympics, culminating in qualifying for the 2004 ten-thousand-meter-run.
- Our men's baseball coach, James Hines, achieved four hundred wins in 2016.
- ELAC's women's badminton team won the state doubles title in 2016.
- Former student and athlete John Mosley has coached ELAC's men's basketball team to the state playoffs in each of the five years he has coached. In his 2016–2017 season, he coached them to a best-ever 26–4 record. His crowning achievement in the past two years is that 100 percent of his sophomores have transferred to four-year universities, including NCAA Division I schools.
- ELAC's women's basketball coach, Bruce Turner, in 2017 established the best record in the seventy-year history of the school, at 28–3. His team played for a state title against perennial state powerhouse Mt. SAC (San Antonio College) in 2017.
- There have been many other state and national accomplishments by ELAC's athletic teams under the administration of now retired Athletic Director Al Cone, former ELAC baseball coach. Al is as competitive as the athletes who compete on the college teams he administered.
- Most recently, ELAC Athletics has been blessed to have had Toni Harris join our football team and inspire so many young girls and women to believe in themselves and follow their dreams. Toni played free safety on our football team and has been one of the first women to have received a football scholarship to a university. She will be attending Central Methodist University in Missouri in the fall semester 2019. She aspires to be the first woman to play in the NFL.

PART TWO

Classroom Techniques

Positive Changes

———◆———

The health classes I taught over the years became my favorite to teach. I learned to incorporate meaningful, life-changing supplemental assignments into the subject at hand to enhance learning and effect positive change in their lives. This is the section of my book that contains many of my self-help suggestions and information for my readers as a guide to behavior change, or as perhaps a classroom instructor's guide for teachers to create a more effective atmosphere for learning.

The textbook I used in each class covered a wide range of health topics and health issues, including information about and discussion of drugs, alcohol, and tobacco, emotional well-being, relationships, and violence against women. My favorite topic and the one in which I believe I created the most positive results in my students was the chapter on emotional well-being. I focused a lot of my time on that chapter because it is the one, based on the material presented, in which students had the best opportunity to create balance and peace of mind in their emotional lives.

The suggestions for change I conveyed to my students came from personal development exercises I conducted in class that corresponded with and supplemented the current chapter information that was being discussed. Many of these self-help and life lessons I brought to my classes and will share with you were from personal and professional development workshops and seminars I personally attended that supported me in making positive changes in my own life that led to more effective, meaningful personal and professional relationships. The information from the workshops and seminars I attended are well-known, previously used formulas and methods of behavior change widely used for decades that you may choose to use and benefit from.

I advocate to my students that you cannot know, love, or respect others unless you know, love, and respect yourself. It is difficult to fulfill the needs of others if your own needs are unfulfilled. That was the premise behind my teaching. It took me many years into adulthood to realize that many needs in my own life were unfulfilled, leading to incompetent and unproductive teaching. Much of what is in this book has been inspired by my own failures in my personal and professional relationships. It was my upbringing that dictated how I related to others. I am not blaming my family for how I showed up in my adult relationships and the subsequent failures within them. How we reacted and responded to each other within my family was the only reference I had for what relationships look like. As I got older, it seemed reasonable to me that all relationships were like those developed in my childhood.

I have willingly chosen to take the necessary action to create and maintain healthier, more meaningful relationships in my life. It is only as I strive to become whole and vital that I am able to support others in doing the same. Often, it was while I was explaining self-improvement objectives and exercises to my students that I would have my own "aha" moments of self-discovery that garnered opportunities for change in myself.

From day one, my intent in class has been to encourage my students, chapter by chapter, to willingly identify and change their negative behaviors and develop positive behaviors in their lives. I tell my students that this health class is not just another class required for graduation or just another three-unit class they need for credit. I want the class to be *that* class in their college career in which they will have learned the most about themselves.

Here are some of the comments and feedback about my health classes that I received from students, many of whom struggled daily to pay for their books and classes, find adequate affordable child care, and find ways and the means to get to and from school:

> From Erika: "I just want to thank you, Ms. Ladd. I have broken all the rules on your syllabus, but was never absent.

And I love the fact you are a disciplined and strict professor because you care about our education. I wish I could keep you as my personal coach!"

From Yvonne: "This class was great and wasn't what I expected. I found a deeper inner part of me I didn't pay much attention to, but now it's different. I focus on things I never thought were important."

Sarah: "I really enjoyed this class. I have been pushed for the better in your class. I am feeling way better about myself."

I will discuss and describe the personal development homework assignments and in-class exercises I conducted that produced results in those students who wanted to create positive changes in their behavior. The changes were generated by the student's own efforts using my exercises as a source for change. What follows are descriptions and explanations of the assignments and exercises that the reader can use to create positive changes in your own behavior, if you choose. Each exercise and assignment is followed by student testimonials, describing the results their efforts achieved. These results have created healthier, happier, and more productive individuals within their families, relationships, and society.

I let my students know on the first day of class, as they walk through my classroom doors, that they can obtain maximum benefits from the lectures and assignments by leaving their baggage at the door. As they exit after each class, they can choose to pick up their current life's challenges, doubts, and past conflicts and hurts that they left at the door before class, or choose to leave some baggage behind, allowing themselves to move forward in their lives. I also ask them to leave their hammers at home—the hammers they often use to beat themselves up when they make a mistake or believe they have done something wrong. I at least encourage them to bring smaller and smaller amounts of baggage and hammers as the class progresses, and that they work to rid themselves of any of their current ineffective behaviors or actions. I also ask them to leave at the door the chips they may have on their shoulders and any past or current anger or animosity they harbor. I want 100 percent of their mental and emotional selves present. I want them to keep an open mind and *trust* the process!

My purpose is to get them thinking from the very start about the emotional hurts and pain they may be continuing to carry that currently control their lives and do not serve them. Becoming aware of these limiting beliefs about themselves may eventually prompt them to get rid of them for good, or to at least to become aware of how much they are affected by their negative self-talk and actions. By leaving smaller and smaller pieces of luggage, hammers, and fewer chips behind in each class, they soon begin to heal from past hurts and start making healthier choices for themselves.

On the first day of class, I also challenge my students to sit in a different seat every class meeting to get them out of their comfort zone and the security of sitting in the same place every week. It has a lot to do with supporting them in the process of taking risks, which I discuss later in the course. When the opportunity arises for them to take risks outside of class, they already have a little experience doing so in class. It can also prevent them from becoming complacent, giving them an opportunity to experience the class and perhaps life from a different place and location.

I ask if they know or are friends with another student in the class. Once they admit to their friendship with another student or students in the class, I ask them from now on not to sit together. Sit at least two rows away from someone you know. This helps eliminate distractions. If they sit next to someone they do not know, they are less likely to talk and get diverted away from listening. I need their full and complete attention, as I believe a lot of the information and topics discussed contain potentially life-saving information.

On the first day of class, I write the following on the board:

      Discover   Change   Results

As each chapter is discussed, and as they complete each associated supplemental personal development exercise, I encourage them to make note of what they have discovered most about themselves in that chapter. What I encourage them to do as the class progresses with what they discover about themselves is to make changes based on those discoveries. Lastly, I tell them to make note of the results they created based on the changes they made. I give them an opportunity on their class final to receive three points of extra credit toward their class grade by letting me know what they discovered most about themselves in this class, what changes they made based on those discoveries, and what results they got based on the changes they made.

For instance, in my Women's Health class, one of the first topics we discuss is diet. Many women *discover* that they have a poor diet. I then encourage them to make *changes* based on what they discovered about their current diet, and then make note of the different *results* they get after changing. Most of the students usually discover that they eat too much fast food and sugar, and change their diets to eat more fruits and vegetables or fish and poultry. Typically, their results, by the end of the semester, are that they have lost weight, they have more energy, and they feel better about themselves. They have also often been able to get their families and children to make better food choices as well.

The more a particular health topic impacts a student, the more likely she or he is to make profound discoveries, changes, and results. The topics and supplemental exercises discussed and completed during the chapters on relationships and emotional well-being seem to garner the most far-reaching, heartfelt results in their lives, more than the other topics and chapters.

Some of what the chapter on "Relationships" discusses in the textbook I typically used, which was *Our Bodies, Ourselves,* are the following:

- What are you looking for in a relationship?
- How do you define and express intimacy?
- How does it affect your relationship when you are with someone who the world gives more or less power than you have, because of race, gender, income, or disability?
- What effect do children have on dating or staying in a relationship?
- What are some of the obstacles that can get in the way of relationships?

To support them in taking action to make changes in their lives, there is a formula for change I write on the board when we begin our discussion on the unit in our textbook on "Relationships":

The Formula for Change
1. Notice the negative behavior
2. Ask why I behave that way
3. Change the negative action

The first step to making changes in our lives is to be *willing* to start *noticing* when your actions are not serving you. Notice when you are continuing to be jealous in your relationships. Notice that you are an emotional eater. Notice how often you get angry and impatient because things are not getting done in the time and the way you would do things, or you discovered or noticed that the reason you are doing drugs is to wipe out emotional pain. Notice how often you need to control everyone and everything. Notice how much and how often you procrastinate or arrive late to your commitments. Be willing to notice all those actions you do that have you paying prices in your relationships, your finances, or your career.

The next step in the formula is to *ask yourself why you are behaving in a negative way*. Why you feel the need to get jealous, why you feel the need to overeat, why you get impatient or anger easily when things don't go or get done your way. Why do you procrastinate or arrive late all the time? Why do you feel the need to control just about everyone and everything in your life?

An added discovery here that you will find is that your needs are driving your actions. Two needs that I discovered that drive my negative actions are: *my need to be right* and *my need to look good*. I have paid big prices in my relationships both in and outside the classroom for my need to be right. My need to be right drives my need to look good. I won't look good if I admit I am wrong. After I was finally willing to ask myself why I need to be right, my answer was: *I don't need to be right*, or *I am not being right about anything, I just need to be right!* I was paying too many prices for my unnecessary and unwarranted need to be right. What I realized is that my need to be right was driving my negative actions of impatience, controlling others, and not holding others capable. All these actions on my part were ruining my relationships with just about everyone in my life, both personal and professional.

A willingness to notice negative nonproductive behavior, then doing something different, can be life-changing. This was illustrated to me many years ago while I was watching one of the early episodes of the current TV series *Cops*. The scene was what I remembered years later when I was finally ready to change and get rid of my needs to be right and look good.

In the episode, there was a social worker who was called to the scene of a drive-by shooting by the local police, who wanted him to talk to a young teenage male who had just killed another young man from a rival gang. The teen was in handcuffs behind the police car and was exhibiting defiant, aggressive, confrontational behavior, dictating to law enforcement and anyone else that he had no intention of admitting that what he had done was wrong or that he cared about taking the life of another human being. As I watched his demeanor play out on TV, it appeared, despite the pleas of the social worker, as if the teen was proud of what he had done and would now *look good* in the eyes of his neighborhood gang.

The social worker was quietly pleading with him to take a look at what he had just done; that he had senselessly taken a human life, ruined his victim's family, changed lives forever, including his own, and for what? The young man continued to be defiant and rebellious until the social worker told him to look him in the eyes and answer this question: "At what age were you when it became more important for you to be right than human?"

The young man stared at the social worker, and several seconds later the young man's entire demeanor changed. His chin dropped to his chest, his shoulders slumped forward, and he fell very quiet. I could tell that it was at that very moment that he realized the gravity of what he had done. What a price for an innocent human being to pay for his need to be right and look good. I was moved by that painful, disturbing, profound scene, and have played it out in my mind many times since. I have used that line on a few occasions when making a point to a student of similar demeanor or to a health class when we are discussing the chapters on relationships and violence against women. It was a question that I would ask myself many times when my need to be right was rearing its ugly head. That question has been the catalyst to change for me and my students as we continue to discuss the formula for change.

The final step to the formula is to *change the negative action* that is not working; those negative behaviors that you discovered are not serving you. If you discovered or noticed that you are paying prices in your relationships for getting impatient and angry because things are not going your way, instead change the action and become more sympathetic and obliging. That action could be to hold others capable once you have explained clearly what you want. Allow them to make mistakes without getting angry or impatient, which you already know does not serve you or support them. Change by delegating so that you are not upset about having to do everything yourself, because you believe you are the only one who can do it right. You will be surprised how your relationships will improve and how good you will feel about yourself when you have successfully used this formula for change.

Here are some of the responses I have received from male and female students with regard to their discoveries, changes, and results achieved using the formula for change:

> The beautiful, lovely brown-eyed Raquel said: "What I discovered most about myself is that I should never give up and to better myself by striving for balance and peace of mind in my life. I tried my best to get my goals. Although I felt like I couldn't do it, I kept going. My results are that I believe in myself more, and I have more balance and peace of mind, and I will keep going until I'm a 10!"

> Bright and focused Aimee says: "I need to take risks in life and never give up. To always be myself and let no one tell me what I can't pursue in life. I am more confident in myself. I came into this class with low self-esteem and doubts within myself. But now, based on what I learned about myself in this class, it showed me that I myself am a strong woman, and no one can break me. Results: I have high self-esteem, confidence, and more happiness in my life. Even in this very moment I'm going through a tough situation, and I'm still remaining strong."

> From outgoing and fun-loving Jori, one of the men in my Women's Health class: "What I discovered most about

myself through this class is that if I have confidence in myself, I'm able to tackle obstacles that normally seemed out of reach or unobtainable. The biggest change I made was to quit doubting myself. To have confidence even with the unknown in my life. With confidence in myself, I can achieve most anything."

From a recharged and encouraged Martha: "What I discovered most about myself is that I'm not as weak as I thought I was. I have more strengths than weaknesses, which I really need to know at this point in my life. Changes I've made are to think more positively about who I am. I've also learned to let certain things go."

From quiet but determined Phillip: "I have potential. I can and will be less critical of myself, which will benefit me in the future. I have become more confident in myself and motivate myself to take chances. I am closer to my goals than I have ever been in my life. I am now independent and can push forward with my life."

Four Agreements

Each semester is four months in length. That gives me the opportunity to introduce the book by Don Miguel Ruiz called *The Four Agreements*. His book allows the reader to take a look at their self-limiting beliefs and create better relationships with others, including themselves. His book corresponds beautifully with the healthy living principles taught in my classes.

I write one of the four agreements from h is book on the board at the beginning of each of the four months in the semester, and after a brief discussion, I ask my students to actively and consciously follow that agreement. The first agreement I discuss during the first day at the same time as I discuss my class rules from my syllabus is: *Be impeccable with your word.*

impeccable: free from fault or error

At the end of discussing each class rule, I ask the students if they are in agreement with that rule before moving on to the next rule, until the entire class is in full agreement with each of my ten rules. I don't tell them when, but I let them know that they will have an opportunity sometime during the semester to take a look at what their relationship with their word is. I encourage them to use the class rules as a way to practice being their word. These four agreements remain written in one corner of the board throughout the semester.

Some of my class rules discussed from the class syllabi include: Be on time, Turn cell phones off during class, Do not talk while I am talking, and No food or gum in class, only water. I encourage them to take care of their personal needs before class so they are not getting up to use the restroom, are not eating in class, or on their phone during class. I let them know that these are all distractions, that my rules are designed to eliminate distractions during class so that only maximum learning takes place.

About mid-semester is when I present the class with that opportunity to take a look at what their relationship with their word is. I have every student stand up next to their desk. I read each of my ten class rules from my syllabus again, one by one. As I read each rule, if the student broke that rule, even after they agreed to follow that rule on the first day of class, I instruct the student to sit down. Even if they did not break any of the subsequent rules as I read them, they are told to remain seated. After reading all ten rules, I usually have between one and three students out of forty-five or so still standing. This means forty-plus students were not *impeccable with their word* for ten simple rules in one of their college courses. If they are breaking simple rules in my class, where else in their lives outside of class are they not being their word? How a student shows up in my class is often how they show up outside class. I let them know before I read the rules that this exercise is not meant to embarrass them in front of others or make them feel bad about themselves. It is designed to allow them to take a look at what their relationship with their word is.

This exercise also gives the student an opportunity to be honest with themselves. Honest in being willing to sit down in front of others, acknowledging wrongdoing instead of remaining standing when you know you broke that rule, which would show an unwillingness to be honest and probably a need to look good. Many realize they broke several of the rules, not just one, and that they do indeed admit that they also break their agreements outside of class.

I encourage them to remember the broken agreements perpetrated against them by others in their lives and how they felt when someone promised to read them a story tonight but never did, or promised to stop beating their mother but never did, or stop doing drugs, or cheating on them, but never did. Based on results, this agreement allowed my students to get honest and to be their word.

In one of my 2007 fall semester health classes, a student, Terrell, who dropped my class after about a month and a half, told his girlfriend, also in my class, after agreeing to the class rules, that it was time for him to get honest with himself and with her. So he told her that he has been doing PCP for the past six months. He began seriously working on his addiction after that admission to his girlfriend.

Another student, a female, decided to get honest and be her word by telling her boyfriend that she has been cheating on him. One other student told me that she stopped doing methamphetamine the day in class she agreed to be her word.

It was always rewarding to me that many of these exercises prompted students to take life-changing action in their lives. My hope is that the reader here is willing to take a look at the effect that agreements you broke have had on others, or how others' broken agreements have affected you. I encourage and challenge you to take action to get honest, if you believe you need to, and develop a better relationship with your word. Here is an opportunity to develop healthier, more meaningful relationships, especially the relationship with yourself.

I always wanted my students to know that what we did in class may not impact them right now, that they may not "get it" right now, that it may be years later in a similar situation that they will look back at what was discussed in class and the lightbulb will *then* go off and produce results in behavior change.

The next agreement, for month number two, is *Don't take things personally*. This agreement is always big for me and for many of my students, especially those who have had a lot of parents or people of influence in their lives who were overly critical and never satisfied with anything. As a middle child in a large family, with four older brothers and a difficult-to-satisfy father, I always felt a compulsion to defend myself against what I felt was their criticism. I could never, according to them, do anything right.

I grew to realize and imparted to my students that I have a choice as to how I either react or respond to comments from others; that my upbringing does not have to define who I become as an adult; that I don't always need to see others' comments as criticism but rather to see it as feedback. Seeing their comments as feedback rather than criticism has allowed me to stop taking what they say personally. Most people you know don't sit around thinking of ways to anger you or upset you with their comments. Often their comments are based on their experience of you and are not always meant to hurt your feelings.

reaction: an action or attitude that shows disagreement with or disapproval of someone or something

response: action taken in answer to something (*Webster's Dictionary*)

What the above definition of *reaction* means to me is that when I *react* to others' feedback, that is me defending my behavior, with no intention of changing. *Reaction* is to revert back, to act again, a desire to repeat an ineffective behavior or a refusal to change a behavior that someone is bringing to your attention or attempting to help you change.

There *are* people who go out of their way to make you feel bad about yourself. They go out of their way to make you feel as miserable as they are. "Misery loves company." These are the kinds of people you want to negotiate out of your life. I know this one because many people negotiated me out of their lives because I was always nagging and controlling and sarcastic to them. Overly critical people like me and my dad never want to be about solutions. I did not want to take responsibility for my behavior. It was much easier to play a victim and blame others, and rationalize or defend my behavior. That way, I didn't have to take any responsibility for it!

Response to feedback is taking action to change. Remember that *response* is the root word for *responsible*. The first action I took, which was not easy for me at first, in response, not in reaction, to the person giving me feedback, was to say, "Thanks for the feedback. Let me think about what you just said." Once I was willing to get myself out of the way and respond, take action to feedback, I came to realize that nine times out of ten, that person giving me the feedback was right. What I had to learn is that it is *just* feedback. What's the worst that could happen if I gave myself permission to take what others say as an opportunity for change, or just take it in stride and not become upset by it? I was defending my behavior by reacting instead of changing my behavior by responding!

Of the four agreements, I believe the second agreement is the one that seems to profoundly affect more students than the other three.

> With regard to the second agreement, Joselyn wrote: I needed to stand up for myself, which helped me see that I have a voice and a mind of my own. I took things personally, but the second agreement allowed me to just brush off what everyone says or thinks about me. It's not my concern to please others and not myself. Now I am first on my list! Also, if you know the real truth, what difference does it make what anyone else thinks?

> Maria said: I let everything get to me and let it affect me and let others take advantage of me, but that is not going to happen anymore. I changed by realizing that I shouldn't always take things personally. Enjoy everything; don't regret anything. What has resulted is that I think more positively about myself and my decisions.

> Leslie wrote: I have discovered many things in this class. I feel this class has made me recognize the areas in my life that were lacking some strengths. I also work a full-time job, and the tip of not taking things personally has been helping me throughout the course of my work.

The third agreement for the third month of class is ***Do not make assumptions***. This is big for me and my students to practice as it is easy to presuppose or presume others know what you know. This agreement has helped me tremendously in all my relationships. I challenge myself and my students to practice this and all the agreements on a daily basis. I believe and have seen these agreements create more balance and peace of mind in the lives of my students.

One classic incident where I made an assumption that cost me, but was a learning experience, was when I was parked at a curb waiting to pick up a nephew of mine from school. There was a post located just a few feet away from where I parked at the curb. When he opened the car door, he hit the post with the passenger door.

He cringed because he knew he probably dented the door, and I was going to yell at him for doing that. Instead of yelling at him for hitting the door, I took responsibility for my part by admitting to him that I shouldn't have parked so close to that post, or should have let him know the post was there instead of *assuming*, taking for granted, as we can all do, that he knew the post was there and wouldn't hit it. This made him feel better knowing that it wasn't his fault. I was practicing learning to take personal responsibility for my mistakes and not blame others as I had always done in the past and what others sometimes did to me.

To illustrate this agreement further, I vividly remember watching a television documentary one time about a foster parent's first encounter with a young incorrigible youth that they took into their home. The angry child picked up a kitchen knife and threw it at the foster father. Instead of assuming that the child should know better and get angry and then punish him for throwing the knife, he instead told the child, "I never should have left those knives there for you to get at them." It was probably the first time in that child's life that an adult took some responsibility for their actions and didn't negatively blame him for outcomes.

When we are about to make a left turn on a yellow light, can we assume we can go ahead and safely turn left in front of drivers coming at us in the opposite direction, that they will slow down and not run through that yellow light? Can we assume our children or others in our personal and professional lives know what we know? Making assumptions will get us into trouble every time. These kinds of scenarios and conversations take place many times a day, so my students have many opportunities to practice this agreement.

> Santos wrote: "Something I discovered about myself is that I shouldn't make assumptions, and now I no longer make assumptions. I am more conscious, and I realize the mistakes that I'm making."

The fourth agreement for the fourth month of the class is *Always do your best*. No matter what, as a parent, teacher, brother, sister, coworker, manager, teacher, no matter what—*always* do your best.

If you are not going to give life your best, why give your life and everything in it any effort at all?

Why get married if you are not going to be the best husband, wife, or partner you can possibly be? Why become a parent if you are not going to be the best parent you can possibly be? Same goes for being the best possible son or daughter, or aunt, uncle, student, or coworker you can be. I tell my students to apply this and the other three agreements to everything they do. Always do your best at your job, at doing a homework assignment or a test or task, at anything you do in life.

Where this particular agreement can be further demonstrated is when we are discussing the "Violence against Women" chapter in my Women's Health classes. I suggest that they take a self-defense class to build their confidence and learn to protect themselves. If they ever have to use these learned self-defense techniques on an attacker, they wouldn't use them or fight back at only 80 or 90 percent of their effort or strength to save their lives; they'd better give a hundred percent then, and in all they do in life, or don't fight at all. Always do your best!

Clarity and Consequences

———◆———

This quote and others supplemental to the textbook classroom exercises that follow are well received by my students and have produced results in their everyday lives:

> Be clear, in agreement, and establish consequences.

Apply these suggestions in your conversations with anyone in your life and you will find that all your relationships will become more effective and meaningful. As the semester progresses, I ask my students to notice if using the above statement seems to improve their relationships.

Give all the details; make sure the person understands clearly what you are saying. It is helpful to ask them to repeat back what you just said so that you are both on the same page and are both clear in what needs to be done. If the agreement is broken, hold that person accountable for the consequences discussed previously.

The example I give the class to illustrate this lesson, if you will, is to visualize a parent who is talking to their child about cleaning their room. Often, all a parent might typically say is, "You have thirty minutes to clean your room or you don't get to watch TV tonight." When you show up thirty minutes later and the room, to you, is not cleaned, and you have your child suffer the consequences by not letting them watch TV, and then she or he insists their room *is* clean—what happened?

The following, I believe, demonstrates how you as a parent

can have a successful conversation with your child that produces results. First, be clear with your child as to what a clean room looks like. "Do you understand that all your clothes go here? Am I clear that your books go over there, and your toys go here, and what your properly made bed is to look like?" After being clear with what a clean room looks like, ask your child to repeat back to you what you both agreed on as to what a clean room looks like. When you are both *clear* with what a clean room looks like, then get into *agreement* as to the amount of time it will take to clean their room, and then, finally, discuss the *consequences* the child will incur if the room isn't cleaned in the time and manner agreed upon.

Most important in all of this is to stick to your consequences. If you allow them to watch TV anyway, even if they broke their agreement with you, and maybe you can't stand hearing them cry because they don't get to watch TV, you will lose their respect. They have just learned that they can break an agreement with you and not have to suffer any consequences if they cry or throw a tantrum. You only have to hold them to your consequences once and they or anyone else in your life will *get* that you keep your word, that you follow through with consequences, that you do not let others cross boundaries without consequences.

This is how, I believe, many of our children today learn ineffective behaviors that will get them what they want without paying any consequences. They have not been held accountable when they break their agreements. As they get older, these behaviors often show up in the form of lying, cheating, and crying, because those behaviors have gotten them what they wanted without keeping their agreements.

If they cry or throw a tantrum, or if Mom won't give them what they want, they will ask Dad. They may believe this same behavior will work as an adult in their adult relationships. It will work if they end up with someone like one of their parents who doesn't hold others accountable for broken agreements. Otherwise, that child will have real difficulties in their adult relationships in holding themselves responsible for their agreements.

My mother held us accountable, and we paid the consequences for our broken agreements with her. My dad did not hold us accountable for agreements we broke with him, like coming home after dark when he told us not to. We knew Mom would give us a spanking if we broke an agreement with her, and we knew that we could often cross boundaries with Dad without consequence.

During our chapter "Violence against Women," the discussion often turns to talking about the women in class who themselves or their mothers were being abused in the home. Many have admitted that when a line is drawn for the abuser to stop the abuse, and he is allowed to continue to cross that line without consequence, he doesn't stop. The more often the line is crossed without consequence, the more difficult it becomes over time to hold him or her to any kind of agreement to quit the abuse, which typically gets worse.

When I discuss the ten class rules with my students on the first day of class, I make sure I am clear with them on each rule. For instance, I let them know that if they break their agreement to be on time, the consequences are that they will be held accountable for anything they may have missed in those minutes they were late. When my students suffer the consequences after breaking their agreement to be on time or turn in an assignment when due, they soon get that breaking agreements is not acceptable. My hope is that they follow the "Be clear, in agreement, and have consequences" concept in their daily lives and hold others to it as well. Their relationships will be more meaningful and effective from that day forward, and they will become an example to others.

As a parent or anyone in a position to trust others or gain their trust, this concept can become very effective in establishing and maintaining that trust. Begin by being clear with your children, your students, your friends, and your family that you will always trust them and they can always trust you, no matter what. You will always defend them against others as long as you are clear with them that they better be telling you the truth and that there will be consequences if they aren't. That one time they break that trust or an agreement with me, it is important that I let them know that the consequences are that it will take a long time for me to build that trust with them again. When those in your life know that you keep your word and you are honest, they are likely to want to create and maintain your trust and honesty by keeping their agreements with you.

I received some feedback from a mother in the class who used this concept with her children. She said that she was getting tired of always being late for my health class because her children were never ready on time to leave for school in the morning. She decided to get in agreement with them that the next time they were not ready on time, the consequences would be that she would leave without them. The next morning, they were not ready, as usual, and broke their agreement to be on time, so she backed down the driveway and into the street. They all came frantically running out of the house, putting their jackets on while they ran, holding their shoes in their hands, their backpacks hanging from one shoulder. She stopped, of course, and said that now they have been ready to go on time ever since!

I remember Bill Walton of UCLA and NBA basketball fame being interviewed one time after he had retired from his pro career. He told the story of his coach, John Wooden, who told his players on the first day of practice that one of his rules is that they were to cut their hair short while playing for UCLA. The next day, Bill Walton showed up for warm-ups with his long hair. He was called into his coach's office, where he was reminded by John Wooden that the rule was that all players were to cut their hair short while playing on the team. Bill said he liked his hair long. John Wooden simply said, "The team is going to miss you." Bill immediately got on his bike and quickly rode down to the nearest barber, got his hair cut, and made it back just in time to start practice that day.

Asking Questions

Another effective concept and one that I believe is one of the most important of the lessons I teach, which goes hand in hand with the "Be clear, in agreement, and have consequences" concept that I write on the board is to:

Make "I" statements and ask questions.

About half of what I say on a daily basis in the classroom and elsewhere is in the form of a question. To me, asking questions gives my students and others a chance to build confidence in themselves and creates responsibility. This concept leads to win-win situations in your relationships. Making "I" statements followed by a question does not put them on the defensive or make them feel like they have done something wrong, or worse yet, make them feel inadequate.

This exercise works well with the "Be clear, in agreement, and have consequences" concept just discussed, and it also works well with a homework assignment I will discuss.

A female student in one of my Women's Health classes said she used the "Make 'I' statements and ask questions" and the "Be clear, in agreement, and have consequences" concepts with her boyfriend and said her relationship with him and others in her life improved tremendously.

First I tell my students to work on getting the words *can't*, *won't*, *shouldn't,* and other negative words out of their vocabulary. When I use these negative words when speaking to a student, it puts the student on the defensive or makes them feel they are wrong, often leading to "I'm right; you're wrong; I win; you lose" situations. By contrast, this concept can create win-win conversations for everyone involved.

Instead of saying things like "You can't do that," "You shouldn't put that there," or "Don't spill that," what if we spoke the previous by making an "I" statement followed by a question, as opposed to saying them as a negative demand or reprimand? Understand that this would create more effective, less contentious relationships with everyone in your life. Instead of "You can't do that," what about saying instead: "I talked to you about this topic before, and what was our agreement about that?" Instead of "You shouldn't put that there," what about asking, "I believe you should put that over there. What do you think?" "Don't spill that" could instead be asked and stated in one "I" statement *and* a question, such as, "Can I help you carry that?" Making "I" statements and asking questions allows your speaker to feel capable. It opens the door to more effective, win-win relationships.

Sometimes you know others are not doing what they should be doing. Giving them the opportunity to see that for themselves, without demeaning them with a *don't* or *shouldn't*, will create win-win relationships. Making the "I" statement followed by a question is a positive way to avoid potentially negative outcomes. This concept gives your speaker an opportunity to come up with their own answers without you taking away that opportunity from them, thus potentially creating defensive posturing or hurt feelings.

My point here is that making "I" statements and asking questions, and being clear, in agreement, and establishing consequences in just about everything you do prevents others in your life from ever being able to say, "I didn't know; you didn't tell me." I use my class rules from my syllabus, which I clearly discuss and get into agreement with, as an example in which my students will never be able to say, "You didn't tell me; I didn't know I would be paying consequences for being late or for missing a test." Since I have been setting up my classes this way, rarely does anyone ever come back to me to discuss or question a final grade or why they received what they got on an assignment. Nor do I get complaints about a consequence they received for breaking an agreement.

I set up the "'I' statements, ask questions" and "Be clear, in agreement, and have consequences" scenarios in everything I do and say, whether I am talking to and asking questions of everyone from the bank teller to a stranger at a bus stop to one of my students, a colleague, or close family members and friends. I do need to mention that the "I" in your statements can be replaced by "my." For instance, if I am talking to someone about their behavior I might say, "*My* experience of you in that situation was ...," and then I would follow that up with, "What do you think about what I just said?" Using "my" instead of "I" can still garner positive results without putting your speaker on the defensive.

I tell my students who are parents in the class that they can set up these same win-win scenarios with their children and others in their lives. Even each night when saying good night to their children, they can set things up for the next day. "What time did we say we are all getting up tomorrow morning?" "What did I say we are going to do on the way to school tomorrow?" "How long did I say we are going to stay at McDonald's on our way to school tomorrow?" On and on in this manner each day, every day, sets up win-win situations all day long, and no one can ever say, at any time, "I didn't know; you didn't tell me," when you had clearly and previously discussed it all.

One of my students in a recent semester was struggling with her father-in-law, with whom she and her boyfriend live. Her father-in-law insisted on feeding his granddaughter—her daughter—food and snacks that she believed were unhealthy for her. She felt she should dictate what her daughter should or should not eat.

I suggested she go home and address the issue differently with her father-in-law by asking him, instead of telling him, "Do you understand why I want my daughter to eat the diet I have provided for her?" and "Can we come to an agreement on the foods we believe are healthy for her?" or "What foods do you believe she should eat?" followed by suggested compromises on those foods on which they can both agree. I then suggested she state clearly to him that, if he feeds her foods that are not what they had previously discussed and agreed upon, the consequences would be that she would take her daughter out of his future care when it involves feeding her. Several days later, when she returned to class, she said, "It worked! My father-in-law and I were able to come to a mutual, friendly agreement about feeding my daughter. Thank you, Ms. Ladd!"

Another of my students came to me and was distraught over her concern for her young daughter, who was continually waiting outside the after-school pickup gate, where my student told her daughter numerous times it was an unsafe place for her to wait. It seemed no matter how or what she said to her daughter, she would be waiting for her after school outside the schoolyard gate.

I suggested she sit her daughter down and begin by asking her questions instead of continuing to reprimand her for her unsafe behavior. She would tell her daughter things like, "I thought I told you not to wait outside the gate when I come to pick you up," and "You are going to be punished if I catch you outside that gate again."

I told her to start by asking her daughter, "Do you know why I ask you to wait inside the gate?" or "Can you tell me some of the things that could happen to you when you wait outside the gate?" or "Have I made myself clear why I want you to wait for me inside the gate?" and "What did I say would be the consequences if I find you waiting outside the gate again?"

These questions are asked in a clear, nonthreatening, yet firm manner that gives her daughter an opportunity to respond with an *answer* to her mother's questions as opposed to *being told* in what may be a menacing way. She told me her daughter changed and began to wait inside the gate after their discussion because her daughter felt she had some input and a better understanding as to why she should wait inside the gate.

If I break one of my own rules by accepting late homework from a student, then she or he now knows that I do not keep my agreements and that I allow previously discussed boundaries to be crossed. I believe I lose their respect when I do this. I want them to understand they will be paying consequences for their broken agreements. I did not always set boundaries in my own life in many areas. I continue to work on setting boundaries and holding others accountable. As an enabler, I still struggle with holding others capable and following through with consequences for their broken agreements, but I am working on it!

Our class textbook indicates, and my students agree, that

effective communication is the key to meaningful long-term relationships. We discuss what safe and equal relationships look like and how to attract what you want in a relationship by being and possessing that positive trait or behavior yourself.

I conduct an in-class exercise during our chapter on "Developing Successful Relationships." I ask the class to take out a piece of paper and number it 1 to 10. I then ask them to list the top-ten qualities, behaviors, characteristics, and attitudes that they would find attractive in a mate. If that person possessed all ten listed, they would be the person with whom my student would want to spend the rest of their lives in a long term, committed relationship. I ask them to rank their desirable qualities in a mate from one to ten, with one being their top most desirable characteristic or trait.

I like to see what qualities and characteristics they find attractive in another person, so I ask the entire class to let me know some of their top choices, and I write several of them on the board. What I look for and hope they find attractive are qualities like honesty, integrity, trustworthiness, and compassion—a more attractive value system than physical or emotional qualities they might list, such as an attractive smile, a good job, being well educated, and being goal oriented, to name a few. These are certainly admirable qualities to possess, and are often in their top ten, but they usually do agree that a strong value system should be higher on their lists. As the class looks at all the qualities on the board, at their direction and agreement, I circle the class's top ten. They agree that those ten qualities, which everyone agreed to circle, would indeed create a successful, long-term, committed relationship. Students have indicated that this exercise, along with the "Healthy Relationships" chapter discussions and readings, did help and support them in developing and maintaining their current healthy relationships, and that they planned to use those top ten to create a "10" relationship in the future!

The most important part of the exercise is when I ask my students to take a few seconds to look at their own top-ten list and, with honesty, circle those qualities they believe *they* possess. This part of the exercise gives them the opportunity to understand that if they expect to attract a life mate with healthy, positive traits, they should possess the same or similar qualities. How can you expect to attract someone in your life who is honest if you aren't? How can you attract someone you can trust if you are not trustworthy? Actually, you can attract someone who is honest and trustworthy, but once they find out you aren't, they probably won't stay long. At about this time, I see a lot of lightbulbs going off in my students' heads. They begin to understand that law of the universe that "You attract what you put out there."

Effective Listening

The next topic of discussion is about effective listening, which creates win-win relationships. Listening is at the crux of creating meaningful, successful communication in relationships. To set my students up to become effective listeners, I distribute and discuss a handout on the rules of effective listening that I have extracted from their textbooks. After going over the handout, I ask them to incorporate and follow these rules of effective listening into their daily conversations for the next week. The assignment is called "My Experience of Me as an Effective Listener." They submit a typed two-page double-spaced report on how they showed up in those conversations using the do's and don'ts of effective listening.

I believe one of the most important do's of effective listening is to avoid interrupting your speaker; *let* your speaker finish. Another important rule is to avoid giving your speaker your advice or opinion unless asked. Work to avoid correcting your speaker or finishing your speaker's words or sentences for them; be about their experience, their story or concerns. Demonstrate understanding by accepting their ideas and feelings. It also helps to maintain eye contact with your speaker and avoid looking at their clothes, jewelry, or other possibly distracting things. Many of my students indicated that the most difficult rule of effective listening for them to follow was: "Avoid using your cell phone when you are supposed to be listening!"

I know it has helped me to follow the rules of effective listening because, in the past, I can say I have been one of the world's worst listeners. This assignment has helped me and countless numbers of my students in developing more effective listening skills. For some of my students, the effective listening homework makes the biggest impact in their relationships with others.

Marta says: "I discovered that I was not practicing great relationship skills. I was not practicing great listening habits. I feel that this class has made me recognize the areas in my life that were lacking some strengths. Slowly I do see changes in the conversations I have with others. When I began the class, at the same time I began dating someone as well. I was afraid things were not going to work out, but some of the tips from this class, like being a better listener, have helped me."

Candace writes: "I am not as good a listener as I thought I was. The listening homework had to be my favorite assignment because it made me aware of how I was not making the person speaking to me my main focus. I used the good listener techniques (open body, eye contact, *no* texting) and now I have better conversations, especially with my dad." She draws a smiley face.

José writes: "In the beginning of the effective listening assignment, I noticed that I wasn't a good listener when I would talk to my friends or family. I had problems of interrupting them while they were telling their story to me. Since I started to follow the rules of being a good listener, it has helped change my way of listening. Now I let my friend talk while I'm listening to every word he says, and not interrupting the conversation, and making him understand that he is important."

From Cindy: "The greatest discovery about myself in this class is that I am not an effective listener. I discovered how I interrupt another person while they are talking about something important and talk about my experience, and that is something that I already started working on."

Janet said: "I discovered that I wasn't a great listener with everyone around me, especially with my mom. And that has changed now; we have a very high level of communication, and it feels so great."

Gloria: "I discovered I was a bad listener! I was paying more attention to my cell phone than I was to my daughter when she was trying to talk to me. I now give the person who is talking to me my full attention. I make eye contact and listen; I only give my opinion if asked for it. I pay my daughter more attention. I stay off my cell phone more. Being a better listener has resulted in better communication and understanding with my loved ones and people in general."

Kimberly: "I learned that I wasn't a good listener. I would only listen to whatever would benefit me. I didn't care much for what other people had to say. I have worked on my listening. I do not only think about myself but of others. I have a better relationship with my mom. I could talk to her more and listen to her. Also with friends and family, which now they say they love the change I have made."

Empathy versus Sympathy

Effective listening is achieved through empathy. Empathy is "genuinely understanding the inner experience of another human being" (*The Lost Art of Listening*). To understand another person's point of view, you must put yourself in their shoes, see through their eyes, feel what they are feeling.

This assignment is a great exercise for those, like me, who need to stop thinking so much when listening and start feeling more. When listening to others, I work to balance my head with my heart. Getting myself out of the way and being all about my speaker has benefitted my relationships tremendously.

Sympathy is "a capacity to share in the interests of others." It is a positive action in supporting others. Sympathy might include holding the hand of your speaker or crying with them while they are sharing their feelings. Sympathy is not the same as understanding their inner feelings when they speak. Speakers do not necessarily want to be held or cried over when they are speaking to you; they just want to be heard. They just want you to listen!

Codependent Behavior

Like my dad, I am a fixer. I like to *fix* things. I like to rescue others. I like to "do for others at great cost to my own self-esteem and well-being." I am codependent. This definition of *codependent* is by Melody Beattie in her book *Codependent No More*. Codependency is an excessive reliance on other people for approval and a sense of identity. I learned to be the caretaker in my family at a very young age, which absolutely gave me the approval and sense of identity I craved in a large family. I was not aware of how codependent I was until I read Melody Beatty's book and began teaching about codependency during my health classes chapter on "Drugs, Alcohol, and Tobacco."

Because I am a fixer and a rescuer, and don't hold others capable, I do for others those things that they are perfectly capable of doing for themselves. I have *discovered* that it takes a lot of time, energy, and money to rescue—time, energy, and money I no longer choose to give to others. The *change* I made was to start saying no and start holding others capable. The *results* I got were a lot more time, energy, and money for myself! To make these changes, I used the formula for change mentioned earlier. I began to *notice* how often I automatically say yes to everything and to everyone; even if I know I don't have the time or money to do so.

In using the formula for change, noticing how many times each day I rescue or fix others was quite an eye-opener. The "Ask why" was easily answered when I realized that I rescue and fix others for the compliments and adulations I get from them for my efforts. The "action to change" by saying no to others was the most difficult part of the formula for change for me. I had spent nearly a lifetime rescuing and doing things for others. It was difficult to pull away from them and hold them capable. It took some time, but I and those I enabled eventually began to become responsible for their own lives and actions, and I allowed them to do so. It was a win-win choice!

An unforeseen life-changing incident occurred several years ago that involved me and a young, sassy, independent little female dog. The encounter with this stubborn little headstrong stray turned out to be a catalyst for change for me. The adventure with her forever changed my enabling, codependent behavior once and for all.

She was a small multicolored dog that I first caught sight of standing defiantly on the double yellow line in the middle of traffic on a busy four-lane street in Pasadena, boldly barking at passing cars. I decided I wanted to save her from her inevitable demise, whether she wanted me to or not, much like those students in my health classes that I insist on helping because I believe they are headed, in my mind, like this little dog, toward their own inevitable self-destruction.

I pulled over and got out of my car, and started to walk toward her, when she bolted away from traffic in the opposite direction, much like some women have done when I come at them offering tools to regain control over their lives. I continued after her, across the street and down the sidewalk, for several yards, when she suddenly ran out into the street and to the other side, narrowly avoiding getting hit, just as some students have successfully navigated through risky, potentially life-threatening behaviors and situations despite the dangers.

She headed up a residential street north toward Altadena. I got back into my car and started driving after her. I decided to call the Pasadena Humane Society to help me catch her, much the same way I would call a local agency or organization to assist me in offering help to a student. Twice within the next ten minutes of chasing her, I nearly cornered her, once after she entered someone's yard and again as she entered another person's driveway, narrowly eluding me each time. Similar to when I think I have almost talked my student into getting help and she disappointingly declines services or support that may help her.

She continued heading north, and again I called the Pasadena Humane Society to find out where they were in locating me and my female runaway. I solicited the help of a couple of teenage male skateboarders she'd just run by, as I might look for an alternate agency to help when other attempts to get assistance have failed. The skateboarders eventually gave up, just as the Pasadena Humane Society called me to let me know they were on their way. When I told them that my female canine friend had just crossed from Pasadena into Altadena, they informed me that since she was no longer in Pasadena, there was nothing they could do because she was now in Los Angeles County territory. Sometimes those agencies I depend on to help my students cannot come through with their assistance, and I have to seek support from another source.

Forty-five minutes had passed and I now found myself on my own to catch her. By no coincidence, she was running along one side of a cemetery, in my mind literally in the run of her life. She was on the sidewalk on my left, calmly and casually trotting along, looking over her right shoulder at me as defiant as ever in her commitment to make sure she didn't surrender to my desire to rescue her. I continued my chase for several more minutes, until she finally gave me the slip in a neighborhood two miles from the start of our original encounter. She won. She rejected any and all of my attempts to save her from herself.

It was very difficult to accept defeat that day, just as it was difficult to lose that occasional student to a drug habit or a bad relationship or a dangerous life on the streets. I resigned myself to the fact that I can't win them all. I can offer the tools available for their salvation or a better life, but it is up to them to make the choice.

The next day I drove back to that busy four-lane street to look for her where I had seen her the day before, and guess what? There she was, up on the sidewalk, barking as audaciously and boldly as ever at me and others. No one would ever change her ways or tell her what to do! I never saw her again.

I can make change simple or I can make change difficult. All I know is that once I gave myself permission to be responsible for myself, I began to stop focusing so much on taking care of others and began, little by little, to take care of myself. It feels great now to take care of myself and hold others capable of being responsible for themselves once the tools for success have been presented to them. I don't allow myself to get upset when they choose not to use those tools.

In my health classes I discuss and ask my students to listen to some of the characteristics of codependent behavior as I read them. I want them to listen instead of taking notes or distracting themselves with something else. I want them to own what they hear if they believe they exhibit these characteristics and codependent behaviors from living their lives with people whose ineffective or inappropriate behavior has affected them. Without realizing it, they begin to care for their troubled family or relatives and probably others in their lives. I attempt to encourage my students to notice how they cope with the problems and behaviors of others, which can lead to their codependency.

Often what they discover is how their codependent behavior attracts people with troubled lives. Some of the common characteristics of a codependent behavior I have listed below are from Melody Beattie's book *Codependent No More* that I reference during our "Healthy Relationships" chapter. A codependent person:

> thinks and feels responsible for others.
> finds themselves saying yes when they mean to say no.
> tries to please others instead of pleasing themselves.
> finds needy people attracted to them.
> overcommits themselves.
> feels they are being taken for granted, unappreciated.
> comes from dysfunctional families.
> takes things personally.
> tries to help other people live their lives.
> appears rigid and controlled.
> centers their lives around other people, and then ...
> loses interest in their own lives.
> finds it difficult to have fun or be spontaneous.

I know these characteristics because I have possessed many of them at one time or another. After I read Melody Beattie's book at the suggestion of a friend, I was tempted to change my middle name to codependent: Marilyn Codependent Ladd! Her book was written for and about me. I can only hope that others will get as much out of this codependent section of her book as I did.

Changing my codependent behavior allowed me to hold others in my life capable of solving their own problems, to grow and be responsible for their own lives. My self-esteem increased because I stopped taking others' rejection of my ideas or decisions as a reflection of my self-worth. I stopped rescuing my alcoholic brother by no longer spending money on him when I felt sorry for him. I stopped overcommitting myself and doing everything by myself on projects and events and started delegating and asking for support from others. It was difficult at first to say no instead of always saying yes, but it did get easier with time and practice. I stopped attracting needy people and centering my life around others. I started having more fun and began pleasing myself instead of others. It did not happen overnight, and to this day, on occasion, I find myself tempted to revert back to codependent behavior.

The *dys* in *dysfunctional* means "painful" or "difficult." I was raised in what I would call a mildly dysfunctional family where it was painful or difficult to live in our household. Painful enough that either I did not want to come home sometimes, or I wanted to leave sometimes because it was too chaotic, noisy, or difficult to focus on my own needs or tasks, like homework or having some quiet time for myself.

When I was younger, if things got too chaotic around the house, I went outside in the backyard and climbed up into the large avocado tree just outside the back door, to the highest place I could safely find, and just spent several minutes looking out over the neighborhood, listening to the sounds of the birds or airplanes or other nearby activity, until I felt calm enough to return to the fray. When I got older, I drove down to the South Gate Park and just sat in my car or walked around the park for a while before returning home.

Some of the results my students created after discussing codependency are:

Samantha from the Winter 2008 session writes: "My greatest discovery about myself in this class was that I am a codependent person. Although it is a good thing to help others, most of the time I do it before helping myself. I know I need to change the way I do things if I want to accomplish my goals. I am going to do what I have to do for myself; then I can help someone else. I can't help someone with their problems if I have my own. Once I can do this, I'm sure my life will be less stressful and more successful."

Valerie from the fall semester 2007 said: "I need to stop putting everyone's needs before mine."

Diana wrote: "My greatest discovery about this class was that as a woman I have the power to say no to whatever I want. I also learned that taking care of others and putting me last is not good, because people get used to it, then I am the one with all the worries and stress."

Kathy said: "If I don't do things for myself, no one will. So I need to do things for myself instead of doing things for other people. I know it might sound selfish but I need to do it in order for me to accomplish my goals."

Miriam said: "I discovered that I never want to leave my comfort zone. I'm terribly afraid of risks and disappointing others. People have always had expectations and I'm sorry to say I've always met them for them, not me, which is why I stopped going to Cal State Los Angeles: to take school easy and to figure out what is it that *I want*. Now I realize how much I do for others and how I need to stop being an enabler."

If my students express a desire to choose to change their behavior to achieve different results in their lives, I tell them that choice is based on another word I write on the board the first week of class:

Commitment

---◆---

One example of commitment I give is that marriage is a commitment.

commitment = making a choice and surrendering to it.

You are making a lifetime choice to get married to someone and are surrendering one hundred percent to that marriage. If you are not committed to that marriage, more than likely it will not survive, and what we know about marriage in this country is that about half of all marriages in the United States end in divorce. Based on results, it looks like we may start out committed to our marriage or relationships but it doesn't look like we *stay* committed. We must commit and surrender to our choices. Otherwise, if there is any doubt whatsoever, we need to rethink our level of commitment when making any choice.

When she gets pregnant and chooses to have or keep that child, a woman must surrender to that choice. That child needs her to give it everything she's got; she must surrender to the care of that child, 24-7, for at least eighteen years. Career choices, taking on a cause or activity, making a promise, vow, or pledge to someone or something all require complete and total commitment. Commitment is resigning ourselves to our choices.

Taking my health class is a choice. Surrender to doing the best you can in the class, or any class, or why take it? Yes, I know we are all busy and things get in the way of doing our best, but remember, we all have the same twenty-four hours each day. What you do with those twenty-four hours, I tell my students, is your choice.

Maybe it is procrastination that gets in the way. Maybe you don't feel you deserve good grades. I don't know. These are the conversations we have when we get into our chapter on creating emotional well-being.

At the beginning of the second week of class, all my students fill out a behavior change contract in which commitment will be the key to achieving their behavior change goal. Our behavior, or our physical, action side, is one of the four sides of our nature. The other three sides are our emotional, mental, and spiritual sides. All sides must be in balance for us to achieve peace of mind in our lives. The first of the four sides I discuss is our behavior side. Our early family dynamics can often dictate how our behavior, our actions, and things we do can play themselves out later in life, in both a positive or in a negative way.

The beauty about a college health class is that all the chapters within the textbook discuss the four sides of our nature. That is why I am glad that health and physical education courses are requirements for graduation. Fortunately, colleges know the value and importance in developing a well-balanced student.

After I have discussed and described our physical side, I ask them, and then I write on the board, all the negative behaviors, actions, and things that they do that do not serve them. One of the negative behaviors that is often one of the first mentioned by students is overeating. Dangerous and ineffective eating habits are part of our physical side that a student can choose to change. If she or he believes that their poor eating habits are the action they feel they need to work on most during the semester to achieve balance, they will fill out their behavior change contract to address ineffective, unhealthy eating habits.

Another negative behavior often mentioned is procrastination, which is something we do, an action we take, or in the case of procrastination, an action we don't take but should, that does not serve us. Like our eating habits, people pay prices for procrastinating. It has us putting things off until the last minute. It can affect our quality of work, educational success, relationships, and many other areas of our lives.

Doing drugs is a behavior, something we physically do, an action we take. Most people who abuse drugs pay prices for that behavior. Overeating and procrastination, abusing drugs, and other such ineffective behaviors do not support us in creating balance and peace of mind in our lives. My students decide which behavior they want to change. We then get into small groups and discuss in detail their desired change. Each student makes a commitment by signing their contract. At the end of the semester, after working on their contract using the class health textbook, their family, their classmates, myself, and other suggested entities as support, they sit in their groups again to discuss if they achieved their behavior change goal.

It is at this time that I tell my students to maintain confidentiality. Sometimes students do not want others outside class to know about the behavior or action they want to change. What is said in the class stays in the class. Confidentiality is especially essential when students divulge a behavior they want to change that is sensitive or delicate in nature and not easy to talk about, let alone work to change.

One student, sensitive to his confidentiality, indicated in his behavior change contract that he wanted to stop doing methamphetamine. It was ruining his life; he was paying huge prices for using it. He never completed his contract, and dropped the class about halfway through the semester. It appears that his meth use along with other life challenges got the better of him. I urge the students in their behavior change contract groups to help their fellow students throughout the semester to achieve their goal. When I asked his group members how much help and support they gave him, they said none. I believe he would have had a better chance if he would have had more active support from his classmates and me as well. As soon as I initially read his contract, I should have sought him out and provided more support and help.

Behavior change student results:

> From Kandy: "With a set plan, I'm able to work better in accomplishing my goals. The behavior change contract helped me pay off my debts, save money, and now finally I'm going to be able to purchase a car by myself with my own effort."

> Elizabeth writes: "The changes that I made most were from

the behavior change contract. Making myself actually do something that was really hard for me was amazing. The behavior change contract was probably the biggest thing that changed me."

From Erika: "I learned that I could do anything if I put my mind to it and stick with it. If I don't like something about myself, I could change it, like quitting smoking cigarettes. I am now eating healthier, *not* smoking, and accomplishing my goals."

Elijah: "I stopped smoking and drinking."

This brings me to the discussion of another side of our nature: our emotional side. Our emotional side includes our feelings and our attitudes. How we feel about ourselves can dictate how we behave.

Just as we list on the board behaviors and actions that do not serve us, I ask my students to list feelings, emotions, and attitudes that do not serve them. For instance, if you *feel* bad, depressed, confused, jealous, and any number of other negative feelings and emotions, these could lead to negative behaviors such as overeating, or procrastination, or drug abuse. What this means is that how we feel, how our emotions and attitudes play themselves out in our lives, determines how we behave. It stands to reason then that changing your attitude or how you feel can change your behavior. A positive attitude change can lead to a positive behavior change.

When I talk about attitudes, I am talking about an "I don't care," a "so what," or a "too bad" posture or stance we can take with just about everyone and everything. These are the kinds of attitudes that affect our behavior in a negative way. If I don't feel like or don't care about doing my homework, and I don't, the resulting action will be to suffer consequences for that behavior. If the homework doesn't get done, my grades will suffer. If I change my "I don't care" attitude to "I do care," I will ultimately change my behavior to *doing* my homework. Thus, changing a negative attitude changes negative behavior, resulting in more balance and peace of mind in your life.

The third side of our nature is the way we *think* about ourselves.

"I'm not enough," "I'm not important," "I don't matter" can affect how we *feel* about ourselves, which in turn affects our *behavior*. For instance, in my case, when I bought into this belief about myself at a young age that I'm not enough, that belief began to automatically dictate how I felt about myself, which was to doubt myself and feel inadequate or incompetent. Those feelings then dictated my behavior. Whenever I encountered a challenge in life, I automatically went to "I'm not enough," "I'm not capable. So why try?" I believe my self-doubt and feelings of inadequacy prevented me from achieving and reaching my goals sooner in life. When I finally chose to believe that I was enough, I stopped doubting myself and started feeling more confident and self-assured, which created better results in my teaching, my relationships, and other areas of my life.

By looking at and changing any one of the three sides of our nature discussed so far that you feel is not serving you, it will alter the other two. You can first choose to change your behavior, like to stop overeating. This will change how you feel about yourself; getting compliments about your weight, wearing a smaller clothing size. Feeling better about yourself because you have lost weight changes your thinking about yourself that you are capable, that you *are* beautiful!

The fourth side of this concept I have not yet explained is our spiritual side: that side of us that believes there is something out there that can support us in achieving things in life that otherwise appear impossible to accomplish on our own. Call this fourth side an energy, a spirit, our higher power, God, Yahweh, or any other name or entity that you would be willing to hand things over to, allowing this energy or higher power to be your means of support. Allow it to assist and spiritually abdicate on your behalf.

Part of our spiritual side is our value system. Values refer to those guiding principles or ideals that are the estimate of our worth as individuals: integrity, honesty, trust, self-love, compassion, etc. When our values are out of alignment, we are not trustworthy, we do not operate from integrity, we are not honest. All this can lead back to the first side of our nature we discussed, our behavior side, resulting in inappropriate or ineffective behavior and actions toward others or ourselves.

The premise behind these four sides of our nature is: Changing to positive, more effective values (spiritual side) changes how we treat ourselves and others (behavior side), which makes us feel better about ourselves (emotional side), which changes how we think about ourselves (mental side), which brings us full circle back to our spiritual side. We have now created more balanced and peaceful lives.

After discussing each of the four sides to our nature, I ask my students to rate each of their four sides with a number between 1 and 10, with 10 being best and one being the worst. That number is based on their personal current assessment of that side of their nature. I then ask them to add all four numbers and divide that total by four. If a student felt she or he was a 5 on their behavior side, a 5 on their emotional side, a 6 on their mental side, and a 6 on their spiritual side, that equals 22, which divided by 4 equals 5.5. This example of 5.5 means out of the possibility of being a ten in life, they are showing up as a five and a half.

My next question is: how do you expect to attract a ten in your life when you are a five and a half? You could probably attract a ten, but once they see you operating as a five and a half, they probably won't stay long. Either that or you will bring them down to the five and a half that you are. Or, if you are a ten and happen to attract a seven, you either, by example, show them what a ten looks like and they work to become a ten also, or they bring you down to the seven that they are. Let's say they bring you down from a ten to a seven by talking you into using drugs like they do. By using drugs all four of your sides, you could potentially suffer in a negative way and drop in numbers, bringing you down to that seven, possibly resulting in a life that is out of balance and starts to lack peace of mind.

Using the textbook, class assignments, especially the behavior change contract, and any other campus or outside help, I challenge them to focus first on improving that side with the lowest number and bring it up as close to a ten as they can by the end of the semester. I encourage them to work hard to eventually achieve a ten in all four sides of their nature.

I work on my spiritual side because I have had an early history of having a poor, ineffective set of values and little belief in asking for support from anything or anyone to improve them. I have not always been honest, trustworthy, or displayed much integrity in my affairs with others. It became easy for me to lie, to cheat, or to steal from others. My poor set of values stemmed from a program, a belief about myself that I discovered I had on my mental side, that affected my values on my spiritual side. On my mental side, as mentioned earlier, it was important for me to look good to myself and others even if it meant compromising my values.

I could have cookie crumbs coming out of the corner of my mouth and I still wouldn't admit, when asked, that I had eaten a cookie I wasn't supposed to eat. I never apologized for anything; even when I was wrong and I knew I was wrong, I would still insist I was right. I would lie or do anything to make myself look good. I stole money from my mother's purse and never told her. I was OK with cheating on most of my partners in my relationships. I would cheat at cards or Scrabble if I could get away with it, and then deny any wrongdoing, even if I was caught red-handed. I stole some valuable coins from an older brother's coin collection and spent it on candy and ice cream. On a number of occasions, I stole small toys, candy, and other items from the grocery store or the five-and-dime store. What a terrible value system I possessed—something I am not proud of and continue to work on to this day. Those old, ugly, ineffective, and inappropriate behaviors, feelings, and beliefs about myself still rear their ugly heads at times. Through teaching, personal development seminars, reading self-improvement books, and lots of action to change for the better, I recognize those behaviors sooner, and I move off them faster now.

When I think of individuals who have created balance and peace of mind in their lives, people who are a ten, I think of individuals like Maya Angelou, Oprah Winfrey, Ellen DeGeneres, Martin Luther King, John Kennedy, Dr. Phil, Bill Gates, Iyanla Vanzant, and Indira Gandhi, to name a few. I believe they all possess total symmetry, complete harmony, balance, and peace of mind in their lives. Many of those I have listed had challenges in their lives that they overcame that could have been their demise or affected them negatively. They have all been positive role models for others. Other individuals with balance that I think of are some of our more successful college and professional coaches whose coaching style instills discipline, teamwork, a tough work ethic, life lessons, and a sense of fair play. Coaches like John Wooden of UCLA fame and the highly successful Pat Head-Summit from Tennessee Tech come to mind.

Some of the results from the behavior change challenge have been:

> A powerful young African American woman named Brittnee writes: "My greatest discovery in this class was my behavior change. I didn't know that having patience can pay off for me in the long run. Now I understand that the meaning of having patience is good for the future."

> Jackie says: "My greatest discovery was that I'm a very aggressive person, and because of reading and listening to you, I've found a different way of approaching things and situations."

> Shy but determined Omar writes: "What I discovered from myself is that I could make changes in my life if I put my mind to it."

> From Elias: "In this class, I discovered a lot of things about myself. One of them was that I had to change my way of seeing things. I also learned that I have no excuses for not having time to do what I have to do to accomplish my goals and responsibilities. I also learned that the way I live and whatever I do will always depend on the choices I make, so I have to think about what I really want from me and from life and make the right choices and decisions."

> Jessica says: "What I discovered about myself is that I was very impatient and that, for the many problems I have at home, I was becoming very angry at everyone around me, but especially myself. I have been changing a lot from the beginning of the class. I am not as impatient or angry as before because I know how to control myself. The results I've gotten are that my family is much closer to me and I feel much happier with myself."

From a strong and determined Rebecca: "What I learned about myself in this class was that I was a really angry person. To stop being angry, I stopped taking things personally, and now I ignore comments that get me mad. Also, I talked to the people that I had anger toward and cleared everything out. Now, I don't get angry, and I just feel better about myself."

Kendra writes: "I learned that I really can make a change if I try and really put my mind to it. I'm so glad I took this class. I know how to understand people now and how to listen to others and not just think I'm right all the time. That's what makes me happy now, now that I can talk and listen to my family and friends. I'm not controlling anymore, and that made me and my boyfriend have a better relationship. This class really meant a lot to me because it *changed my life*."

From an intelligent and likeable Alejandro: "What I have discovered about myself is that there should be no reason why I can't do things on time and get things done. If I want to be a well-educated progressive person, I need to stop procrastinating, which I did. I have learned my lesson and now, I'm getting my license this month."

And the last one is from quiet, good-looking Roland: "While in Health, I discovered about myself that I procrastinate a lot and suffer at the end for doing it. Now, at the end, I don't procrastinate on my school work. I get it done 'there and then.'"

Earlier I discussed a chapter on "Relationships" from the book I used in my Women's Health classes, *Our Bodies, Ourselves*, written by the Boston Women's Health Collective. This book, about women's health and sexuality, was written by women, for women. It reflects the work and contributions of over four hundred women and quite a few men since its first publication in 1970. It was featured and actively promoted and endorsed by Oprah Winfrey during one of her earlier shows. The chapter on "Emotional Well-Being" discusses useful, lifesaving sources to help someone get through those difficult, frightening, sad, or confused periods we experience at various times in our lives. The chapter offers strategies, activities, and other means of support to help us feel better. The following supplemental classroom exercise is assigned during our discussion on emotional well-being.

Ridding Ourselves of Resentment

One of the last and most powerful classroom exercises my students are assigned is called "Ridding Ourselves of Resentment." It offers the opportunity for my students to let go, once and for all, of any negative emotions they may still have toward someone. That current, existing resentment has been holding them back from moving forward in their lives. *Resentment* is any negative emotional reaction to what was said or done to you. The example I give is, if someone cheated on you by having an affair outside your relationship, your negative emotional reaction to their cheating would probably be anger.

Resistance precedes the resentment you are feeling. *Resistance* is "not accepting what is"; in this case, not accepting the cheating going on, which has led to your resentful anger. It is not accepting something that was said or done to you. What follows the resistance and the resentment to the cheating is revenge. *Revenge* is the "get back"—getting back at someone for what was said or done to you. In this case, revenge may be to cheat on them, slash their tires, or any other negative behavior carried out to get them back for cheating on you. "Take *that* for cheating on me!" It does not serve us to hold on to resentment, thus the purpose for this assignment.

Resistance, resentment, and revenge can also happen when you *thought* something was said or done to you when it was not. Depending on our emotional state or our current life challenges, we sometimes read volumes into what someone has said or done.

After the smoke has cleared, we come to find out that they didn't say or do what we thought. We have often held a grudge (resentment) toward them unnecessarily for years only to eventually find out the incident did not occur in the manner and way we originally thought.

Just the other day at school I started to go into resentment unnecessarily. I noticed that after Plant Facilities waxed the floors in my office during our winter recess that my personal portable heater was missing. I immediately went into the first R, resistance. I was upset and would "not accept" someone stealing my space heater to what I automatically thought was one of the facilities workers. I went into the second R, resentment. My "negative emotional reaction" to the perceived theft was anger at whoever stole my heater. My "get back" was to let the Facilities Manager know that I did not appreciate my heater being stolen from my office by one of his staff.

Turns out the heater was placed in the foyer of the gym while they waxed the floor in my office, and they forgot to put it back when they finished. For about a week the heater had been sitting in the foyer, which is right next to my office. The custodian discovered it and brought it back to my office. It had never been stolen; it had been misplaced after my office floor was waxed. But there I was, into resistance, then resentment, and then into revenge over nothing; over something I *thought* was said or done to me. It made me think how resentment plays itself out in our families, our communities, our cities, states, and sometimes countries against other countries and how it does not serve anyone to be in resentment, whether the event happened or not.

I next ask my students to think of a past or present situation or experience that has resulted in resentment. A student, Gloria, gave her resentment story. She and her boyfriend, Carl, were sitting at a restaurant celebrating their first year together. She went to the restroom and, before returning to her table, happened to unexpectedly run into her brother at the restaurant. She had not seen him for some time, and her boyfriend had never met him. Her boyfriend saw her from across the restaurant, coming back from the restroom, and watched her hugging and having an animated conversation with this other man. The boyfriend went into resistance. He was getting upset that she was, in his mind, having a relationship with this guy behind his back! He now went into resentment by getting angry at her for what he believed was her cheating on him.

By the time she says good-bye to her brother, who had to leave, and sat back down at her table with her boyfriend again, he was now into his revenge "get back" mode, and went off on her. He raised his voice and ranted about how could she embarrass him like that in front of everyone; she was supposed to be with him; how could she do this to him after all he has done for her. She was finally able to calm him down and tell him that the guy was her brother that she hadn't seen in some time, and she would have brought him over and introduced him, but he had friends with him and had to leave.

If he had just held back on his negative emotional reaction and waited until she returned to the table and explained who the guy was, he could have saved himself a lot of unnecessary grief and possible damage to their relationship. It does not serve us to automatically think and feel the worst when these situations present themselves.

My students' homework assignment on getting rid of resentment is to write a page or two about where in their lives they are still experiencing resentment—where in their lives they are still holding a grudge, still harboring negative energy or thoughts toward someone or others from the past or present.

When they bring their assignment back to class the following week, I set up a solemn nondistracting atmosphere in the classroom, conducive to the assignment, before I ask them to read their resentment paper silently to themselves. I want them to give themselves permission to feel whatever they want to feel as they read their paper. My goal is to support them once and for all in ridding themselves of that lingering, damaging resentment that continues to consume them long after the incident or person have left their lives.

The most important step comes next: I ask them to see themselves wishing that person or persons well. Forgive them for what they did to cause the resentment. See that person turn their back and walk away from you, off into the distance, taking your resentment with them, never to hurt you or cause you pain ever again!

Understand that if that person could have brought something different to their relationship or experience with you, they would have. That person probably doesn't even know that you still have negative energy about them or that they are still ruining or running your emotional life, and could probably care less if they were aware. If my father could have brought something different to my life, he would have. What he brought was all he knew to bring. If you do not want to forgive them, that's OK. If you can do anything to support yourself in getting rid of your resentment once and for all, it would be to at least let go of your negative emotions toward that person. Maybe forgiveness will eventually happen another time.

This is my resentment story that I tell my students: My feelings of inadequacy and self-doubt began when I was twelve years old. It was early evening and I was out front just finishing mowing the lawn. All I had left to do was to finish sweeping the sidewalk. I was thinking to myself, Wouldn't it be great if my dad came home right now to see me doing a great job of mowing the lawn? Not two minutes later, there he was. I saw him driving down the street up to the house and up the driveway to park his truck. Now I was thinking, Wouldn't it be great if he came out here to see me finishing my great work on the front lawn? There he was, striding down the driveway, walking directly toward me. I stopped to absorb his praise and compliments on a job well done, when instead, without saying a word, he took the broom out of my hand and started sweeping the last of the grass off the sidewalk.

No words of praise, no acknowledgment of my work, only what seemed to me to be quiet disgust that he has to come home from a long day of work only now to have to sweep the sidewalk. Maybe he felt I needed his help to finish. Maybe he felt I wasn't sweeping it right and he needed to sweep it for me. All I know is, that was the incident that had me believing that I wasn't good enough: I can't even sweep a sidewalk right; my dad has to come home from a long day and sweep it for me because I'm not able to sweep it as well as my dad can.

That is why I did this exercise with my father, who was that person toward whom I had resentment. I wished him well, and then began to move forward in my life, letting go of my resentment toward him. It was exhilarating and exciting to let go of the resentment and stop spending so much unnecessary negative energy on him, and stop letting that resentment run my life long after he was dead. Until I did this exercise, a lot of my decisions and actions were dependent on my belief about myself, that I was not good enough, which I bought into based on how my dad treated me and made me feel that day. For many years after that incident, I would not make a decision or act on opportunities because "Why should I? I am not good enough, so why try? I'm only going to prove dad right again." I do not blame my dad for my limited negative thinking. *I* chose to buy into it. I chose to let what he said to me that day affect how I felt about myself.

Like many of my students, I became emotional during this exercise when I did it. Some of them cry during the exercise, some of them are relieved and grateful to let go once and for all, and some are still unable to forgive. To them I suggest they continue to work on forgiving that person. If that is still not possible, I ask them to go into www.forgive.org and give it some more thought and work. Otherwise, the resentment will continue to affect their lives and may create negative results and behavior.

To take ridding my students of their resentment one step further, I ask them to take their resentment papers they wrote outside the classroom, where I had readied and placed an old empty two-wheeled barbecue. In that barbecue they quietly, solemnly, and ceremoniously burn their resentment papers in a symbolic gesture of seeing their resentment go up in smoke: gone forever, never to affect their lives again. This exercise is quite exhilarating and cleansing, if they choose.

Here are some of the student comments from the resentment assignment:

> From a relieved and rejuvenated Brenda: "My great discovery about myself was that I am a person who keeps all these resentments inside of me, and that I need to let them go, and even though it is really hard to do so, I'm trying."

> From Esmeralda: "I discovered that I am worth more than what any man or anyone has valued me. I changed

my resentment I had for men, and I'm currently learning how to maintain a safe and not so jealous relationship. The resentment activity took so much weight off me. It has been one of the best things that I have felt since my heart was broken."

Martha says: "My greatest discovery in this class was that I was in such denial about myself. When we did the resentment paper, I was able to own that and change myself."

From a now more powerful and courageous Luisa: "I discover a lot of things about myself in this class. I discover that I'm worth a lot, and to just let go of the past and move on; that I can do what I want if I focus and do my best. The resentment assignment helped me a lot to let go of the person that hurt me the most, and I know it's not my loss, it's their loss."

From a relieved and more confident Tamara: "I discovered that I was holding a grudge against someone, and that it wasn't OK, because that grudge affected my life and how I lived it. What I changed was that I forgave the person I had a grudge against, and let it go. The results were me talking it out with the person and with me letting go. I felt a weight being lifted from me. The activity we did in class of the resentment paper made me realize I was holding a grudge, and it was time to let it go."

This last comment is from a much happier and trusting Robert: "I discovered that I was very unwilling to let things go and just live on. I decided to trust my parents in lieu of *noticing* that I would not change the way I was, which obviously wasn't working. The result I got was that I trust them now and feel much happier. I let go of a lot of resentment that was initially dragging me down. Thank you for helping me realize this through your behavior change work."

During our discussion on the chapter on relationships, I give another assignment to be done over the weekend. I assign this exercise after we have discussed and cleared off resentment. The assignment is to clear off a relationship—a relationship that ended badly, a relationship on which you still have negative energy. I have them clear off this relationship because often that still-brewing bad blood or negative energy, that either you or the other person caused, continues to drive the results in a person's life. The clearing-off does not have to be with the person toward whom they had the resentment in the previous assignment.

I chose to clear off my relationship with my dad. What I did was to write him a letter acknowledging my part in our relationship. The part that says I bought into the limited thinking that I am not enough. That what I had to do was come to terms with the fact that I had a controlling dad who was never wrong. I read the letter to him at his gravesite. Even though he had passed many years earlier, it was still a relief to get that off my chest. It allowed me to clear off my relationship with him once and for all. The purpose was not to make him wrong for what he did; it was for me to work on letting go of the ineffective behaviors that I continued to display that I needed to acknowledge, that my failures were not his fault, as I had convinced myself to believe.

When my students are doing this assignment with that other person in the relationship, they are only acknowledging their part in how the relationship ended, even if they believe that it is clearly the other person's fault or behavior that caused the bad blood or negative energy. The assignment is not to blame or accuse that person one more time in hopes they will agree to and accept responsibility for the way things ended. I have them do this assignment *only* if it is safe for them to do so. If contacting that person puts them in danger, they are either to find someone else in which to clear off, or to use another means, like talking to a picture of that person. They can email that person and have an email conversation with them. They can invite them to lunch and talk. They can write them a letter but not mail it, because at least they were able to release themselves of their negative feelings, even if the letter didn't get mailed. They don't mail it because they already indicated to me that the person wouldn't "get" nor acknowledge their part in what the student is trying to accomplish with that person, so why bother.

A few of my female students write letters to their fathers who abandoned them and were always promising but never delivering at being a part of their lives. A few of their fathers are in jail or are doing drugs or have been murdered because of their behavior and are not willing or able to hear what their daughters have to say. I believe that some of their fathers wouldn't care to hear what their daughters have to say anyway, even if these women were to mail the letter or call them. Some people never change; they are given plenty of opportunities, but some refuse to "get it." It has become more important for them to be right than to be human!

I am always amazed and pleased at how hard my students work at ridding themselves of resentment, especially the many women in my class who have suffered personally at the hands of the perpetrators in their lives. Statistics show that one in three girls and one in five boys experience sexual assault or are sexually molested in childhood.

Typically, our student population at East Los Angeles College is about 65 to 75 percent Hispanic, and the remaining students are an even mix of Asian, Armenian, African-American, and Caucasian. The majority of our Hispanic students are the first to attend and graduate from college.

I love the students at East Los Angeles College. They have always been very respectful and grateful for the knowledge and education they receive. When I attended ELAC, it was at a time of social turmoil. The students at local Garfield and Roosevelt High Schools walked out in early 1970 in protest of the lack of a proper equal education. Rioting and looting in East Los Angeles followed, in which a few of my ELAC friends I knew at the time participated. There were many dissatisfied minority members of society at the time that were very unhappy with the social injustices being perpetrated upon minority populations. The Watts riots had just subsided months earlier.

I believe that if anyone had the right to be resentful for the kind of treatment they were getting, it is the many women over the years in my health classes who acknowledged receiving inhumane treatment from others. I can't tell you how many women in my classes have been abused and have suffered silently at the hands of another. Several have been molested by their brothers, fathers, or uncles. Some are still instructed to endure domestic violence from their partners because "it is your turn now, *mija*" (daughter) to be in a violent relationship.

I have participated in a vigil held each October during Domestic Violence Awareness Month for nearly twenty years. It is called Mujeres de Paz (Women of Peace). The vigil takes place on the ELAC campus, where survivors of domestic violence can speak in front of the assembled students and community about their story of abuse. It has helped bring a tremendous amount of awareness and attention to domestic abuse. It has also generated a lot of recent support and involvement of men to help women end domestic violence. Society cannot bring the kind of awareness and prevention needed to stop the abuse without men working with other men to stop relationship violence. Prevention is the key!

Women benefit from my classes. It is they who realize that despite what they have been told, they do have a choice: a choice to negotiate the use of a condom when having sex, a choice to get out of a violent relationship, a choice to stop using drugs or alcohol to numb their pain. And finally, they realize they have a choice and ways to end their depression and emotional pain from the abuse. I met several students who revealed that they are bulimic. What I know about the history behind many of those who are bulimic is that the majority of them have been molested. One woman suffering from bulimia revealed having been molested by her brother for about ten years.

When we talk about eating disorders in the class, what comes to light is that while being abused, most women are unable to control much of anything in their lives. They are unable to control the threats and the intent to do harm to loved ones if she tells anyone about the abuse. They are often unable to control their environment where boundaries are being crossed and trust is not present. But the one thing they can control is what they eat. So not eating enough, or eating too much, then purging themselves, gives them some sense of control over their lives, albeit destructive in nature and dangerous to their health.

I design all my health classes around creating healthy, meaningful, balanced lives. All the textbook information along with the supplemental exercises and personal development supplemental assignments we do in class let my students know that I care about them and that I am committed to their growth.

I give my students a reward for their efforts in creating positive change in their lives. After they have worked so hard to clear off a relationship, to rid themselves of resentment, and to see themselves forgiving their perpetrators, I ask them to go do something personal and fun for themselves over the coming weekend. They can just lock the bathroom door and have a nice long candlelit bath. They can get their nails painted, go for a walk on the beach, go see a movie, take themselves out to dinner—any number of things they can choose from to do something pleasant and rewarding for themselves. This is the most difficult assignment for some, who are always putting others before themselves. I simply ask them to give themselves permission to do something nice for themselves and not feel guilty; they earned this special treatment.

The "Do something nice for yourself" assignment usually concludes our unit on relationships and creating emotional well-being in my health classes. It is a great way to segue from relationships to other topics that follow, like making choices about having protected sex, or about the concerns of becoming pregnant, or what to do if you contract a sexually transmitted infection. These are scenarios that take communication to negotiate positive outcomes within your relationships. Since we have already discussed ways to develop successful relationships through effective listening and communication, things like the aforementioned get resolved easier.

Here are more results from students who have completed my health classes and have made changes based on what they discovered about themselves:

> A happier, less angry Diana writes: "I learned that I had an anger problem. I learned that the person I hurt the most was me, so I needed to change my anger and learn how to control it. I started to go to anger management, and I went to see a psychologist two times a week. She helped me to understand that I needed to let go of all my resentment from my mother and father, to start seeing life with other eyes, and to start seeing that I had two kids and a boyfriend that love me. So, at the end, I change the way I talk to my two kids and my boyfriend; now I talk with lots of respect."

From small but mighty Marta: "What I discovered about myself in this class is that I was a terrible listener, and I had trouble with anger. I was able to control these things when I acknowledged my problem, and through the assignments I went through a changing process. Now I can handle situations with a smile and not get upset."

Michelle explains: "I learned many things in this class, from family to sex, but the one thing that I learned about myself is that I was always really angry. I was always angry not only with myself by always putting myself down but with other people by putting them down. After this class, I have noticed that I don't go off on people much. I stop and talk myself out of problems. I also have a lot more confidence in myself. I don't take things personally, I don't make assumptions, and I always do my best in whatever I can. This class has helped me become a better person, not only with friends and family but with people out in the street. I would like to thank you, Ms. Ladd, for helping me."

From Nora: "What I discovered about myself is that I have some negative people in my life, and that drags me down and makes me negative and antisocial. The change I made was that I already eliminated the person who drags me down the most. Life is too short, and I have no room for negativity, and no time to waste on it."

Guadalupe says: "My greatest discovery about myself was to believe more in myself and to overcome any obstacle."

Sylvia: "My greatest discovery in this class was that I do matter. I am important, and I need to acknowledge that. I need a lot of me time, and I don't have to settle."

Carmen: "What I discovered about myself was that I do need to take care of myself even more so as I am getting older. Especially because I have lupus, I know that my health is my priority in my life. I am a very energetic, busy person, both at work and at home (and also at ELAC), but thanks to this class, Ms. Ladd, I have learned to say no, and just relax."

From confident Christina: "Well, taking this class has opened my eyes to a lot of things in my life. I noticed that I had a problem with self-value, and my self-worth was low. I also learned that my home situation is not healthy, and I need to do something to change it before it continues to affect my life, and I now began to change my old habits and focus more on my self-worth."

Rene: "My greatest discovery was that I truly can achieve anything I can possibly dream. It was difficult at times to keep going, yet I found a way to dig deeper and continue on. I also discovered there are truly people in this world who care about the well-being of others. I feel so blessed to have chosen the classes that I did."

Gabriela: "My greatest discovery about myself was my lack of self-awareness and self-appreciation. I have learned that I need to take care of myself and others around me in order to live happily. This class has helped me have no resentments toward the people that have hurt me in my past and to allow myself to be loved and be appreciated of all the good things life has to give but also to protect myself and others by being aware."

Olga: "I discovered that I can be an OK student if I tried. I just have to put myself first. I know one thing next semester I will be is a great A student. I had a few obstacles this semester and almost gave up! I know I'm making changes because the old me would have dropped from school. I even changed the way my kids eat now!"

From a renewed and revitalized Kendra: "My greatest discovery in this class is that I can do anything if I put my mind to it. I know a lot of older people told me that before, but I didn't really believe it. But now this class made me realize it's the truth. Because I always told myself I don't want to be controlling anymore, but I never stopped until I got this class. I never thought one class would change me when I have been trying all my life."

From shy but determined Gabriela: "I didn't give up. I tried really hard on everything I did in all my classes this semester. I found strength, and I believe in myself. I did everything in my power to feel comfortable and accept myself. People who were putting me down didn't win. I keep fighting and proved them wrong."

Cristina writes: "Something that I learned about myself is that I need to stop taking things so personally because not everyone is out there to make me feel bad. When people say things, they don't always say them to hurt me. I believe that if I change that about me, I will live a little happier and in peace."

And from lovely, beautiful Kenya: "I discovered that no matter what I have been through, it doesn't have to continue to be a part of my life. I learned in this class and I am also going through the same lessons at church to learn to let things go instead of holding on and allowing it to affect me for the rest of my life. I learned everyone that is around you is not for you, and I also learned everyone around me may not be out to harm me. I am continuing to be my word; I am working on avoiding taking things personally. My biggest task to overcome will be to learn how to avoid making assumptions, and I have picked back up a good habit, which is to always do my best."

A more confident Alfredo says: "One thing I learned about myself in this class is that my problems are created because of me. I always seem to have that little voice in my head telling me that I can't do this, can't do that. This class has taught me to believe in myself because if I don't, no one will. Self-confidence is one of the most important attributes a person can have, and I feel that this class put me closer in terms of gaining that attribute."

Small but mighty Claudia writes: "What I did discover about myself was that I am a closed person and I have a rough time dealing with other people's feelings and emotions.

One of the things that I managed to change was the relationship toward my friends and family. I've become more considerate of other people's feelings, and I've become more aware of how my behavior might impact them. Though I may have changed my personality, I must admit that I still have a tough time dealing with other people's feelings; not only that, but I've also come to discover that I might have trouble dealing with my own feelings and emotions."

From beautiful Joanna: "The greatest discovery that I had in this class about myself is that now I do know and understand how much I need to work on myself. I need to start thinking about the future and get right to it and stop procrastinating."

The determined Anthony writes: "The greatest discovery about myself in this class was that now I can stand up to people a lot more. Back then I really wouldn't care and I would let people walk all over me."

And from shy, beautiful Yosajandi, from my 2008 winter session class: "What I discovered about myself was that I am worth it, and I matter. I found the courage in me to forgive my ex-boyfriend, and to believe in myself. I feel more confident in my choices and in who I am as a person."

Epilogue

After I stopped drinking in 1988, I continued to stay sober over the next several years and had a few brief relationships, but they did not last. One of those relationships did last a few years, with a fun-loving, adventurous woman who worked with at-risk youth, teaching them to maintain and ride dirt bikes. After teaching me to ride, we either trailered or rode bikes to the upper and lower deserts near Victorville, Baker, and Barstow, sometimes staying overnight in the desert in complete and utter darkness, staring at a beautiful, clear night sky overhead. I ended up having an affair with another woman, which ruined our relationship. We got back together for a while until she developed a wandering eye and cheated on me. We broke up shortly after her affair was revealed and went our separate ways. I loved the free-spirited, test-the-limits personality she possessed that I often wished I could have had.

In 1997, I enrolled in several employee personal and professional development workshops that dramatically changed my behavior and helped me create more meaningful, effective, and successful relationships with my family, students, colleagues, friends, etc. In those workshops, I finally began to get to know, love, and respect myself. It took several years of these workshops, self-help books, and consciously making better personal changes to finally develop and build successful results in the classroom and elsewhere in my life.

What finally drove me to attend these personal development workshops was another woman, whom I had been seeing briefly, who walked out of my life. As she was angrily walking away from my house, closing my front gate as she left, she turned to me and said, "You are nothing but an insensitive, controlling bully!" Now, I had been called all of those terms at one time or another in my relationships with women, but not all in the same sentence, as she so rightfully proclaimed.

It was at that moment that I realized my relationships failed because of me, that it was my need to be right and to look good that drove my ineffective behavior. Looking back, even when I was wrong, I was right. I would do anything to look good in the eyes of others, especially the women in my life, even if looking good meant lying or cheating in my relationships. I learned the hard way that my negative actions and needs were not working in my adult relationships.

Based on the positive behavior changes I finally made in myself, by the year 2000, when I turned fifty, I was creating in my students those same positive behavior changes. These student discoveries, changes, and results are evidenced in the testimonials you have been reading thus far. I not only created better results in my health classes but also in my activity classes I was teaching and in my relationships with my coaching and athletic staff as Athletic Director.

I was more flexible in my teaching, I was allowing myself to have fun and not taking myself so seriously. I was more patient and easygoing. I was finally able to get myself out of the way and be about others! All areas of my life were firing on all cylinders. I was more present and gave myself permission to be in the moment, to get out of my head where I had been hanging out all those years. I finally developed a balance between my head and my heart. I stopped thinking so much and began feeling more.

I now see that I displayed similar behaviors that I saw in my dad growing up. He and I were very task-oriented: we focused on getting things done, creating results, making things happen, because I believe it was expected of us. We kept busy so we didn't have to feel. We avoided being emotional. I believe we felt that allowing ourselves to be vulnerable or too thin-skinned would make us appear to others as less than, not enough. I know that if any one of us siblings cried while watching a sad, touching movie, we were made fun of by others in the room. I learned that showing emotions was not OK, especially as I grew into a position of responsibility at an early age. I became my dad at ten years old when I stepped into a co-parent position with my mom. It wasn't until I completed those personal development workshops in my late forties that I became what I believe I am today: the best of both my parents.

As a result of the positive changes I was making, I was able to enjoy a high level of self-esteem and self-confidence, I began to think about creating multiple streams of income. I no longer wanted to trade my time for money. I wanted to have a conversation with someone and calculate, after five minutes of talking to them, how much money I made during that conversation. As of the writing of this book, I am still, slowly but surely, working on creating multiple streams of income.

In 2001 I was helping at a personal development seminar, called PSI Seminars, by working at a sign-up table for people interested in attending one of the seminars I attended. I suddenly spotted a real head-turner of a woman. She was a beautiful, energetic blond with an ear-to-ear smile surrounded by a small group of interested friends she was hoping to sign up to take the same seminar she had just finished attending. At that instant I could only admire her from afar. As fate would have it, a few weeks later, I saw her again as part of another seminar that she and a female friend of hers were attending. It turns out her friend was the woman she was dating at the time. To my surprise, she broke up with her during the seminar.

It was shortly after her breakup with her former partner that she and I developed a mutual interest in each other. After the seminar was over, we began dating. She moved in with me about nine months into our relationship. We had a commitment ceremony at a local church with about a hundred of our friends and family in attendance in April of 2003. The ceremony was followed by a celebration at our house. We were eventually able to receive all the benefits of a married couple when the Los Angeles Community College District recognized her and me as domestic partners in 2005.

For the first few years, things were going great. We got along well; we vacationed abroad with members of her family. With two good friends of ours we took a cruise along the East Coast; we bought and rode horses together; we also enjoyed getting spas and facials, attending plays and musicals in the LA area, and many other fun and exciting things. Before I knew it, I began to realize that I was spending so much money on all these activities that I was starting to go through money faster than I was making it. I eventually took out an equity loan on the house to keep up with our expensive lifestyle. What I found difficult to do was to tell her we should cut back on our spending and expensive activities. I just couldn't seem to find a way to say no to her, which, to me, would be admitting that I was not capable of providing her with the finer pleasures and things in life that I felt she deserved and that she was now used to having.

I kept my concerns to myself, but unfortunately, I found myself turning to alcohol again to cope. I always have, and often still do, feel that I *have to* be productive, that I *have to* take care of and provide for others as I have done since I was a young child. It was assumed that I could take care of myself, that I didn't need anyone's help, so I never asked for it. If I did, in my mind, it meant that I was not capable. These were feelings I had battled before but didn't do anything to address, but to drink solved nothing. And now for the first time in my life, I was unable to provide for or take care of the one person who meant more to me than anyone else.

In an attempt to create another stream of income, we started a gay and lesbian greeting card company in 2004. We thought it was a novel idea, and would be successful, and would help with our mounting debt. To finance all the start-up costs, I used a good portion of my tax shelter monies.

She knew I was a recovering alcoholic when we got together in 2001, and now, in 2004, she could tell that I am drinking again. My behavior began to frighten her, so she moved out. This put even more of a financial burden on me, as I was now paying for everything to do with the house and the continuing start-up costs of our greeting card company. I quit drinking shortly after she moved out, realizing the drinking was not helping the situation and was only making things worse. After about ten months, convinced that I was no longer drinking, she moved back in, and things went well for a while.

She was employed by a bank in their human resources department. She was good at what she did and made pretty good money. Looking back, I should have, could have, asked her to help more financially, or found the courage to start saying no to our spending. For several years I gave her the impression that I had the money for us to enjoy our lifestyle. Little did she know that I was suffering financially and emotionally over this dilemma.

I was still in a lot of debt as 2006 came to a close. Our greeting card business was not doing well. Our gay and lesbian cards were contemporary, tasteful, and sophisticated, but we found that men want "beefcake," sexually edgy cards that we were not interested in creating. There were already plenty of that type of card out there. We also found that women are less likely to buy greeting cards than men. That hurt our sales, and ecards were becoming popular, so greeting cards were starting to become less popular. There just wasn't the demand nor the social acceptance of mainstream gay and lesbian greeting cards. I continued to work the business, selling cards at several gay boutiques and gay-owned businesses in West Hollywood, a traditionally heavily populated gay area. As hard as I worked at it, the company never did make a profit. I stopped selling in 2009, and the inventory has been stored in my garage ever since.

I began drinking again in 2008, just after my life partner and I got married in June during that window of opportunity when it was legal in California to do so and before it was repealed in November that year. Maybe it was the constant feeling that the world was continuing to cave in on me financially that life began to become more and more difficult to face. Drinking was an easy escape, as it had been in the past. I believe I would not have started drinking again if I had attended an alcohol treatment program when my drinking first got out of control in 1988 because I know it would have helped me address the feelings that led to my drinking. Needless to say, she moved out again, fed up with my renewed drinking and me doing a poor job of trying to hide it. She felt betrayed and did not want to have anything more to do with me.

I quit drinking in early 2009 and wisely sought support for my drinking this time instead of thinking I could remain sober on my own. Fortunately, my bouts of drinking stints between my times of sobriety were short lived. I began attending AA meetings with other alcoholics, and by mid-2009 my wife and I were going to couples' therapy to resolve some of our continuing differences that were preventing us from bonding and getting along like a married couple should. The sessions did help with understanding ourselves better and the reasons why we were struggling to get along. We went individually at times. Those sessions helped me realize how much of an enabler I had become and how that was a big part of the problems within the relationship. I was taking on a lot by myself without speaking up and asking for help, like carrying the financial burden that we should have been sharing together. This caused me great anguish that I could not express.

Another area of contention in our marriage that my wife tried to discuss and bring to light early on was how much time and energy I continued putting into my family, sports, and school, and how little time and energy I was giving her. She needed more of my attention and loving care, and I was oblivious as to how important that was to her. I was acting like a single person, spending more time away from home than at home with her. We had many great times together, but I am sure those good times were few and far between compared to what they should have been.

Things were going fairly well for us, so in late 2009 she moved back in. Every time my wife moved out, I would reluctantly refinance the house to keep up with the current bills I alone was paying, and to pay all the past bills that we had both accumulated. I took out all the equity in the house each time and ended up with lower-interest home loans but ended up with higher monthly payments and owing more than twice the original price I first financed. Each time she moved out, she would accumulate a lot of debt, paying all the start-up costs in first and last months' rent, buying a few new pieces of furniture, and paying for anything else that went with her being on her own financially. That is why it was difficult for her to help with our debt when she moved back in, because she accumulated a lot of personal debt each time she moved out. Each time she moved back in, I picked up where I left off financially, which was to remain in and increase my already seriously mounting debt. Since I felt it was my fault that she moved out each time, I felt I alone was responsible to continue to pay for our financial debt, which only increased my silent anxiety and tension.

By the end of 2010, I had stopped attending my AA meetings, believing I had my drinking under control again and no longer needed support. As had happened in the past, instead of seeking professional help to cope with times of personal distress, I started drinking again off and on. I would quit for a few weeks only to drink again for a few days or weeks, and then quit again. I talked myself into believing my drinking was not affecting my teaching or my relationships when, in fact, it definitely was. My wife knew and did not like me drinking but tolerated it. It was those times when I knew she knew that I would stop, only to cave to temptation and stress and drink again.

This went on until July 2011, when late that month I drove down alone to a small town near the Mexican border to pick up my mother-in-law and bring her back to stay with us for a while. I drank all the way down there, I drank while I was there, and I drank all the way back with my mother-in-law in the car. I would put a lot of vodka in a clear sweet carbonated drink in an attempt to mask the smell of the alcohol. I had drunk so much in those two days that I was falling asleep while driving back and had difficulty keeping the car in its lane. When I thankfully and finally arrived home, I remember that horrible look of disgust on my wife's face that I got when she immediately recognized the drunken state I was in and promptly turned away from me and walked her mother to her room.

There was no anger and no discussion from her. Based on the past, she knew it would do no good; this was my problem and it was up to me to do something about it. That date was July 31, 2011, the day I took my last drink. I got my butt right back to AA and dove in head first, and haven't looked back. I have stayed sober, one day at a time, ever since that decisive, momentous day. I finally addressed my feelings of inadequacy and my perceived failures. It took several years to feel good about myself again, but I can say I am that positive, productive, diligent person I was many years earlier.

What disappoints and disgusts me the most about my drinking, besides the fact that I never needed it to cope in the first place, was the many times I drove my mother, family, friends, and pets while drunk. I was so fortunate to have never injured anyone while driving drunk. I wished I'd had the courage to ask for help sooner.

Unfortunately, sober now or not, my unfaithful drinking and betrayal each time I started drinking again took its toll on our relationship, and my wife moved out one last time in the spring of 2012. She stayed in the area and we kept an amicable relationship with each other, walking our dogs together, going out to dinner on occasion, and going out to the horse ranch together to ride and compete in barrel racing. We did eventually get a divorce that became final in February 2015. She retired in March 2015 and moved south shortly after to be with her sister and brother-in-law. We still maintain friendly contact with each other and visit each other whenever we can.

My debt is still there, but if I begin to get upset over it, I no longer feel the need to drink to numb my anxieties. I apologize to those I may have hurt or put in danger over the years while drinking. I hope my family, friends, and colleagues can forgive my past behavior. I need to make amends to my students and athletes who were shortchanged by giving them less than my best teaching and coaching. My family and fellow recovering alcoholics have always been there for me, supporting me through my disease. They have always been understanding and nonjudgmental. They loved me no matter what. I am so fortunate to have had the loving support of my brothers and sisters throughout my ups and downs in life—one of the many reasons why I am so *Glad to Be a Ladd*!

I retired from teaching in June 2013 after a thirty-nine-year teaching career. I continue to teach physical activity classes at ELAC to the students with special needs two days a week. Each and every one of my students is a gift to me. I have remained active on a few committees at school and volunteer my time and energy to the East Los Angeles Women's Center, which provides services to survivors of domestic violence, sexual assault, human trafficking, and women who are HIV positive. I recently joined the East Los Angeles Rotary International Club, in which I enjoy participating in many community projects and fund-raising events. I continue to attend my annual family campouts and summer backpacking trips with my brother Bob and whomever else happens to join us.

I lead a blessed life now, one that took a lot of trial and error and years of personal and professional help to create. The life I have now was worth the emotional and financial ups and downs I experienced. The last piece that was missing, that I needed to become that whole person I longed to be, was recreating my spiritual side that I had lost and lacked for such a long time. I have an empathetic and compassionate side now that allows me to effectively help others. I depend and place faith in my spiritual energy to guide me through difficult, emotional, and stressful times without wanting to turn to drinking. I love my life, and more importantly, I love myself now. I truly believe that I am enough, I am important, and I do matter!

Mom's ninetieth birthday in 2009, the last time all twelve were together. Front row, left to right: Suzanne Ladd Powers, Clarissa Ladd Chambers, Ellen Ladd, Marilyn Ladd. Back row: Mel, Gill Powers (d. March 2011), Marv, John (d. January 2015), Ray, Bob, Mike (d. April 2013), Ralph, Harry, Frances.

I have so many wonderful memories, for which I am eternally grateful. Those happy times were those spent with family, friends, former fellow and student athletes, and the wonderful women I met over the years who gave so much to me in return, at times, for unfortunately so little. I have experienced many unexpected gifts in life, especially that gift to have been born the fifth child in a uniquely special family of fourteen. What I wouldn't give to be back in the girls' room at ten years old getting tucked into bed by my mom, looking over at my two tired and sleepy sisters across the room from me in their bunk beds, hearing my brothers settling in for the night down in the den below, my dad rising from the kitchen table, rolling up a finalized set of sprinkler plans for a customer, and then watching him and my mom turning out lights as they made their way down the hall to their bedroom.

Index

A
Aceves, Laura 221
Adelman, Rick 178
All-American Red Heads 182
Allen Theater 24
Amateur Athletic Union (AAU) 180, 181, 182, 183, 194
Arroyo Seco 209, 214

B
Bachman, Gwen 182
backpacking skills 207
Brussa, Flora 191, 192, 203
bulimia 279

C
California Lutheran College 200
California State University, Fullerton 180, 191, 198, 221
California State University, Long Beach 191
Camarillo 37, 165, 198
Camp Hoegee 211, 212
change. *See* formula for change
Chantry Flats 211, 212, 213
codependency 255, 258
commitment 261
Compton College 184
Cone, Al 222
Connecticut Brakettes 194
Costas, Bob 192
Curry, Denise 196

D
DeGeneres, Ellen 216, 267
Dell, Helen 181
Del Mar Fair 160
Delta Pi Gamma 185
Dodgers 28, 180
domestic violence 279
Downey 19, 25, 108, 175
Drysdale, Ann Meyers 180, 193, 196
Dunkle, Nancy 194

E
East LA high school walkouts 278
East Los Angeles College 146, 190, 202, 206, 218, 278, 279
East Los Angeles Women's Center 217, 292
eating disorders 279
Echo Mountain 210
empathy 254

F
Farnell, Mary 202, 204
Flying Queens. *See* Wayland Baptist College Flying Queens
formula for change 230, 255
The Four Agreements 234
Fullerton 194, 195, 196
Fullerton College 67, 194

G
Galvan, Margaret 146
Good Humor ice cream 64
Gould Mesa Campground 209

295

INDEX

H
Harris, Toni 222
Head, Pat.
  See Summitt, Pat
Helm's Bakery 64
Hines, James 222

I
Immaculata
  College 195
Ito, Nancy 194

J
Jones, Ed "Too
  Tall" 200
Joyce, Joan 194

K
Knickerbocker
  Hotel 13
Knott's Berry
  Farm 167

L
La Costa State
  Beach 158
Lazarus, Stephanie
  202
Leo Carrillo State
  Beach 161
listening 251
Lompoc 38, 44
Long Beach City
  College 194
Lopez, Dave 53
Los Altos Intermediate
  School 198, 199, 200
Los Angeles City
  College 218, 221
Lynwood 52, 56, 90,
  166, 175, 178

M
McAlister, Maurice 25
Meyers, Ann.
  See Drysdale, Ann
  Meyers
Meyers, Patty 180
Miller, Cheryl 192
Mitchell, Mary 182
Moore, Billie 191, 193,
  194, 195, 196, 200
Mosley, John 222
Mosqueda, Sylvia 222
Mujeres de Paz 279

N
Naismith Memorial
  Basketball Hall of
  Fame 181
Nashville Business
  College 182
National Basketball
  Association (NBA)
  178, 180, 193, 244

O
Olympics 179, 180,
  191, 192, 194, 196,
  197, 222
O'Neal, Shaquille 183
Orange Lionettes 194
Our Bodies, Ourselves
  229, 269
Oxnard 35, 36, 37, 128
Oxnard brothers 37
Oxnard, Henry T. 37
Oxnard, Robert
  "Bob" 37

P
Parnassus, Monsignor
  George J. 176
Pink 216

Pius X High School
  19, 53, 108, 173,
  175, 176, 177, 178,
  179, 184
polio 89, 136
PSI Seminars 287

Q
Quintana, Gloria 203

R
Reagan, Ronald 201,
  218
Redin, Harley 181
Reeves, Betty 204
resentment 271
Riley, Pat 193
Ruiz, Miguel 234

S
Santa Ana Valley High
  School 199, 221
Schaafsma, Fran 191
Shank, Teresa 195
Sharp, Linda 192,
  193, 194
Simi Valley 201, 202
Simi Valley High
  School 200, 201, 202,
  205, 221
Sisters of St. Joseph of
  Orange 88
Soledad Canyon 148,
  155, 156, 161, 163
Southern Pacific
  Railroad 156
South Gate 18, 24, 68,
  69, 110, 128, 185
South Gate
  Educational
  Center 190
South Gate High
  School 25, 66, 70

South Gate
 Intermediate
 School 38, 66
South Gate Junior
 High School 69, 146
South Gate Park 20,
 62, 259
South Gate Press 128,
 170
St. Don Bosco High
 School 51, 122
St. Emydius Catholic
 School 51, 52, 53, 56,
 58, 89, 90, 94, 95, 98,
 108, 125, 146, 172,
 175, 179
Summitt, Pat 196,
 197, 268
sympathy 254

T

telephone 105
television 99, 100, 174
Thousand Oaks 200,
 205
Title IX 181, 191, 192,
 194, 203
Topley, Shirley 194
Turner, Bruce 222
Tweedy Boulevard 19,
 22, 23, 24, 25, 29, 77,
 83, 170, 171, 173

U

University of
 California, Los
 Angeles (UCLA) 40,
 128, 180, 196,
 244, 268
University of
 Southern California
 (USC) 193

V

Vandenberg Air Force
 Base 39, 135
Vandenberg Village
 39, 43
Vasquez Rocks 162
Vega, Sally 100
Ventura 13, 35, 36, 37,
 80, 161, 166, 198, 201
Ventura College 17,
 107

W

walkouts. *See* East LA
 high school walkouts
Walton, Bill 244
Watts riots 104
Wayland Baptist
 College Flying
 Queens 181
Welsh, Bill 100
*Where to Watch
 Trains* 129
Women's National
 Basketball
 Association
 (WNBA) 192
Women's Recreation
 Association 185
Wooden, John 40,
 244, 268

Y

Yosemite Fire
 Falls 153
Yosemite National
 Park 150

www.ingramcontent.com/pod-product-compliance
Lightning Source LLC
Chambersburg PA
CBHW071302110526
44591CB00010B/749